# 50 HIKES

## IN SOUTH CAROLINA

# 50 HIKES
## IN SOUTH CAROLINA

SECOND EDITION

Johnny Molloy

THE COUNTRYMAN PRESS

A division of W. W. Norton & Company

*Independent Publishers Since 1923*

For information about permission to reproduce selections from this book,
write to Permissions, The Countryman Press,
500 Fifth Avenue, New York, NY 10110

For information about special discounts for bulk purchases, please contact W. W.
Norton Special Sales at specialsales@wwnorton.com or 800-233-4830

Library of Congress Cataloging-in-Publication Data

Names: Molloy, Johnny, 1961- author.
Title: 50 hikes in South Carolina / Johnny Molloy.
Description: Second Edition. | New York : The Countryman Press A divisionof W.
W. Norton & Company, [2016] | Series: 50 Hikes | "Distributed by W. W. Norton &
Company, Inc."--T.p. verso. | Includes index.Identifiers: LCCN 2016020222 | ISBN
9781581573473 (paperback)Subjects: LCSH: Hiking--South Carolina--Guide-
books. | Trails--South  Carolina--Guidebooks. | South Carolina--Guidebooks.
Classification: LCC GV199.42.S58 M66 2016 | DDC 796.5109757--dc23 LC recor-
davailable at https://lccn.loc.gov/2016020222

The Countryman Press
www.countrymanpress.com

A division of W. W. Norton & Company
500 Fifth Avenue, New York, NY 10110
www.wwnorton.com

978-1-58157-347-3

1 2 3 4 5 6 7 8 9 0

*This book is for the hikers of the Palmetto State.*

# 50 Hikes in South Carolina at a Glance

| Hike | City | Distance | Views |
|------|------|----------|-------|
| 1. Big Bend Falls via Big Bend Trail | Walhalla | 7.0 | |
| 2. Ellicott Rock via East Fork Chattooga | Walhalla | 8.2 | |
| 3. Ellicott Rock Wilderness Loop | Walhalla | 19.3 | √ |
| 4. Foothills Trail Vistas via Sassafras Mountain | Pickens | 9.4 | |
| 5. Hidden Falls | Walhalla | 5.0 | √ |
| 6. Hospital Rock | Cleveland | 2.2 | √ |
| 7. King Creek Falls/Big Bend Falls via Burrells Ford | Walhalla | 7.6 | |
| 8. Laurel Fork Falls and Lake Jocassee | Pickens | 9.8 | |
| 9. Lick Log Falls/Pigpen Falls via Chattooga Trail | Mountain Rest | 9.2 | |
| 10. Little Pinnacle Mountain Loop | Cleveland | 5.4 | √ |
| 11. Lower Whitewater Falls/Coon Den Natural Area | Salem | 6.0 | √ |
| 12. Miuka Falls/Secret Falls via the Winding Stairs | Walhalla | 4.6 | |
| 13. Opossum Creek Falls | Long Creek | 4.6 | |
| 14. Pinnacle Mountain Loop | Pickens | 7.6 | √ |
| 15. Raven Cliff Falls Loop | Cleveland | 7.9 | √ |
| 16. Raven Rock Loop | Salem | 3.9 | √ |
| 17. Rim of the Gap Loop | Cleveland | 9.1 | √ |
| 18. Station Cove Falls Loop via Historic Oconee Station | Walhalla | 2.3 | |
| 19. Sulphur Springs Loop | Greenville | 3.8 | |
| 20. Upper Saluda River Loop | Cleveland | 5.5 | √ |
| 21. Whitewater Falls There-and-Back | Salem | 5.8 | |
| 22. Aiken State Natural Area Loop | Aiken | 2.6 | |
| 23. Blackstock Battlefield Passage of the Palmetto Trail | Cross Anchor | 1.7 | √ |
| 24. Buncombe Loop | Whitmire | 26.7 | |
| 25. Cheraw State Park Loop | Cheraw | 4.2 | |
| 26. Dreher Island State Park Hike | Chapin | 2.4 | √ |
| 27. Horn Creek/Lick Fork Lake Double Loop | Edgefield | 6.6 | |
| 28. Kings Mountain Loop | Blacksburg | 15.1 | √ |
| 29. Long Cane Loop | Abbeville | 22.9 | |
| 30. Oakridge Loop at Congaree National Park | Gadsden | 6.5 | |

| Water-fall | Camp-ground | Trail Camp | Kids | Comments |
|---|---|---|---|---|
| √ | √ | √ | | Most powerful falls in South Carolina |
| √ | | √ | | "Gorge-ous" scenery to a historic spot |
| √ | | √ | | Backpack the state's largest wilderness |
| √ | | √ | √ | South Carolina's highest point, great views, high-country trek |
| √ | √ | √ | √ | This hike has a little bit of everything |
| | √ | √ | √ | Historic rockhouse |
| √ | √ | √ | √ | Superlative Chattooga River scenery |
| √ | | √ | | Isolated approach to the falls and a mountain lake |
| √ | | √ | | Bag two falls in one hike. Bring your camera! |
| √ | | √ | | River-and-ridge trek |
| √ | | √ | √ | Old-growth forest and a massive waterfall |
| √ | √ | √ | | The trail really does wind to two cascades. |
| √ | | √ | √ | Cataract near lower Chattooga River |
| √ | √ | | | Views, falls, large elevation change |
| √ | | | | Spectacular but challenging |
| | √ | √ | √ | Natural bridge, lake views |
| √ | | √ | | Cliffs, huge bluffs, waterfalls |
| √ | | | √ | 200-plus-year-old house and waterfall |
| | √ | | √ | Climb Paris Mountain |
| √ | | | | High-country trek |
| √ | | √ | √ | 400-plus-foot falls |
| | √ | | √ | Botanically rich area |
| | | √ | √ | Historic Revolutionary War site |
| | √ | √ | | Best Midlands backpack loop |
| | √ | | √ | Red-cockaded woodpecker habitat |
| | √ | | √ | Water water everywhere |
| | √ | √ | √ | Fine overall recreation destination |
| | √ | √ | √ | Beauty at the battlefield |
| | √ | √ | | Big trees, backpacking |
| | | √ | √ | Huge trees at South Carolina's only national park |

| Hike | City | Distance | Views |
|---|---|---|---|
| 31. Parsons Mountain Loop | Abbeville | 4.2 | √ |
| 32. Peachtree Rock Nature Preserve Loop | Columbia | 2.2 | √ |
| 33. Palmetto Trail near the Broad River | Pomaria | 7.2 | √ |
| 34. Poinsett State Park Loop | Wedgefield | 1.7 | |
| 35. Sesquicentennial State Park Hike | Columbia | 4.8 | |
| 36. Stevens Creek There-and-Back | Edgefield | 11.2 | |
| 37. Timmerman Trail at Congaree Creek | Columbia | 4.0 | |
| 38. Tates Trail at Carolina Sandhills Refuge | McBee | 5.1 | |
| 39. Turkey Creek There-and-Back | Edgefield | 9.4 | |
| 40. Awendaw Passage of the Palmetto Trail | Awendaw | 8.4 | √ |
| 41. Caw Caw Interpretive Center Loop | Ravenel | 3.6 | |
| 42. Dungannon Plantation Loop | Hollywood | 3.7 | |
| 43. Hunting Island State Park Loop | Beaufort | 3.1 | |
| 44. Ion Swamp Interpretive Walk | Awendaw | 2.0 | |
| 45. Old Santee Canal Loop | Moncks Corner | 2.3 | |
| 46. Sandpiper Pond Nature Trail and Beach Walk | Murrells Inlet | 4.8 | |
| 47. Santee Coastal Reserve Loop | McClellanville | 3.3 | |
| 48. Santee State Park Loop | Santee | 7.3 | √ |
| 49. Spanish Mount Trail at Edisto Beach State Park | Edisto Beach | 3.9 | √ |
| 50. Swamp Fox Passage of the Palmetto Trail | Awendaw | 48.1 | √ |

| Water-fall | Camp-ground | Trail Camp | Kids | Comments |
|---|---|---|---|---|
|  | √ |  | √ | Old gold mines |
| √ |  |  | √ | Unusual geological features |
|  |  | √ | √ | Rail trail with views of Broad River |
|  | √ |  | √ | Good loop at an underutilized state park |
| √ |  | √ |  | Cruise through sandhills and along spring-fed streams and a lake. |
|  |  | √ | √ | Wildflowers |
|  |  |  | √ | Greenway travels through Congaree Creek Heritage Preserve. |
|  |  |  | √ | Wildlife and lake views |
|  |  | √ | √ | Wildflowers, bluffs |
|  | √ |  | √ | Views of tidal marsh and the Intracoastal Waterway |
|  |  |  | √ | Birding at a well-kept park |
|  |  |  | √ | Wildlife area |
|  | √ |  | √ | Gorgeous maritime setting |
|  |  |  | √ | Explore a former rice-plantation-cum-swamp. |
|  |  |  | √ | Human and natural history |
|  | √ |  | √ | Walk along an interdune pond and the Atlantic. |
|  |  |  | √ | Wading bird rookery |
|  | √ |  | √ | Lake Marion vistas |
|  | √ |  | √ | Tidal creek and live oak woods |
|  | √ | √ |  | Great backpack in the Lowcountry |

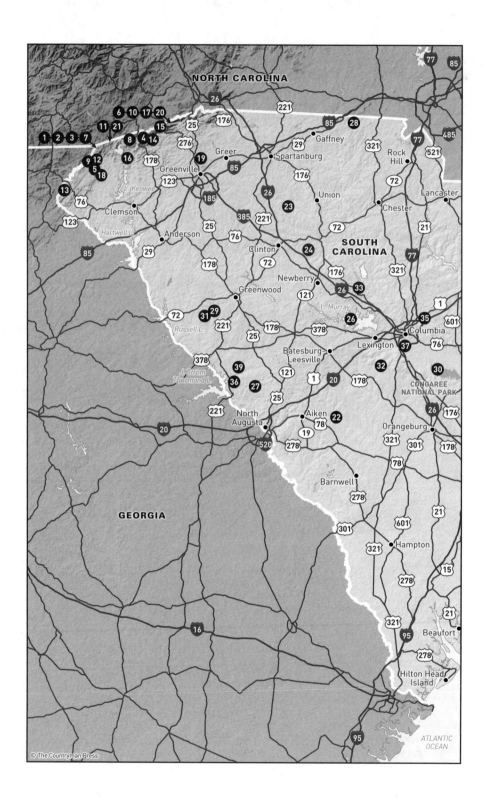

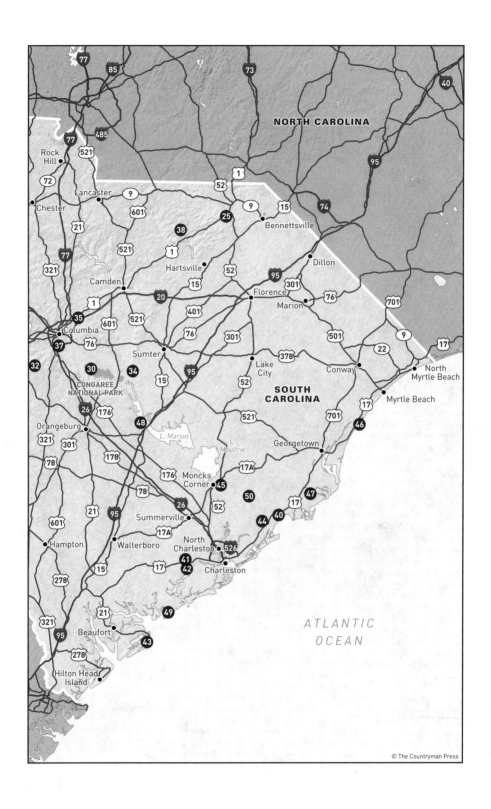

# CONTENTS

----------------------------------------------------------------

## III. LOWCOUNTRY | 195

# Preface

Welcome to the second edition of this guide. I have been lucky enough to explore South Carolina's natural wonders for more than two decades. Most of my early adventures were mountain and coastal trips, but a trip to the Midlands demonstrated just what a beautiful and ecologically diverse place the Palmetto State is. With admittedly low expectations, friend Aaron Marable and I backpacked the Buncombe Loop, located in the Sumter National Forest's Enoree District. The area, near Newberry, was simply a place halfway between our two homes at the time. That three-night trip blew me away. I still remember the fall colors shining over Flannigan Branch, the other creeks flowing over wide rock slabs, the majestic pines backed against a crystalline sky. Then and there I realized how much beauty the Palmetto State offers, from the mountains to the sea.

Off-and-on adventures preceded my next watershed moment. While writing a book titled *Long Trails of the Southeast*, I decided to include Foothills Trail, South Carolina's main mountain path. This time I had high expectations. And they were exceeded. I still maintain that Foothills Trail has the best 80 miles of track in the entire Southeast. It is that good. Later, while writing *The Best in Tent Camping: Carolinas*, I systematically explored the Palmetto State and found destinations aplenty. During the research, paddling, and writing of *Paddling South Carolina*, still other gorgeous South Carolina scenes were revealed, adding to the mosaic of superlative scenery found in this southern slice of Heaven. Inspired by all this beauty, I longed for others with whom to share it. I pitched the idea for this guidebook; then, using my background in the Palmetto State, I began systematically exploring South Carolina for all of its best hikes. It was a real pleasure (most of the time) to travel the trails of South Carolina, from the quiet Blackstock Passage of the Palmetto Trail, to busy Mountain Bridge Wilderness, to the wetlands of Santee Coastal Reserve. Not all the hikes I made were included here. Along the way I found some unexpected joys—Hospital Rock, for one, pleasantly surprised this grizzled veteran. And to update this book, adding new exciting hikes, has been an honor and a joy. And with the joy of completing a book and the sadness of an adventure ended, I finished my additional research. But I will continue putting my lessons to work, enjoying more of South Carolina in future outdoor adventures.

THE MOUNTAINS OF UPSTATE ARE OFTEN CLOAKED IN GRANITE

# Introduction

This book details 50 of South Carolina's best hikes, from Opossum Falls near the Georgia state line to Huntington Beach State Park on the Atlantic Ocean—and all across the state between. Specific emphasis was placed on the most scenic destinations and unique places that make South Carolina so special—spots like the Chattooga River, Congaree National Park, and Hunting Island. In addition, South Carolina has two long trails, the Foothills and the Palmetto. Foothills Trail traverses the mountain corner of the state, while Palmetto Trail is slated to head from the Southern Appalachians, through the Midlands, to the Atlantic Ocean. Many hikes in this book include parts of these two trails. South Carolina offers three distinct regions in which to trek: the Upstate, Midlands, and Lowcountry. I have included hikes covering all three areas, of assorted lengths and difficulties, to add to the variety of experiences. Sometimes you feel like going on a rugged hike; other times, an easy stroll will do. Time constraints, companions, and time of year are just some of the considerations when choosing a hike. Grandma is not going to feel like fording remote rivers. A weekend backpack with your old Scout buddy, on the other hand, will likely entail more challenging terrain.

Many hikes take place in South Carolina's national forests—the Sumter and Francis Marion. These federal lands span portions of the entire state. The Sumter includes mountain highlands and rolling piedmont, while the Francis Marion offers coastal terrain. These forests boast not only hiking trails but also campgrounds, waterways to float and fish, special scenic areas, botanical areas, hunting, and more. South Carolina state parks and forests also dot the landscape and are destinations for those who want to explore. Table Rock State Park harbors a famous state landmark. Santee State Park makes the most of its setting and offers recreation of all stripes, including, of course, hiking. Edisto Beach State Park has oceanside palms and maritime woods. These are but three examples of a fine state park system of which South Carolinians should be proud.

No matter what entity manages the land, there is plenty to see in this state, from old gold mines, to dramatic falls where whitewater is framed by rich forests, to rock outcroppings where panoramic views extend from high peaks, to dark swamps where nature's beasts find retreat. You must reach these places by foot. The rewards increase with every footfall beneath stately pines on a sunny knoll, or within deep gorges where waterfalls roar, or along the flats of a waterfowl-laden wetland. A retreat into the "real" South Carolina will revitalize both mind and spirit. Climbing a rock slab overlook, contemplating pioneer lives at an old homesite, or peering into a cypress swamp will put your life in perspective.

That's where this book can come into play. It will help you make every step count, whether you're leading the family on a brief day hike or undertaking a challenging backpack into the back-of-beyond. Your time is precious, and the knowledge imparted to you here will allow you to realize your outdoor experience to its fullest.

This book includes many classic South Carolina treks, such as Ellicott Rock and Big Bend Falls. Many others, however, are off the beaten path, offering more solitude as you travel toward lesser-known yet equally scenic sights, such as Tates Trail in the Carolina Sandhills and Dungannon Plantation Wildlife Area. This will give you the opportunity to get back to nature on your own terms.

Two types of day hikes are offered: there-and-backs and loops. One-way hikes lead to a particular rewarding destination, returning via the same trail. The return trip allows you to see everything from the opposite vantage point. You may notice more minute trailside features on the second go-round, and returning at a different time of day may give the same trail a surprisingly different character. Still, for some hikers, returning on the same trail just isn't as enjoyable. Many can't bear the thought of covering the same ground twice, given the miles of South Carolina trails awaiting them. The loop hikes help hikers avoid this. Most offer solitude to maximize the experience, though, by necessity, portions of some hikes traverse popular areas.

Day-hiking is the most popular way to explore South Carolina's trails, but for those with the inclination, this book also details some of the best locales for overnight stays, allowing you to see the cycle of the backcountry turn from day to night and back again. Backpackers should follow park regulations where applicable and practice "Leave No Trace" wilderness-use etiquette.

The wilderness experience can unleash your mind and body, allowing you to relax and find peace and quiet. It also enables you to grasp beauty and splendor: an overlook with a window to the wooded valley below, a bobcat disappearing into a thicket, a live oak hill marking an old homestead. In these lands, you can let your mind roam free, going where it pleases. So get out and enjoy the treasures of the Palmetto State.

# How to Use This Book

The 50 hikes in this book are divided into three basic areas: Upstate, Midlands, and Lowcountry. Each hike is contained in its own chapter. An information box is included at the opening of each description. Following the hike name you'll find its total distance, hiking time, vertical rise, and maps. Like this:

# Awendaw Passage of the Palmetto Trail

**TOTAL DISTANCE**: 8.4 miles round trip

**HIKING TIME**: 4.5 hours

**VERTICAL RISE**: 20 feet

**RATING**: Moderate

**MAPS**: USGS 7.5' Awendaw; Awendaw Passage of the Palmetto Trail; Francis Marion National Forest

**TRAILHEAD GPS COORDINATES**: N33° 1.795', W79° 36.179'

**CONTACT INFORMATION**: Sumter National Forest, 112 Andrew Pickens Circle, Mt. Rest, SC 29664, (864) 638-9568, www.fs.usda.gov/main/scnfs

From the box, you can discern that the hike is 8.4 miles long. In determining distance, I walked (and in many cases rewalked) every hike in this guidebook using a Global Positioning System (GPS) tracker. You may notice discrepancies between the distances given in this book and those listed on trailhead signs, in other books, or in the literature distributed by the governing bodies administering the trails. Sometimes trail distance is passed down from one government body to the next until, eventually, no one knows where it came from. The same goes for trail signs. I have full confidence in the mileages given in this book, since I obtained them myself from my own hiking—field experience, if you will—with GPS in hand. Distances to the destination are given from the trailhead, not from the parking area.

This example is a there-and-back hike, meaning that you walk to the destination, then return to the trailhead on the same footway. Other hikes are loops or end-to-ends. An end-to-end hike requires an auto shuttle between the ends, whereas there-and-back and loop hikes start and end at the same trailhead.

The hiking time listed here is 4.5 hours. I based all these times on the actual hours spent on the trail by an average hiker, plus a little time for orientation and breaks. These times are intended to be a baseline from which you can plan your trek; actual times will of course be different for each hiker and hiking group. Before taking on a trip, think about the physical fitness levels of your group members, the rest times desired, and eating and drinking breaks, as well as relaxing and contemplating-nature breaks; work all of these into your projected hiking schedule.

The vertical rise of our sample hike is 20 feet—inconsequential. However, for other hikes—especially in the Upstate—vertical rise is an important consideration. Vertical rise is calculated as the largest uphill vertical change during the hike. It may come anywhere along the hike, and not necessarily on the first climb from the trailhead. It is not the sum of all climbs during the hike. I obtained vertical rise figures from my elevation profiles, which I in turn derived by plotting the GPS tracks I created while on the hike onto a mapping program.

This hike is rated moderate, what with its minimal elevation change and the fact that it's a well-marked and well-maintained trail that is easy to follow. Hikes can be given ratings ranging from easy to moderate to difficult. The difficulty rating is based on the following factors: trail length; overall trail condition, including maintenance; trail followability; and elevation changes. Longer, rougher hikes with large elevation changes will be rated difficult. By contrast, a short, level, and well-marked nature trail, such as the Ion Swamp Interpretive Walk, is rated easy.

The "Maps" entry informs you of maps that could be used for the hike, in addition to the one provided in this book. The first map or maps mentioned are the United States Geological Survey 7.5' quadrangle maps. These "quad maps," as they are known, cover every parcel of land in this country. They are divided into highly detailed rectangular sections. Each quad has a name, usually based on a physical feature located within the quad. In this case the hike traverses one quad map: Awendaw. Quad maps can be obtained online at www .usgs.gov. Next, other helpful maps are

included. In this case the Awendaw Passage of the Palmetto Trail map will be useful, as well as the Francis Marion National Forest map. Other hike descriptions may list more detailed maps of wilderness areas, or state park hiking trail maps. All can supplement the map included here—but you will find the book map sufficient. I created these maps by interfacing the GPS tracks I made for each hike onto a mapping program. Many governing bodies and organizations offer online trail maps. In this case you can download the pertinent map for this hike from the Palmetto Trail website, www.palmettoconserva tion.org.

"Trailhead GPS Coordinates" gives you the latitude and longitude of the trailhead location. Therefore you can simply punch the coordinates into your navigational phone or GPS and reach the trailhead. However, readers can easily access all trailheads in this book by using the directions given. But for those who wish to navigate via GPS, the necessary data has been provided.

"Contact Information" gives you mailing addresses, phone numbers, and Internet resources to help you learn more about the hike, should your curiosity extend beyond what is given in the book, or if you desire information about the destination beyond the scope of hiking.

Following the information box is an overview of the hike. This paragraph or two gives you an overall feel for what to expect, what you might see, trail conditions, or any important information you might need to consider before undertaking the hike, such as permits needed, river fords, or challenging driving conditions. "Getting There," which follows the hike overview, offers detailed directions from a known and identifiable starting point to the trailhead. Finally, "The Trail" is the meat and bones of the trek—a running narrative that gives detailed descriptions of the trails used in the hike, including trail junctions, stream crossings, and interesting bits of human or natural history along the way. This keeps you apprised of your whereabouts as well as making sure you don't miss the trail's most critical and interesting features. With the information included in this guide, you can enjoy a better-informed, better-executed hike, making the most of your precious time.

## WHAT IT'S LIKE—HIKING SOUTH CAROLINA

It's the quiet of the Wadboo Swamp broken by a white-tailed deer;

It's walking Stevens Creek Trail in a misty rain;

It's watching snow fall from Foothills Trail on Sassafras Mountain;

It's gaining views of green forestlands from Tamassee Knob;

It's fording Stillhouse Branch and noticing the crystalline clarity of the water;

It's Turkey Creek reflecting the green density of the forest;

It's smelling the damp, rich soil of Ion Swamp;

It's listening to King Creek Falls echo off stone walls;

It's looking out on the Broad River from a former railroad bridge;

It's the sheer numbers of hikers at Caw Caw Interpretive Center on a spring Saturday;

It's imagining the Revolutionary War clash at Blackstock Battlefield;

It's backpacking the entire Swamp Fox Passage of the Palmetto Trail;

It's being eaten up by mosquitoes at Santee Coastal Reserve;

It's being awed by the massive trees at Congaree National Park;

It's traveling the maze of trails at Dungannon Plantation;

It's feeling infinitely sore from hiking while camped near Chattooga River;

It's absorbing the raw power of Big Bend Falls;

It's trying to identify the pines while at Cheraw State Park;

It's wondering if you can get any hotter on Tates Trail on a scorching afternoon;

It's looking out on barren winter trees from Governors Rock;

It's strolling amid cathedral cypress and gum trees along Cedar Creek;

It's watching the fall colors reflect off Lake Marion on a calm evening;

It's eating lunch on the bench overlooking tidal Scotts Creek;

It's reading the interpretive information on Old Santee Canal Loop;

It's identifying delicate spring wildflowers on the Saluda River;

It's being disheartened at trash left by thoughtless hikers;

It's passing an old hardscrabble homestead and wondering what life was like back then;

It's missing Chattooga River Trail as it turns off an old roadbed;

It's the constant birdsong along South Edisto River;

It's seeing the ruggedness of the Rim of Gap Trail;

It's falling asleep to a mountain stream while snug in your sleeping bag;

It's seeing tree after tree after tree and appreciating them all;

It's being amazed by the rock walls and slabs of the Mountain Bridge Wilderness;

It's watching turkeys scatter on a wooded hill;

It's just being on a South Carolina trail.

## CONTACT INFORMATION

Francis Marion and Sumter National Forests
4931 Broad River Road
Columbia, SC 29212
(803) 561-4000
www.fs.usda.gov/main/scnfs

South Carolina State Parks
SC Department of Parks, Recreation & Tourism
1205 Pendleton Street
Columbia, SC 29201
(803) 734-0156
www.southcarolinaparks.com

Congaree National Park
100 National Park Road
Hopkins, SC 29061
(803) 776-4396
www.nps.gov/cong

Carolina Sandhills National Wildlife Refuge
23734 US Highway 1
McBee, SC 29101
(843) 335-8350
www.fws.gov/carolinasandhills

# I.

# UPSTATE

# Big Bend Falls via Big Bend Trail

**TOTAL DISTANCE**: 7.0 miles there-and-back

**HIKING TIME**: 4 hours

**VERTICAL RISE**: 380 feet

**RATING**: Moderate

**MAPS**: USGS 7.5' Tamassee; Sumter National Forest—Andrew Pickens District; Chattooga National Wild and Scenic River

**TRAILHEAD GPS COORDINATES**: N34° 56.478', W83° 5.390'

**CONTACT INFORMATION**: Sumter National Forest, 112 Andrew Pickens Circle, Mt. Rest, SC 29664, (864) 638-9568, www .fs.usda.gov/main/scnfs

This hike takes you from high and dry Chattooga Ridge to Big Bend, the most powerful falls in the Upstate. At this 30-foot waterfall, the entire Chattooga River musters its power, then drops loudly in ragged stages and in a frenzy of whitewater, finally slowing as it falls into a pool below. The name Big Bend comes from the 180-degree southeast-to-northwest turn the river makes upstream of this roaring demonstration of natural power. The walk starts near Cherry Hill Campground, in the Sumter National Forest, and descends from Chattooga Ridge, winding ever downward to reach a feeder branch of the Chattooga. Enter this moist environment, continuing downstream to meet Chattooga-Foothills Trail just upstream of Big Bend. Continue downstream, walking along the sharp slope of the river valley, passing rock bluffs and outcrops, switchbacking where the slope mandates it. Finally the roar of the waterfall lets you know it's there. Two very rough and challenging spur paths access different parts of the falls. The upper spur path passes under an impressive rockhouse, while the lower allows an up-close view of Big Bend Falls.

## GETTING THERE

From Walhalla, drive north on SC 28 for 8.5 miles to SC 107, then turn right. Follow SC 107 for 8.5 miles. The trailhead is on the gravel pull-off on your right, just before the right turn into Cherry Hill Campground. Big Bend Trail starts on the left side of the road, in the woods and opposite the gravel trailhead parking area. Winding Stairs Trail starts on the same side of the road as the gravel parking area.

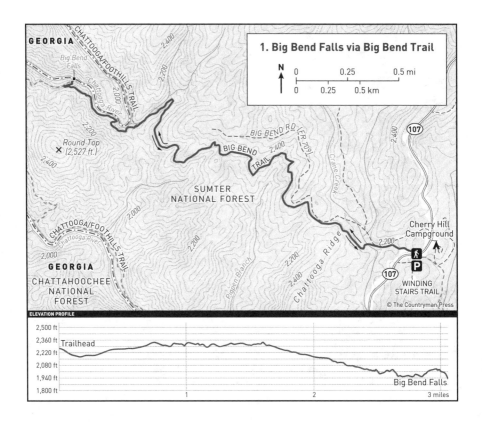

## THE TRAIL

Leave the SC 107 trailhead and head west, crossing the paved road. (You can bag two hikes at once from this trailhead; see Hike 13.) Begin descending into an intermittent tributary of Crane Creek. Enter shady woods, coming near gravel Forest Road 709, Big Bend Road. Crane Creek is falling loudly to your left. You are heading upstream along Crane Creek. Pass a few warm-up cascades, mere drops compared with what awaits you. Notice the large white pines towering overhead in this valley. Cross Crane Creek on a footbridge at 0.2 mile. Large white pines are especially prevalent here. Continue upstream, then away from Crane Creek, reaching a gap

in Chattooga Ridge. You are now in the Chattooga River watershed. The forest road has cut through this gap, too.

Big Bend Trail now curves into a sharply sloped hollow where tall mountain laurel shades the path. The laurel's crooked arms and spindly trunks look like props for a horror movie. Cross an intermittent branch on a footbridge. The trail is skirting the uppermost part of the Pigpen Branch drainage, which flows into the Chattooga miles downstream from Big Bend Falls. Continue winding around hollows feeding Pigpen Branch, divided by drier ridgelines in oak-dominated woods, with some pine. One ridgeline in particular, which you will cross at 1.3 miles, is rife with beard cane. Young pines also grow here.

BIG BEND FALLS

After the beard cane, enter a deeply incised hollow with a footbridge crossing the intermittent stream. Look for another big white pine at the bridge. Notice how the tree divides into twin trunks about 15 feet up, reaching high into the sky. The trail bisects an old road leading from Big Bend Road along a ridge down toward the river. An old fishermen's survey box is located up the road. Begin curving into the immediate Chattooga Valley; even through the trees you can get a sense of this valley's size and depth. A steady descent ensues, and the path passes another straight-line shot to the river. This trail comes from the end of Big Bend Road. Big Bend Trail takes an easier and less jarring route to the river as it dips into a feeder branch of the Chattooga. The feeder stream makes a much different sound from the low roar of the Chattooga below. Reach the feeder stream and rock-hop, then immediately cross the stream a second time on a footbridge built by Girl Scouts in 2004. The forest is lush overhead. The valley tightens, forcing the branch to tumble over cascades just before you reach a trail junction at 2.7 miles. Here Foothills Trail is making its trek up the Chattooga Valley, bridging the stream you've been following. A sliding cascade noisily heads toward the river just below a footbridge at the junction. Stay left here, not crossing the plank bridge over the stream, and you will shortly pass the unmaintained trail coming from Big Bend Road.

Travel along the Chattooga on Foothills Trail, reaching some switchbacks that work above rough rock bluffs, unseen through the rhododendron below you. The river descends loudly in several ledges. The trail is on the sloped mountainside, curving in and out of little hollows, bordered by classic mountain beauty of Fraser magnolia, black birch, and other moisture-tolerant Southern Appalachian species. Negotiate the last two downward switchbacks before coming to the falls—this is your second set of switchbacks. The roar of the falls becomes clearly audible at 3.0 miles. Your last steps before the spur trails to the falls will be over rock, going downward.

The first spur trail heads down and to the right, leading to the upper drop.

It eventually passes under a large rockhouse with many fallen boulders at its base. When it rains, water flows and drips down the inner side of the rockhouse, though there are a couple of areas where you can stay dry. If you want to view the upper part of the drop, the last stretch leads down over slippery rocks, so be careful. The convergence of the river into the main chute is easily visible from here, as is the initial drop.

The "trail" to the base of the falls is more difficult. From Foothills Trail, it leads slightly left and down through rhododendrons, then beside a trickling branch, then over a ledge to reach an open rock mere feet from the falls. Mist drifts in the air as you gaze up at the river dropping into the swirling catch basin of the falls. Standing here will teach you to respect and understand the power of water. The nexus of gravity and water is the essence of Big Bend Falls. The falls drop at once across the river, then morph into a jumble of whitewater, pinched in by boulders, to regroup in a swirl below. Be careful around this powerful display.

# Ellicott Rock via East Fork Chattooga

**TOTAL DISTANCE**: 8.2 miles round trip

**HIKING TIME**: 4l hours

**VERTICAL RISE**: 450 feet

**RATING**: Moderate to difficult

**MAPS**: USGS 7.5' Tamassee, Cashiers (NC); Sumter National Forest—Andrew Pickens District; Ellicott Rock Wilderness, Chattooga National Wild and Scenic River

**TRAILHEAD GPS COORDINATES**: N34° 59.155', W83° 4.322'

**CONTACT INFORMATION**: Sumter National Forest, 112 Andrew Pickens Circle, Mt. Rest, SC 29664, (864) 638-9568, www .fs.usda.gov/main/scnfs

This hike combines human and natural history into one fine trek. Start at Walhalla State Fish Hatchery, first built by the Civilian Conservation Corps (CCC) in the 1930s, to enter the Ellicott Rock Wilderness, then head down the rugged East Fork Chattooga River Gorge, passing waterfalls and an immense rock bluff before you reach its confluence with the Chattooga River. Here the trek turns north and travels along the wild and scenic river. Circle Bad Creek and return to the Chattooga on a tough track, gaining up-close looks at the river, where gravel bars and sand beaches form. Rocks, thick vegetation, and uneven terrain make it a challenge to reach Ellicott Rock. This rock, insignificant in its own right, forms the border where the states of South Carolina, North Carolina, and Georgia meet. Here you can clamber down to the streamside where, back in 1812, Andrew Ellicott etched the exact boundary in stone while surveying the Carolinas. Interestingly, Ellicott helped survey the capital city of Washington, DC, the western boundary of Pennsylvania, and "Ellicott's Line," which divides Alabama from Florida at 31 degrees north. His final act for our country was surveying the border between Canada and the western United States, at 45 degrees north. Part of the border between South Carolina and Georgia follows 35 degrees north. Ol' Ellicott really got around. Also look for Commissioners Rock, etched just a few feet away, which was a resurvey. On your return trip you will doubtless see more exceptional beauty on display alongside these streams. While you're here, visit the hatchery to see the trout of varying sizes in their rearing ponds. And bring a picnic—the hatchery has a nice picnic area, along with a stone picnic shelter also built by the CCC. The hatchery is

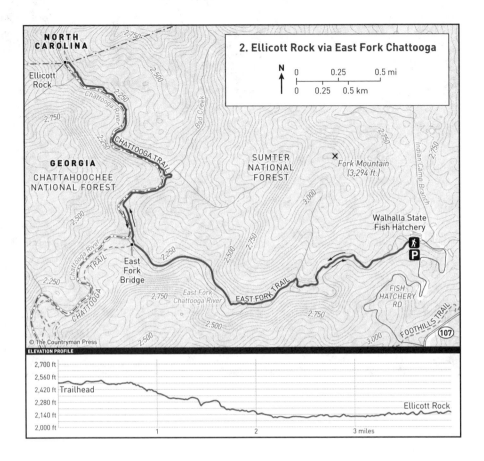

The map shows "2. Ellicott Rock via East Fork Chattooga" with an elevation profile below.

NORTH CAROLINA

Ellicott Rock

GEORGIA

CHATTAHOOCHEE NATIONAL FOREST

CHATTOOGA TRAIL

Chattooga River

Bad Creek

SUMTER NATIONAL FOREST

× Fork Mountain (3,294 ft.)

Indian Camp Branch

Walhalla State Fish Hatchery

East Fork Bridge

CHATTOOGA TRAIL

East Fork Chattooga River

EAST FORK TRAIL

FISH HATCHERY RD

FOOTHILLS TRAIL

107

© The Countryman Press

**ELEVATION PROFILE**

2,700 ft
2,560 ft
2,420 ft — Trailhead
2,280 ft
2,140 ft
2,000 ft

Ellicott Rock

1          2          3 miles

open daily from 8 a.m. to 4 p.m., except for Christmas Day and inclement winter weather.

## GETTING THERE

From the intersection of SC 11 and SC 28 just east of Walhalla, take SC 28 west for 9.5 miles to SC 107. Turn right onto SC 107 and follow it for 11.7 miles to Fish Hatchery Road. Turn left and follow Fish Hatchery Road for 1.7 miles to the hatchery, veering left toward general parking.

## THE TRAIL

From the general parking lot, follow a paved path leading past the restrooms.

The hike soon follows a wooden boardwalk with a side trail leading right to the hatchery. The main trail stays left. At the end of the wooden part of the trail, a footpath goes left, soon leading to the stone-and-wood CCC shelter; the paved path leading forward heads to a wheelchair angling access on the East Fork Chattooga and picnic tables. Note the sturdy yet attractive picnic shelter, with a large stone fireplace inside.

The trail enters Ellicott Rock Wilderness. Wind amidst tall trees to reach a large wooden bridge spanning the East Fork soon. Travel through fern-floored woods, then climb a bit to reach a side trail leading sharply downhill to a waterfall. These falls make a 5-foot, river-wide

COMMISSIONERS ROCK IS JUST A FEW FEET AWAY FROM ELLICOTT ROCK

drop into a plunge pool that would make a nice dunking spot in summer. Back on the hike, the trail—at the same spot as the spur to the waterfall—has now joined a wide old roadbed coming in from your right. At this point, both the trail and the river begin their descent into East Fork Chattooga Gorge. Below you, the East Fork is carving its way down, in falls, cascades, and rapids. The trail begins circling in and out of hollows, passing a drip cascade where the low-flow stream-let drips over a rock face. You get a good view of the cascade from an elaborate footbridge with handrails spanning the watercourse.

Gain views of the East Fork before the path turns into an interesting hollow. The track now crosses a slide cascade on concrete steps that cross the middle of the slide. Note the small falls just upstream of the slide. Ahead, leave the roadbed, aiming for the river in lush woods. Reach an overhanging bluff beside the stream at 1.5 miles. This rock face is slightly overhanging, yet vegetation clings to the cracks. The now narrower trail climbs briefly, then makes an uneven descent, as does the East Fork. The river drops, and the trail chases it downward, all amidst South-ern Appalachian woodland beauty. Drift through rhododendron tunnels, then come alongside the river near a rock slab at 2.2 miles. In the middle of the slab, you'll see an old bridge foundation. The rest of the footbridge was washed away by flooding. Keep moving forward to meet Chattooga Trail at 2.4 miles; a high wooden bridge with handrails leads left to a camping flat. Consider going over there and making your way to the confluence of the two streams, where the rocky and fast-moving East Fork meets the slower Chattooga at the lower end of a long pool. Rapids flow downstream just below the confluence.

This hike, however, keeps forward at the bridge, joining the northbound portion of Chattooga Trail, passing another flat, this one closed to camping for regeneration. Turn north, upstream along the Chattooga, traveling along this strangely silent mountain pool. Doghobble, mountain laurel, and rhododendron crowd the trail, as do rock ledges. Swing into a flat, circling the stream to rock-hop Bad Creek at 3.1 miles. Curve back toward the Chattooga. Note the campsite here; a large, flat rock extending into the Chattooga makes for a good hanging-out spot.

Be careful in the maze of paths around Bad Creek. Chattooga Trail climbs away from the creek and continues up the river, picking up an old roadbed to return soon to the river's edge after passing through a deep, dark rhododendron tunnel. The riverside scenes vary as the river is broken up by islands, shoals, big boulders, gravel bars, and pools in a swirling mosaic of beauty. White pine towers over magnolia, birch, and the ever-present rhododendron, galax, and moss. In places, the trail crosses muddy seeps and tiny feeder streams. The trail, since it's in the wilderness, is managed more lightly; logs left unremoved can become obstacles that may have a cut in them to allow for easier passage.

Come along the river's edge, passing washed-out spots. Cross a small branch on a wooden bridge. Take note here, as Ellicott Rock is not far away. At 4.1 miles you'll reach Ellicott Rock, which is marked with a sign and, sometimes, surveyor's tape. When you get there, you'll wonder where the rock is—there is no significant rock around. Scramble down a mossy, slick slab bordered with rhododendron to the rapids. At the water's edge, you'll see Ellicott's carved inscription, NC. Just downstream, above the water, Commissioners Rock, also carved, states LAT 35, AD 1813, NC + SC.

# Ellicott Rock Wilderness Loop

**TOTAL DISTANCE**: 19.3-mile loop

**HIKING TIME**: 10 hours

**VERTICAL RISE**: 900 feet

**RATING**: Difficult

**MAPS**: USGS 7.5' Tamassee, Cashiers (NC); Sumter National Forest—Andrew Pickens District; Ellicott Rock Wilderness

**TRAILHEAD GPS COORDINATES**: N34° 58.210', W83° 6.918'

**CONTACT INFORMATION**: Sumter National Forest, 112 Andrew Pickens Circle, Mt. Rest, SC 29664, (864) 638-9568, www .fs.usda.gov/main/scnfs

This rugged and scenic loop travels through South Carolina's largest federally designated wilderness. Ellicott Rock Wilderness, located in the corner where the state meets North Carolina and Georgia, has an everywhere-you-look beauty complemented by the superlative scenery of the wild and scenic Chattooga River. You'll leave the Burrells Ford parking area to head upstream along the Chattooga, meeting the East Fork Chattooga River. Continue along the main river to reach the wilderness's namesake, Ellicott Rock. Leave the river gorge along Fork Mountain Trail, traversing piney ridgelines and deep, rich hollows to emerge near SC 107. Here you'll join South Carolina's main mountain path, Foothills Trail, and head south along the East Fork Chattooga, passing several waterfalls, before making Medlin Mountain, on which you'll find your ridge-running return route to Burrells Ford. Backpack campsites are numerous in the river gorge and somewhat scattered out on the rest of the loop, though the last part of the hike has the fewest overnighting options.

## GETTING THERE

From the intersection of SC 11 and SC 28 just east of Walhalla, drive west on SC 28 for 9.5 miles to SC 107, then turn right. Follow SC 107 for 8.9 miles to Forest Road 708. Descend on gravel FR 708 for 2.3 miles. The Burrells Ford parking area will be on your left. The hike starts near the signboard on the south side of the parking area.

## THE TRAIL

Leave the parking area beyond the kiosk. Foothills Trail splits: You head left, immediately crossing FR 708, then

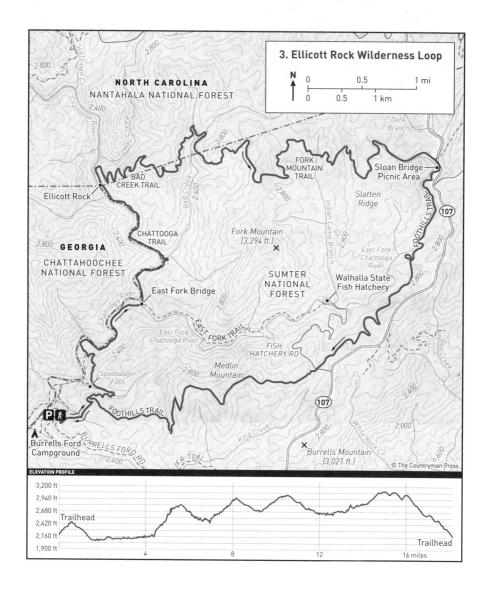

**3. Ellicott Rock Wilderness Loop**

ELEVATION PROFILE

switchbacking up through a dry forest to meet a small stream above a low-flow, 40-foot waterfall over a rock face at 0.4 mile. Squeeze past a fallen rock to reach a trail junction at 0.6 mile. Here Foothills and Chattooga Trails part ways.

Stay forward as Foothills Trail leaves right; this is your return route. Begin winding toward a small stream. A small campsite is along the stream at 1.0 mile, in a perched flat. Beyond, the

trail slices down along with the creek through a tight gorge, then it curves into the greater Chattooga Valley. The single-track courses along a steep-sided mountain after leaving the creek, crosses an old roadbed, and then dips off the ridgeline to reach a large, heavily used camping flat at 2.1 miles. To your left, the roadbed at the base of the flat leads about 15 minutes downstream to Spoonauger Falls. A spur trail leads to

FALLEN RHODODENDRON BLOOM BESIDE EAST FORK

the actual falls, along a small unnamed stream. The spur trail is 200 yards and ascends via many switchbacks.

Leave the giant flat. Follow the single-track path upstream, gaining river views, to reach another roadbed. Pick up the roadbed and curve along the Chattooga about 30 or so feet above. The trail stays on the roadbed well above the river. Curve around and you can see the large flat of the East Fork on your left. The trail soon enters the flat amid tall white pines and reaches a large camping area. Just ahead, at 2.7 miles, a large wooden footbridge crosses East Fork Chattooga. East Fork Trail leads 2.4 miles right to Walhalla State Fish Hatchery.

Turn left beyond the bridge, joining the northbound portion of Chattooga Trail, passing another flat, this one closed to camping for regeneration. Keep north along the Chattooga. Doghobble, mountain laurel, and rhododendron crowd the trail, as do rock ledges. Swing into a camping flat and rock-hop Bad Creek at 3.4 miles. Chattooga Trail climbs away from the creek, and then it returns to the river's edge. Enjoy the variety of scenery the Chattooga offers. White pine towers over magnolia, birch, and the ever-present rhododendron, galax, and moss. In places the trail crosses muddy seeps and tiny feeder streams. The trail, since it's in the wilderness, is managed less intensively; logs left unremoved can become obstacles. You may have to work around or over them.

Cross a small branch on a wooden bridge. Take note here, as Ellicott Rock is not far away. At 4.4 miles you'll reach Ellicott Rock, marked with a sign and sometimes surveyor's tape. Scramble down a mossy, slick rock slab, bordered with rhododendron, to rapids. At the water's edge you will see Ellicott's carved inscription, NC. Just downstream is Commissioners Rock, also carved: LAT 35, AD 1813, NC + SC.

Enter North Carolina. Chattooga Trail technically ends in the last camping flat at 4.5 miles. The hard-to-find Ellicott Rock Trail comes in from a ford across the river. The hike now joins Bad Creek Trail, which begins switchbacking right, up the ridgeline of Fork Mountain. River sounds fade. White pines and oaks begin to dominate. Crest out after a 500-foot climb to make a junction at 5.7 miles. Here Bad Creek Trail keeps forward to reach Bull Pen Road. This loop turns acutely right to join Fork Mountain Trail, a favorite of mine with its big trees, rich coves, immense rhododendron and laurel thickets, and true wilderness aura. Shortly you'll pass the state line again, back into South Carolina. Galax is prominent in the dry woods, which stand between moist coves. Bad Creek becomes audible below; then the trail turns abruptly right, leaving an old roadbed-cum-campsite, to cross rhododendron-choked Bad Creek at 6.8 miles. Curve away from this cool green watershed to soon reach another dark cove and feeder branch of Bad Creek. A small campsite lies here, too.

Rise to drier woods, passing a large trailside tulip tree at 7.7 miles. Pass through laurel thickets before reaching the crest of Fork Mountain at 8.5 miles. A camping flat without water is located here. The well-graded path begins winding toward Indian Camp Branch, entering a grove of large white pines and some tulip trees before reaching Indian Camp Branch and a quiet campsite at 9.7 miles. Fork Mountain Trail continues winding through scenic coves and piney flats, rising to meet Slatten Ridge, dividing Indian Camp Branch from Slatten Branch, at 10.7 miles. This oak crest is 3,005 feet. From here the trail drops into Slatten Branch and its unbelievable rhododendron thickets, where you and the creek tunnel to reach SC 107 at 12.0 miles. Turn right here, crossing East Fork Chattooga River on the road to reach Sloans Bridge Picnic Area.

Foothills Trail is coming in on the far side of the picnic area. Stay right here, joining the white blazes. A campsite is on your right at 12.3 miles, but traffic from 107 is audible. Just ahead, begin looking for side trails dropping to waterfalls along the East Fork. Some falls are wide with deep pools, others are tall, but all are worth the side trips. Eventually the Chattooga drops faster than the trail, which stays along the west slope of Persimmon Mountain. At 12.9 miles you'll cross under a power line just after passing a pretty multitiered waterfall above a footbridge. Ahead, split a gap at 13.5 miles, then wind through small coves to cross Fish Hatchery Road at 15.3 miles.

Foothills Trail begins curving westerly atop Medlin Mountain, cloaked in hickory, pine, and mountain laurel. Leave the ridgecrest at 17.0 miles, making three wide switchbacks. Begin winding in and out of small hollows, then head down the nose of the ridge before meeting Chattooga Trail at 18.7 miles. Backtrack 0.6 mile to the Burrells Ford trailhead, completing your loop.

# Foothills Trail Vistas via Sassafras Mountain

---

**TOTAL DISTANCE**: 9.4 miles round trip

---

**HIKING TIME**: 5.5 hours

---

**VERTICAL RISE**: 1,000 feet

---

**RATING**: Moderate to difficult

---

**MAPS**: USGS 7.5' Eastatoe Gap, Table Rock; Foothills Trail, Jim Timmerman Natural Resources Area at Jocassee Gorges

---

**TRAILHEAD GPS COORDINATES**: N35° 3.863', W82° 46.552'

---

**CONTACT INFORMATION**: Jocassee Gorges, 1344 Cleo Chapman Hwy, Sunset, SC 29685, (864) 868-0281, www.dnr.sc.gov

---

This hike begins near the crest of South Carolina's highest peak, Sassafras Mountain, at 3,554 feet. While you're at it, you can walk a short distance to reach the high point from the trailhead, travel a bit more to grab a view from a rock, then return to the trailhead and begin your hike southeastward on Foothills Trail. South Carolina's master path will take you past the highland home of an early settler before gradually dipping to reach the historic Emory Gap Toll Road. Your next historic venture will be finding a rockhouse used by Civil War draft dodgers. Be apprised that this rockhouse is hard to find, but findable. Follow this old toll road a short way to pass a stream flowing over sheer rock, making a fall below. A view opens to your right. Pass through a giant boulder field before reaching an old jeep road. To your right, a huge rock slab and a grand vista open to the south and west. Drawbar Cliffs, which offers another vista, is 0.5 mile from the first rock slab vista described in this narrative.

## GETTING THERE

From Pickens, take US 178 north to SC 11. Keep forward on SC 11 for 7.2 miles to Rocky Bottom and F. Van Clayton Memorial Highway, a two-lane paved road. Turn right onto Clayton Memorial Highway and follow it for 4.7 miles to the parking area on your left. The proper section of Foothills Trail begins 150 feet back down the road you drove up. Do not take the blue-blazed Foothills Spur Trail, which begins directly across from the parking area.

## THE TRAIL

Before starting the main hike, consider hiking Foothills Trail beyond the gate

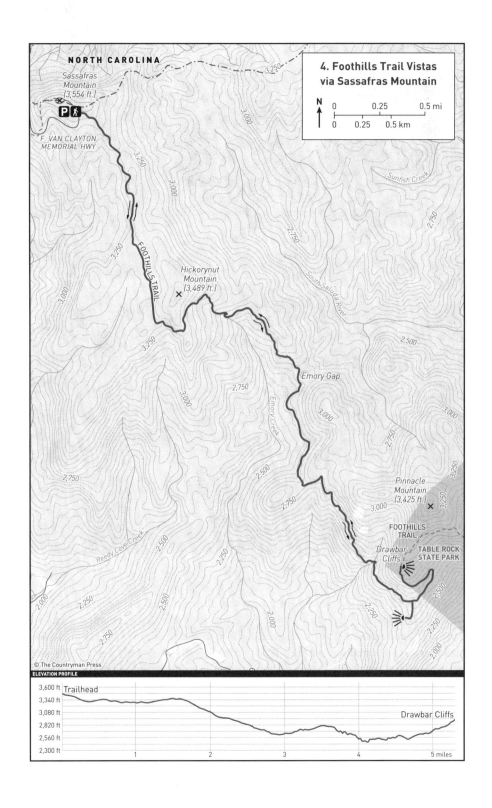

**NORTH CAROLINA**

Sassafras
Mountain
(3,554 ft.)

F. VAN CLAYTON
MEMORIAL HWY

FOOTHILLS TRAIL

Hickorynut
Mountain
(3,489 ft.)

Sunfish Creek

South Saluda River

Emory Creek

Emory Gap

Reedy Cove Creek

Pinnacle
Mountain
(3,425 ft.)

FOOTHILLS
TRAIL

Drawbar
Cliffs

**TABLE ROCK
STATE PARK**

© The Countryman Press

**4. Foothills Trail Vistas
via Sassafras Mountain**

N

| 0 | 0.25 | 0.5 mi |
| 0 | 0.25 | 0.5 km |

ELEVATION PROFILE

3,600 ft — Trailhead
3,340 ft
3,080 ft
2,820 ft — Drawbar Cliffs
2,560 ft
2,300 ft

1    2    3    4    5 miles

MASSIVE ROCK SLAB OPENS TO EMORY CREEK VALLEY

uphill and to your left. The crumbly asphalt track leads to the highest point of South Carolina. Just past the clearing that marks this summit, Foothills Trail continues to a spur trail leading right, heading toward a rock outcrop and vista looking west. Return to the trailhead and descend 150 feet back on the road, turning left onto the white-blazed Foothills Trail leading toward Table Rock State Park to begin the main hike. A nicely graded single-track path winds its way through a highland forest exceeding 3,000 feet. It's almost always cool up here, and often foggy. The trail makes a nice cruise while gently descending past outcrops, ferns, and many holly trees, generally on the west slope of the ridge it follows. Cross an old roadbed; the trail canopy now opens overhead, but is bordered by mountain laurel. At 1.1 miles, look right for the crumbled chimneys marking the homesite of early settler John L. Cantrell. He liked his summers cool and his winters brisk, up here at nearly 3,300 feet.

Continue past the reclaimed homesite-cum-campsite, entering remote woods, tunneling into an evergreen thicket. You will reach a drainage and a low point before climbing a bit. Leave the rhododendron and begin circling the crest of Hickorynut Mountain, bisecting Hickorynut Mountain Gap at 1.4 miles. Keep working around the mountain amid galax galore. Make a gradual descent, passing small rills, which feed Eastatoe Creek, which feeds the Keowee River, which in turn flows into the Savannah River to meet the Atlantic Ocean. And it all starts here, in South Carolina's highest of the high country.

Keep an irregular downhill on an attractive path, with obscured views to your right. You'll reach the southwest side of Emory Gap and the old Emory Gap Toll Road at 2.8 miles. This old toll road once crossed the mountains from Pickens County in South Carolina to Transylvania County, North Carolina. Trace this historic path down to a low point, then turn left and ascend some steps, leaving the toll road, back on a single-track path to bridge a small creek. A few steps lead up to an old logging track, which leaves right and curves around the mountain, climbing to an open cove before making the crest of a ridge and turning sharply left. Continue ascending and, at 3.5 miles, begin looking for an outcrop below the trail to your right. If you reach a bridge over a streamlet, you have gone too far. Before the bridge, the faintest of paths leads right and downhill to Marion Castle's Rock House, which purportedly housed Civil War draft dodgers. The overhang is small, but its angled roof is covered with smoke from past fires and will likely show evidence of more recent use. After crossing the bridge beyond the rockhouse, Foothills Trail crosses Rockhouse Road, an old dirt track. Keep forward, resuming the descent on a steep slope. Pass over another footbridge, then climb past an audible waterfall off to your right. Ahead, at 4.2 miles, you cross the source of the waterfall, a small stream flowing over an open rock slab. Climb away from the stream, looking for a faint trail leading right to a small outcrop. The view opens to Emory Creek Valley below, with Rock Mountain in the distance. The waterfall is below to your right.

Continue on Foothills Trail, entering a world of giant boulders that have tumbled from Drawbar Cliffs above. Keep climbing, passing a campsite amid boulders, then reaching a roadbed in a grassy area at 4.6 miles. Here Foothills Trail makes an abrupt left. To reach the vista, turn right and follow an old, gravelly logging road downhill. Follow the roadbed a couple of hundred yards or so, looking for a short path opening to your right onto a huge rock slab bordered by pine trees. This sloping granite offers great views from the southwest to the northwest, across Horse Mountain to waves of ridges, down to Emory Creek and as far as the clarity of the sky allows into South Carolina. At your feet, notice the rock striations created by water flowing over the rock. The pines form an evergreen frame. To reach Drawbar Cliffs, backtrack to Foothills Trail and follow the path as it switchbacks to the left and uphill, still climbing to reach the cliffs in 0.4 mile, on your left, near the state park boundary.

# 5

# Hidden Falls

| | |
|---|---|
| **TOTAL DISTANCE**: 5.0 miles round trip | |
| **HIKING TIME**: 3 hours | |
| **VERTICAL RISE**: 400 feet | |
| **RATING**: Moderate | |
| **MAPS**: USGS 7.5' Walhalla, Tamassee; Sumter National Forest—Andrew Pickens District; Oconee State Park | |
| **TRAILHEAD GPS COORDINATES**: N34° 51.816', W83° 5.886' | |
| **CONTACT INFORMATION**: Oconee State Park, 624 State Park RD, Mountain Rest, SC 29664, (864) 638-5353, www.southcarolinaparks.com/oconee | |

Hidden Falls makes for a great day-hike destination and also gives a taste of the offerings that can be had along Foothills Trail, South Carolina's master path, which starts here at Oconee State Park. I recommend making this hike in spring, when the water flow will be at its highest. The trek leaves Oconee State Park, a classic Palmetto State getaway established in 1935, then traces Foothills Trail along Station Mountain. Leave the east flank of the mountain, working on a rib ridge that seems to have no water in it, then curve into a feeder branch of Tamassee Creek, where you reach the 60-foot cascade, a drop of a thousand drips, splashing across your viewing site.

## GETTING THERE

From Walhalla, drive north on SC 28 for 8.5 miles to SC 107. Turn right and follow SC 107 for 2.4 miles to the state park on your right. Enter the state park, then veer right, following signs for Foothills Trail. Pass the campground on your right and keep forward to reach a split in the road. Stay forward here, following the signs for Cabins 7–13. You will pass Foothills Trail on your left. The parking area is just around the corner from the trailhead, on your right.

## THE TRAIL

Backtrack a short distance on the road to Foothills Trail. A carved wooden map displays Foothills Trail in its entirety. Make sure to sign in at the self-registration board near the parking area. Begin the trail across the road from the parking area and enter pine-oak woods. Slightly ascend through pine-oak-hickory woods with an understory of blueberry and beard cane. The blueberries will be rip-

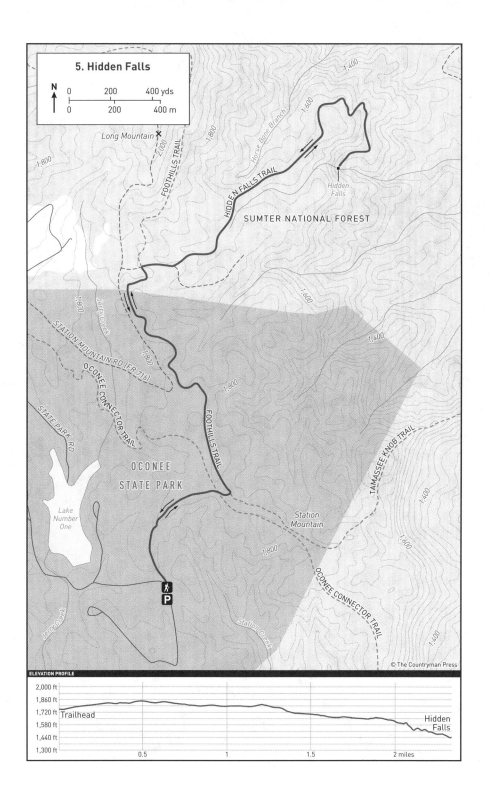

## 5. Hidden Falls

N

0    200    400 yds
0    200    400 m

Long Mountain ✗

FOOTHILLS TRAIL

Horse Bone Branch

HIDDEN FALLS TRAIL

Hidden Falls

SUMTER NATIONAL FOREST

Jerry Creek

STATION MOUNTAIN RD (FR 716)

OCONEE CONNECTOR TRAIL

STATE PARK RD

FOOTHILLS TRAIL

OCONEE STATE PARK

Lake Number One

TAMASSEE KNOB TRAIL

Station Mountain

OCONEE CONNECTOR TRAIL

Jerry Creek

Station Creek

P

© The Countryman Press

**ELEVATION PROFILE**

| | | | | |
|---|---|---|---|---|
| 2,000 ft | | | | |
| 1,860 ft | | | | |
| 1,720 ft | Trailhead | | | |
| 1,580 ft | | | | Hidden Falls |
| 1,440 ft | | | | |
| 1,300 ft | | | | |

0.5    1    1.5    2 miles

HIDDEN FALLS

ening in late June to early July. Work to reach the crest of Station Mountain. Two trail junctions are found at the crest. Here the Oconee Connector of Palmetto Trail is following the Station Mountain jeep track. Keep forward just a few more feet to reach a second junction where Foothills Trail cuts left and onward to Table Rock and Jones Gap State Parks. Tamassee Knob Trail heads east 1.6 miles to a vista, and it is detailed in this guidebook (see Hike 22).

On a personal note, I previously hiked the entire Foothills Trail solo, end-to-end, and remember being at this very spot. After a friend dropped me off at Oconee (I had left my car at Jones Gap State Park, 86 miles away), I got underway on the Foothills but stopped to check the weather on my portable radio. I thumbed through the dial until I got a clear signal. However, all broadcasts were being preempted by news reports of a plane hitting one of the Twin Towers in New York. Puzzled, I kept listening, and within 5 minutes I heard the live report of the second tower being hit. Radio mayhem followed, with wild reports, both true and untrue. I kept hiking as tears welled in my eyes and the bottom fell out of my gut. Comparing the reports with the near-perfect September day in the South Carolina mountains, I was reminded of the H. G. Wells "War of the Worlds" broadcast, the program that fooled so many listeners in the 1930s. But this was real. The reports just kept coming as I walked Foothills Trail. Three days passed before I saw another human being. It took 7 days to reach Jones Gap and my car, a day earlier than planned. Fear is a great motivator.

Back to the hike. Veer left at the junction and travel north around the headwaters of Tamassee Creek. The northeast flank of Station Mountain has a dry aspect, with many hickory trees and pines. But you will likely notice all the fat-trunked mountain laurel up here. The trail grades are moderate. Travel through a grove of planted pines, then hit a closed forest road and Hidden Falls Trail at 1.3 miles. This is the upper end of Forest Road 715, now closed. It used to connect with the forest road that ran up to the closed lookout tower on nearby Long Mountain.

Turn right onto the seeded roadbed, heading downhill just a short distance, then veer left into woods on a narrower path that open onto an attractive fern-floored flat. Cross over a branch—the trickling headwaters of the unnamed stream that creates Hidden Falls. The walking is easy in this perched valley, which you soon leave. Listen for the sounds of falling water on your right. A spur trail leads to an interesting warm-up waterfall. This one drips through rhododendron onto an angled rock slab, flows about 15 feet, then vanishes into the ground. I call it Disappearing Falls, a name that is complementary to Hidden Falls.

The streambed falls away as Hidden Falls Trail stays along a ridgeline that shows evidence of a several-years-old burn. Look for blackened trunks and skeletal mountain laurel. You begin to wonder where the trail is going—and if Hidden Falls truly is hidden, even from those who follow the trail supposedly leading to it. But keep pushing on, as the path delivers winter views from a knob you are circling. Tamassee Knob becomes visible to the south. Start dropping in oak woods with huger laurel trees. Then curve into a hollow. You begin to hear water falling. The fire evidence in this hollow is clear, with the even-aged understory vegetation covering the ground beneath straight-trunked tulip and oak trees. Reach the stream at the base of the falls at 2.5 miles. The low-flow falls spill over a rocky rim, make a straight drop onto a ledge, then make numerous courses over rock, in waterlines that drip and splash to end after 60 feet. In late summer and autumn, the waterfall can become a mere trickle.

On your return hike, consider walking the entire Foothills Trail, which may be the most unsung, underused, and underrated long trail in the Southeast. It traverses the Cherokee Foothills of the Southern Appalachians in North and South Carolina, through state parks, national forests, and state-owned preserves. In these lands you'll find high ridgelines, wild and scenic rivers, deep rock gorges, wilderness areas, mountain lakes, clear trout streams, towering forests, and a number of incredible waterfalls stretching from one end of the path to the other. There are so many cascades along Foothills Trail, such as Hidden Falls, they should have named it Waterfall Trail.

Foothills Trail is in full maturity: Well marked and well maintained, it makes for an excellent extended trek with ample camping opportunities. Several decades back, local folks recognized the sheer number of South Carolina's natural resources, and they realized a path connecting these resources would be a great way to both enjoy and protect them. No one knows the exact originator of the idea, but several people and agencies converged to begin a "Foothills Trail." The first miles were laid out in Sumter National Forest back in 1968. Foothills Trail, extending 77 miles from Oconee State Park to Table Rock State Park, was completed in 1981. Over the years, it has been fine-tuned. No doubt you will notice the carefully built wooden steps, waterbars, and bridges allowing hikers to traverse rugged areas through which the path passes. Since then, an alternative spur of Foothills Trail has been extended along the Blue Ridge of South Carolina to reach Jones Gap State Park. This spur extends the trail to 86 miles in length from Oconee State Park to its end. Many hikes in this book cover parts of Foothills Trail.

# Hospital Rock

**TOTAL DISTANCE**: 2.2 miles round trip

**HIKING TIME**: 2 hours

**VERTICAL RISE**: 700 feet

**RATING**: Moderate to difficult

**MAPS**: USGS 7.5' Cleveland, Standingstone Mountain; Mountain Bridge Wilderness Area

**TRAILHEAD GPS COORDINATES**: N35° 7.614', W82° 34.226'

**CONTACT INFORMATION**: Jones Gap State Park, 303 Jones Gap Road, Marietta, SC 29661, (8640 836-3647, www .southcarolinaparks/jonesgap

Hospital Rock is the most historic destination at Jones Gap State Park, and it is part of the Mountain Bridge Wilderness. And what a hike it is! Though the out-and-back track to Hospital Rock is but 2.2 miles long, it is quite strenuous. It first climbs steeply up Rocky Branch, then turns onto some harshly sloped terrain to clamber and climb over boulders and along the sides of Standingstone Mountain, opening to views before reaching Hospital Rock, the stuff of legend. Though it is rough, it can be hiked by anyone—just take your time. After all, it's only 2.2 miles there and back.

## GETTING THERE

Turn right onto US 276 and follow it for 4.0 miles to River Falls Road. Turn left onto River Falls Road and keep forward for 5.5 miles as it turns into Jones Gap Road to dead-end at Jones Gap State Park. From the parking area, follow the path to bridge the Saluda River. A parking fee and trailhead registration are mandatory.

## THE TRAIL

This trail is set apart from the rest of the paths in the Mountain Bridge Wilderness and only has one short connector path. The first difficult part of the hike is finding the trailhead. From the day-use parking area at Jones Gap State Park, take the trail leading toward the park office, crossing the Saluda River to reach an old fish hatchery pond that harbors trout to this day. Check out the big ones in there. Part of Cleveland Fish Hatchery, the stone-lined fish refuge was built back in the 1930s. You can see the stone wall remains of other pools. After admiring the fish, circle the pool on a paved trail, passing a picnic area

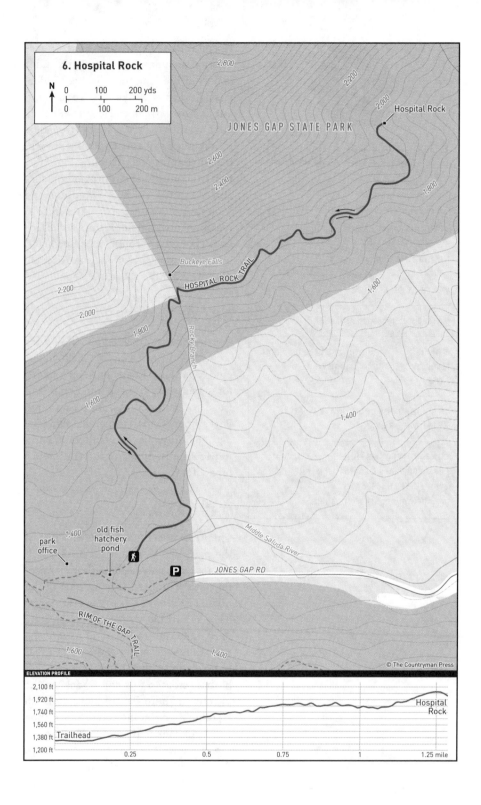

## 6. Hospital Rock

N
0    100    200 yds
0    100    200 m

JONES GAP STATE PARK

Hospital Rock

2,800

2,200

2,000

1,800

Buckeye Falls

HOSPITAL ROCK TRAIL

2,600

2,400

2,200

2,000

1,800

1,600

1,400

Rocky Branch

1,600

1,400

park office

old fish hatchery pond

Middle Saluda River

P

JONES GAP RD

RIM OF THE GAP TRAIL

1,600

1,400

© The Countryman Press

**ELEVATION PROFILE**

2,100 ft
1,920 ft
1,740 ft
1,560 ft
1,380 ft
1,200 ft

Trailhead

Hospital Rock

0.25    0.5    0.75    1    1.25 mile

LOOKING OUT FROM THE SHELTER OF HOSPITAL ROCK

on your left. The pavement runs out and leads to a trailhead kiosk, along with the beginning of Hospital Rock Trail. Sign in at the register. Keep moving forward on an old roadbed, passing Primitive Campsite 1 on your left. Ignore a trail leading right, keeping on the wide track heading uphill through rich woods. The trail is lined with waterbars to prevent erosion. A pipe to your left is used to transfer water from Rocky Branch to the old hatchery.

The trail passes a few more primitive campsites. Turn left as the spur trail to Campsite A leads right and begin ascending along Rocky Branch, which is off to your right. Pass over the water delivery pipe. In summer, the pipe feels cool to the touch as it transfers water from Rocky Branch to the trout pond. To your right you can see a stone dam and intake valve. The trail begins to narrow as the climb proceeds. Park strollers usually turn around at this point. Step over a tributary of Rocky Branch, traveling directly up a rocky rib ridge dividing

Rocky Branch and the tributary stream. At 0.3 mile, watch for a nearly horizontal rock slab that makes a good relaxing spot. Notice the twin-trunked tulip tree with the carved smiley face on it at the far side of the rock slab.

Keep a steady climb through an attractive boulder-laden forest. You are well shaded overhead by streamside trees such as black birch and maple. At 0.4 mile, Hospital Rock Trail crosses Rocky Branch. Here a 15-foot, slide-type, sloped cascade drops just above the trail. Watch the pattern of the water as it spreads wide from the cascade crest to the crossing at your feet. This is your last chance for easy water.

The path now leaves the creek, switchbacking into pine-and-laurel woods before emerging onto a power-line cut. The vegetation is ragged beneath the transmission lines, depending on the last cutting by the power-line crew. Vast views open to your south. Little Pinnacle Mountain stands across the gorge of the Middle Saluda River; looking south beyond the gorge, South Carolina opens as far as the clarity of the sky allows. Don't forget to look up as well, to see the bluffs of Cleveland Cliff.

Leave the bright open area of the power-line cut for woods again. The country is rough with many outcrops. The lack of loop possibilities and the challenging trail conditions keep this trail quiet, even as other trails at Jones Gap State Park are hopping. You're winding through beautiful woods, but the going is slow because of the uneven footing, due to a mix of boulders, rocks, and dirt, all on a sharp slope. At 0.8 mile, the trail turns left and ascends the nose of a ridge, straight up rock bordered by pine and mountain laurel.

This is where the going gets steep. Look back for views here, too. You will use all fours while gaining ground. At one point, a steel cable aids in the climb.

Surprisingly, the path starts dropping steeply. Here the trail slips beneath a rock overhang, then turns 180 degrees to the left, opening to a rock shelter at 1.1 miles. This is Hospital Rock. A full-grown adult can easily walk inside. Centuries of black soot cover the roof of the shelter. Hospital Rock got its name for purportedly being the location of a Confederate army hospital during the Civil War. However, judging by the ultra-rugged terrain and general inaccessibility, this is likely a myth, and maybe even cover for Confederate deserters, who were said to hide here. This seems the more likely story. Others say it was a haven for moonshiners. There is a nearby trickling water source. The mountains around here were notorious outlawed liquor-making areas. Still others say this was a Cherokee Indian camp. Certainly many a mountain trav-eler has stopped here, but it is on the way to nothing and very hard to reach, as is attested by the hike. Nevertheless, Hospital Rock remains the name, and it certainly makes for a fine South Carolina hiking destination. Linger and bring a lunch; it's a good place to be—any time of the year. Take your time on the return trip, and I guarantee you will see more interesting rocks, boulders, mountains, and views before finishing the hike.

You may want to stay overnight at Jones Gap State Park, which covers more than 3,300 acres of rugged mountain terrain. This state park and the adjacent Caesars Head State Park are operated as low-impact wilderness parks. This means they are not designed like traditional parks with big drive-up campgrounds, parking lots, and heavy-usage areas. Rather, the park facilities are integrated into an exceptional mountain landscape, leaving the emphasis on the natural. Tent campers use rustic walk-in campsites. This means: No RVs here. Jones Gap State Park has 29 campsites. Nine are within 0.5 mile of the camper parking area; the other 22 sites are considered backcountry campsites. Four of them are on Hospital Rock Trail. Perhaps you could check them out to get an idea. The only amenity they possess is a fire ring. Showers and restrooms are located near the main visitor center. The campsites fill on the first nice weekends in spring, tapering off when the heat rises. Then, from mid-August until the leaves fall, the campsites can fill any weekend. During the week, you can get a campsite anytime. You will find the accommodations friendlier than those who have spent the night beneath Hospital Rock.

# King Creek Falls/Big Bend Falls via Burrells Ford

**TOTAL DISTANCE**: 7.6 miles round trip

**HIKING TIME**: 4 hours

**VERTICAL RISE**: 240 feet

**RATING**: Moderate

**MAPS**: USGS 7.5' Tamassee; Sumter National Forest—Andrew Pickens District; Chattooga National Wild and Scenic River

**TRAILHEAD GPS COORDINATES**: N34° 58.210', W83° 6.918'

**CONTACT INFORMATION**: Sumter National Forest, 112 Andrew Pickens Circle, Mt. Rest, SC 29664, (864) 638-9568, www .fs.usda.gov/main/scnfs

This hike travels entirely within the Chattooga wild and scenic river corridor, reaching two entirely different yet attractive falls. The first, King Creek Falls, is widely considered the most scenic falls in the entire Sumter National Forest. It drops 80-plus feet over a rock face, ever widening to end at a catch basin bordered by a large gravel bar. The second, Big Bend Falls, is simply the evidence of the power of a large river following gravity: delicate beauty versus raw power. Leave the Burrells Ford parking area, with its primitive walk-in camping area nearby, then cruise downstream along the wild and scenic Chattooga River with its everywhere-you-look beauty to reach King Creek shortly. A spur trail takes you up this creek to its falls. The hike continues in the gorgeous valley, going around the Big Bend of the Chattooga River to arrive at Big Bend Falls. Your return trip will yield more sights and scenes of the river to imprint within your mind an album of superlative memories.

## GETTING THERE

From the intersection of SC 11 and SC 28 just east of Walhalla, drive west on SC 28 for 9.5 miles to SC 107, then turn right. Follow SC 107 for 8.9 miles to Forest Road 708. Descend on gravel FR 708 for 3.0 miles. The Burrells Ford parking area will be on your left. The hike starts near the signboard on the south side of the parking area.

## THE TRAIL

Leave the gravel parking area for Burrells Ford Walk-in Campground, on the access trail by the kiosk. You will immediately meet Foothills Trail. Turn right here, heading away from FR 708, south-

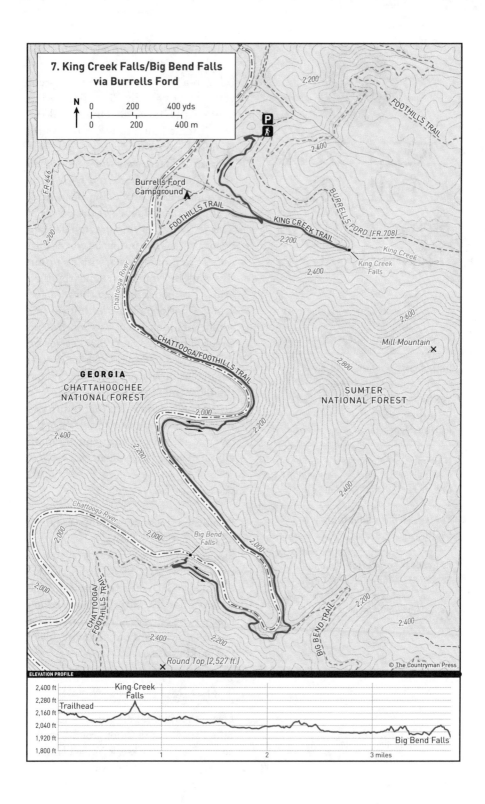

## 7. King Creek Falls/Big Bend Falls via Burrells Ford

N

0      200      400 yds
0      200      400 m

FOOTHILLS TRAIL

FR 646

Burrells Ford
Campground

FOOTHILLS TRAIL

KING CREEK TRAIL

BURRELLS FORD (FR.708)

King Creek

2,200

King Creek
Falls

2,400

2,600

Chattooga River

CHATTOOGA/FOOTHILLS TRAIL

Mill Mountain ✕

2,800

**GEORGIA**
CHATTAHOOCHEE
NATIONAL FOREST

SUMTER
NATIONAL FOREST

2,400

2,200

2,000

2,200

2,400

Chattooga River

2,000

2,000

Big Bend
Falls

2,000

2,000

CHATTOOGA/
FOOTHILLS TRAIL

2,000

BIG BEND TRAIL

2,200

2,400

2,400

2,200

Round Top (2,527 ft.) ✕

© The Countryman Press

**ELEVATION PROFILE**

| | | |
|---|---|---|
| 2,400 ft | King Creek Falls | |
| 2,280 ft | | |
| 2,160 ft Trailhead | | |
| 2,040 ft | | |
| 1,920 ft | | Big Bend Falls |
| 1,800 ft | 1            2            3 miles | |

bound on Foothills Trail, which winds through thick woods of white pine with mountain laurel aplenty. Follow the dug path as it switchbacks through a hollow on a rooty track. Ahead, the trail squeezes through two white pines standing like trailside sentinels.

Descend to reach King Creek at 0.4 mile, crossing the mountain watercourse on a wooden bridge with handrails. The trail then turns upstream in dense rhododendron. A campsite lies to your right. Reach a trail junction ahead. To your left, the spur trail leads 0.2 mile to King Creek Falls. To your right, Foothills Trail leads downstream toward Big Bend Falls. Take the spur upward, toward King Creek, which is crashing to your left, gathering in surprisingly large pools. Keep ascending to get well above the stream, appreciating the declivitous valley this creek has cut. Huge, naked hemlock trunks are a sober reminder of the time when this evergreen reigned in the cool, moist valleys of the Southern Appalachians, falling prey to the hemlock wooly adelgid and possibly going the way of the decimated chestnut tree in the early 1900s, a victim of the chestnut blight.

As you hear the loud noises of water falling ahead and turn the corner, King Creek Falls appears. The spectacular aquatic feature falls over a lip of rock, makes three quick drops, then spreads wide in multiple cascades and flows according to the rule of gravity. Exposed rock stands between the flows of frothing white, all framed in greenery. The plunge pool is limited in depth, but a large gravel bar lies at the falls' base and makes for a good viewing spot. Fallen logs and boulders offer seats in the amphitheater of beauty created by water and time.

Backtrack from the falls, then continue down the Chattooga River on Foothills Trail, swinging around the western edge of Mill Mountain, dipping into occasional hollows. Soon a roadbed comes in on your right. This roadbed-trail leads to the actual Burrells Ford camping area. Follow the old roadbed south as it comes near the Chattooga but stays above the watercourse, passing seeps that feed the river. Rock boulders and bluffs border the trailbed. Small bridges and waterbars have been installed to make the going easier on the rougher areas. Galax is especially fragrant on this steep slope. From this perch you can look down on the river and its attendant gravel bars. The going is rocky, rooty, and slow as the trail works above bluffs below and passes along some rocklines itself. Switchbacks lead you down to the river and a river-wide cascade and recovery pool. This could be a good swimming spot for those individuals so inclined. Pass more exposed rocks, ledges, and shelves that would make good sunning spots when the water is low.

Leave the riverside and climb, leveling off a good 20 to 30 feet above the flow, soon to reach the river again. In places, trail and river are a mere foot or two apart. In these spots the path is ragged, because flood alters the land and the vegetation, making travel slow. Continuing downstream, the trail passes a high-water route, which heads around a section where the trail alternates between rock outcrops and sand. I have been here when this section is under water and walked through it. The high-water route is marked on the downstream end, and hopefully it will be marked on the upstream end when you come here. But you will see the high-

KING CREEK FALLS

water route sign after you have gone the low route. If the trail is flooded, just follow one of the paths that curves up and around this short segment.

The trail climbs away from the river, turning into a hollow and stream to meet Big Bend Trail at 2.8 miles, just above a sliding cascade of an unnamed creek coming from the left. Cross the wooden bridge and stay right on Foothills Trail, which travels above the river, reaching some switchbacks that work along rough rock ledges, unseen through the rhododendrons below you. Head downstream along the river as it spills over ledges. The trail continues on the sloped mountainside, curving in and out of little hollows. Reach a set of switchbacks—your second since the Big Bend Trail intersection. These switchbacks descend to reach the spur trails to the falls at 3.6 miles. You will hear Big Bend Falls before you see it. The spur trail to your right heads to the upper drop. This trail passes under a large rockhouse with many fallen boulders at its base. During a rain, water will be flowing down the inner side of the rockhouse and dripping, though there are a couple of areas where you can stay dry. The last segment—which allows you to view the upper part of the drop—leads down over slippery rocks, so be careful. The convergence of the river into the main chute is easily visible from here, as is the initial drop. The "trail" to the base of the falls is more difficult. It leads down through rhododendrons, then it goes over a ledge to reach open rock, mere feet from the falls. The power of gravity and water in nature is the falls' essence. The descent is perhaps 30-plus feet in its entirety. You will stand there, looking up the drop and down into the swirling catch basin. Be wise as you access this waterfall.

# 8

# Laurel Fork Falls and Lake Jocassee

| | |
|---|---|
| **TOTAL DISTANCE**: 9.8 miles round trip | |
| **HIKING TIME**: 5.5 hours | |
| **VERTICAL RISE**: 1,100 feet | |
| **RATING**: Moderate to difficult | |
| **MAPS**: USGS 7.5' Eastatoe Gap, Reid; Foothills Trail, Jim Timmerman Natural Resources Area at Jocassee Gorges | |
| **TRAILHEAD GPS COORDINATES**: N35° 2.632', W82° 50.319' | |
| **CONTACT INFORMATION**: Jocassee Gorges, 1344 Cleo Chapman Hwy, Sunset, SC 29685, (864) 868-0281, www.dnr.sc.gov | |

This hike travels through Laurel Fork Heritage Preserve, a scenic area that is perhaps the finest mountain valley in South Carolina. It's that scenic. You'll leave Laurel Fork Gap to briefly follow a forest road, soon meeting Foothills Trail. From here the hike winds among thickly wooded steep-sided ridges with copious amounts of mountain laurel. Drop into the Laurel Fork watershed and enjoy the ubiquitous beauty, topped off with a visit to Double Falls. Continuing down the valley, the hike takes you over numerous bridges spanning Laurel Fork and leads to the lip of the gorge over which Laurel Fork Falls drops. The series of watery descents will blow you away. Beyond the falls, Foothills Trail leads to Lake Jocassee, a clear mountain-rimmed impoundment that may just lure you in for a swim. The valley is also a good spring wildflower destination.

## GETTING THERE

From Pickens, take US 178 West to SC 11. Hit your odometer at SC 11 and continue on US 178 for 8.1 more miles to Laurel Valley Road, which is shortly past the community of Rocky Bottom. Turn left at Laurel Valley Road, but stay right and uphill on the gravel road. Follow this gravel road, Horsepasture Road, for 3.6 miles to Laurel Fork Gap. Here the road splits. To the left is a dead end, possibly with gravel stored for future roadwork. To your right the main gravel road continues uphill 50 yards to a second road split, both forks of which are gated. You are at Laurel Fork Gap. Park on the side of the dead road before you come to the two gates. Start walking up the hill and take the right fork, which goes uphill.

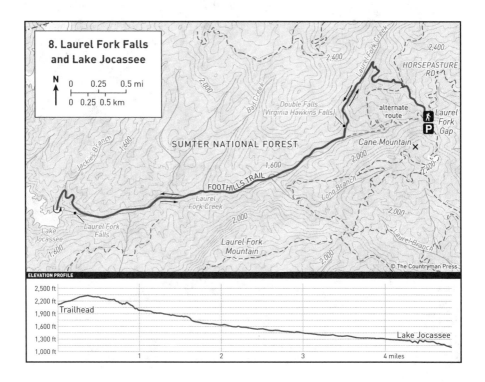

## THE TRAIL

Leave Laurel Fork Gap, reaching the two gated roads. Take the gated gravel road heading uphill and to your right, not the left fork. Neither of these is the dead-end gravel road where you should have parked. The correct gravel track keeps uphill to the northwest, reaching the marked, perpendicular crossing of Foothills Trail at 0.3 mile. Turn left here, joining Foothills Trail and briefly tracing a smaller, nongravel canopied roadbed before turning right into thick woods on a single-track path. Wind along steep-sided hollows, working toward Laurel Fork amid mountain laurel and oak aplenty. Appreciate the trail work, with steps, handrails, and locust logs bordering the low side of the path to keep it level.

As you near Laurel Fork on steep switchbacks, the mountain laurel evolves to rhododendron, and the noisy stream becomes audible. Turn downstream in a tight valley full of tulip trees, black birch, doghobble, and fern. Mossy bluffs protrude from hillsides. Reach the first of five bridges, which span Laurel Fork in quick succession.

After the fifth crossing, you are on the right bank. The valley opens. Keep descending, passing a bench, and reach Double Falls at 1.8 miles. This is a low-flow, multitiered, 25-foot drop. The initial pourover is over a sheer stone slab, followed by shorter, stair-step-like spills. The cataract also goes by the name Virginia Hawkins Falls. Beyond Double Falls, Laurel Fork Trail descends to a camping area and meets a roadbed that has descended from Laurel Fork Gap. You can trace this roadbed back up to the gap on your return if you wish.

DOUBLE FALLS

The very last part of the return is on a foot trail with steps. You cannot see this road from Laurel Fork Gap, but you can see the foot trail heading downhill from the gap. It's about a mile back to the gap from Laurel Fork, but you'll miss all the bridges and Double Falls.

Foothills Trail keeps descending, immediately crossing a bridge to the right bank. The trail hops off and on the old road as it works around side streams and passes through wooded flats. Farther downstream, the trail uses old wooden road bridges to span the creek. At other times, it parallels the old road in woods. Smaller footbridges will span feeder branches while you walk the trail.

The gorge tightens at 3.0 miles, forcing the stream, the white-blazed trail, and the roadbed to squeeze through a slot for about 0.25 mile. The valley opens again. At 3.3 miles Bad Creek comes in on your right. Amid all the hiker and old road bridges the next bridge, at 3.5 miles, will stand out. This is a mini-suspension bridge that crosses over to the left bank. A level campsite is at the bridge. You can get good looks up and down the stream from this point. The forest floor is covered in galax, while white pines form a superstory over the remainder of the lush forest.

Laurel Fork gains momentum as more feeder branches increase its flow. At 3.8 miles the trail meets a closed forest road coming in from the left. There are remains of bridge pilings on both sides of Laurel Fork, along with a large, poor campsite. A hiker bridge leads across the right bank here. The trail immediately cuts into the woods along Laurel Fork but rejoins the main roadbed, still heading downhill and downstream, in an ever-widening valley.

At 4.3 miles a marked spur trail leads left across a suspension bridge spanning Laurel Fork Creek, reaching a campsite and former homesite. The campsite trail, if you follow it downstream, leads to the top of Laurel Fork Falls. Here you can see it slide over the lip of the gorge to reach Lake Jocassee after tumbling downward numerous times, and in numerous forms. It is an impressive fall, and hard to categorize. To gain a better view, continue along Foothills Trail, cruising along a blasted cliff to reach a long vista of the falls through the trees. Near here, unmaintained trails lead very, very steeply down to the midlevel of the falls. You can look up at the first two drops of Laurel Falls, which end in a plunge pool before gathering momentum and dropping even more. At high flows, exploring this midfalls area would be a dangerous proposition—although good rock out-

crops around the falls make it an inviting place once you get there.

To continue to Lake Jocassee, follow Foothills Trail, now on a wide roadbed, as it slices through a blasted gap and works around to reach Jackie's Branch and a trail intersection at 4.8 miles. Stay left here, descending past a few cascades of Jackies Branch to reach the lakeshore and a boat/hiker access for Foothills Trail. The aquamarine water, normally very clear, will lure you in for a swim on a sunny day. Laurel Falls, roaring away farther up the cove, can be heard but not seen from the access. On nice weekends, boaters will motor to this access and reach the falls much more easily than you. However, the beauty of Laurel Fork Gorge will be more than worth the effort.

BRIDGE OVER LAUREL FORK

# Lick Log Falls/ Pigpen Falls via Chattooga Trail

**TOTAL DISTANCE**: 9.2 miles round trip

**HIKING TIME**: 5 hours

**VERTICAL RISE**: 200 feet

**RATING**: Moderate to difficult

**MAPS**: USGS 7.5' Satolah; Sumter National Forest—Andrew Pickens District; Chattooga National Wild and Scenic River

**TRAILHEAD GPS COORDINATES**: N34° 55.029', W83° 10.006'

**CONTACT INFORMATION**: Sumter National Forest, 112 Andrew Pickens Circle, Mt. Rest, SC 29664, (864) 638-9568, www .fs.usda.gov/main/scnfs

This hike travels the lowermost no-boating-allowed section of the Chattooga Wild and Scenic River to visit two waterfalls. The first, 80-foot Lick Log Falls, makes a multiple drop dive to the Chattooga River, while 25-foot Pigpen Falls makes a single drop into a plunge pool. Much of Chattooga Trail works along the scenic slopes above the river; only toward the end of the hike does it travel along the famed watercourse, which forms part of the boundary between Georgia and South Carolina. Chattooga Trail starts on SC 28, then curves into hollows and streamlets flowing toward the Chattooga. About midway, it works along the western slopes of Reed Mountain before dropping to the Wild and Scenic Chattooga. Here you can enjoy the sights and sounds of the big water before the trail turns into the Lick Log Creek watershed, where you will hear the long cascades and descents of Lick Log Falls. Pigpen Falls is a short walk beyond. Hikers can make this a 6.0-mile end-to-end trek by continuing on to the Nicholson Ford parking area.

## GETTING THERE

From the intersection of SC 11 and SC 28 near Walhalla, follow SC 28 for 16.2 miles to a gravel parking area just before the bridge over the Chattooga, on your right. If you cross the bridge, you've gone too far.

## THE TRAIL

The trail starts by Russell Bridge over the Chattooga, and near Ridley Fields. The fields, which were a formerly cultivated flat along the river, are now managed by the Forest Service for crop-

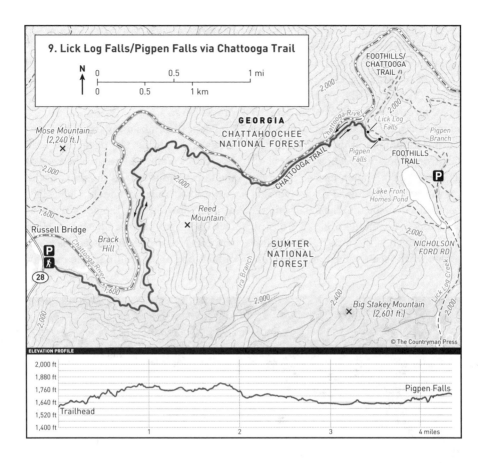

## 9. Lick Log Falls/Pigpen Falls via Chattooga Trail

N

| 0 | | 0.5 | | 1 mi |

| 0 | 0.5 | | 1 km |

FOOTHILLS/
CHATTOOGA
TRAIL

2,000

GEORGIA

Chattooga River

Lick Log
Falls

Pigpen
Branch

Mose Mountain
(2,240 ft.)

CHATTAHOOCHEE
NATIONAL FOREST

Pigpen
Falls

FOOTHILLS
TRAIL

2,000

2,000

CHATTOOGA TRAIL

1,600

Reed
Mountain

Lake Front
Homes Pond

Russell Bridge

Brack
Hill

SUMTER
NATIONAL
FOREST

2,000

NICHOLSON
FORD RD

28

Chattooga River

Ira Branch

1,600

2,000

Big Stakey Mountain
(2,601 ft.)

2,400

Lick Log Creek

2,000

2,000

© The Countryman Press

**ELEVATION PROFILE**

| 2,000 ft |
| 1,880 ft |
| 1,760 ft | Pigpen Falls |
| 1,640 ft |
| 1,520 ft | Trailhead |
| 1,400 ft |

1   2   3   4 miles

land for wild critters. Leave the SC 28 parking area and pass around a gate. A short nature trail heads left, a gravel road keeps forward to Ridley Fields and beyond, and the signed Chattooga Trail travels right and uphill. The single-track path heads along the slope of the valley above Ridley Fields, which you can see below. The forest is rich, with ferns at your feet, along with maple, oak, black birch, and tulip trees; a superstory of white pines towers above all. Shortly you'll progress into the first of many rhododendron-rich coves, where trickling streams cut a course for the river below. Occasional rocks and boulders stand silently planted in the forest,

many grown over with moss, as are the trunks of trees in this lush woodland. Old roadbeds cross the trail at times. The trail is never steep for long and is often level or nearly level.

Pick up a wide and obvious roadbed at 1.1 miles. The track is lined with fragrant galax. The Chattooga is loudly frothing below. Soon you'll turn back into a cove, curving back out onto dry ridges as the trail swings around the west slope of Reed Mountain. Oaks and sourwoods are prevalent up here. The river is no longer audible. At 2.6 miles, at the northernmost point on Reed Mountain, Chattooga Trail makes a big turn back to the east and starts angling for the river. Blueberries proliferate in this locale.

Begin descending to simultaneously reach the river and an old roadbed at 3.0 miles. (You can make your return trip to SC 28 on this old roadbed, but it isn't marked or maintained as a hiking trail.) Turn right and join this roadbed as the Chattooga noisily crashes to your left. The trail will be much nearer the river for the rest of the hike. Pass a riverside campsite, then dip into the flat of greater Ira Branch. Reach the bridged crossing of Ira Branch at 3.5 miles. Enjoy water sweeps of the scenic river before switch-backing to work your way over steep riverside rocks. Return to the Chattooga and along another flat to cross a small stony creek. Pass more campsites that overlook small sandy beaches and gravel bars.

The trail climbs away from the Chattooga and begins to curve into Lick Log Creek Valley. Listen to the roar of the falls to your left. At the point of the curve, at 4.3 miles, a side trail leads left, directly downhill, to the confluence of Lick Log Creek and the Chattooga. Here you can look up at the lowest cascade of Lick Log Falls, spilling wide over an

UPPER CASCADE OF LICK LOG FALLS

angled ledge, from a gravel bar that also offers a close-up view of the Chattooga. Return to the main trail and curve into Lick Log Valley. You can see the middle cascades of Lick Log Falls through thickets of rhododendron. The trail soon reaches the head of the falls in a small flat. A side trail here leads down the rock shelf over which the fall drops to the base of the fall's first drop, a curtain-type fall. A rock outcrop, open to the sun, stands at the base of this uppermost drop. Below, Lick Log Falls keeps descending to the Chattooga in stages. Both the upper- and lower-falls accesses are tougher than your standard trail, but can be easily navigated using precaution.

Your falls viewing is far from over. Continue up Lick Log Creek, passing more flats and campsites to cross the creek on a wooden bridge. Pigpen Falls is just after the crossing. Look upstream at the single-drop waterfall that fills a plunge pool. If you swing around to the left of the plunge pool and stand facing the falls, however, you will see a second waterfall near the right-hand bank of the creek. This other drop, which plunges over the same rock ledge as its left-hand counterpart, is often overlooked. Near here, Chattooga Trail meets Foothills Trail, and they run in conjunction up the Chattooga River for a short distance. Then Foothills Trail continues on its northbound way for 80-plus miles. If you want to make this an end-to-end hike, continue downstream along the right bank of Lick Log Creek just a short distance, to reach the signed junction with Foothills Trail. Turn right here, make a short but steep ascent to span Lick Log Creek twice by bridge, then pass through a pine grove and campsite. Keep ascending to span another small branch before reaching the Nicholson Ford parking area, 0.8 mile from the junction with Chattooga Trail. The directions to Nicholson Ford Parking Area from Walhalla are as follows: From the junction of SC 28 and SC 11, take SC 28 west for 9.5 miles to SC 107. Turn right and follow SC 107 for 3.4 miles, passing the entrance to Oconee State Park, to reach Village Creek Road. Turn left onto Village Creek Road and continue for 2.0 miles to Forest Road 775, Nicholson Ford Road. Turn right and follow Nicholson Ford Road to the parking area.

# Little Pinnacle Mountain Loop

| | |
|---|---|
| **TOTAL DISTANCE**: 5.4-mile loop | |

**HIKING TIME**: 3 hours

**VERTICAL RISE**: 1,150 feet

**RATING**: Moderate to difficult

**MAPS**: USGS 7.5' Cleveland, Standingstone Mountain; Mountain Bridge Wilderness Area

**TRAILHEAD GPS COORDINATES**: N35° 7.522', W82° 34.437'

**CONTACT INFORMATION**: Jones Gap State Park, 303 Jones Gap Road, Marietta, SC 29661, (8640 836-3647, www .southcarolinaparks/jonesgap

This hike explores the southeastern section of Jones Gap State Park, in the Mountain Bridge Wilderness. Caesars Head State Park and Jones Gap make up the Mountain Bridge Wilderness Area. Climb from the classic Southern Appalachian stream that is the Middle Saluda River, winding past big boulders and a rockfall arch, passing a rock slab and open view to make the crest of Little Pinnacle Mountain. The hike then rambles along the mountaintop into moist coves before picking up an old roadbed and descending back toward the Saluda—but not before passing another view, this time of Cleveland Cliff.

## GETTING THERE

From Pickens, take SC 8 north for 15 miles to SC 11. Veer right onto SC 11 and follow it for 2 miles to US 276. Turn right onto US 276 and continue 4.0 miles to River Falls Road. Turn left and proceed forward for 5.5 miles as River Falls Road turns into Jones Gap Road, to dead-end at Jones Gap State Park. From the parking area, follow the path to bridge the Saluda River. Go past the park office on your right. (A trail map can be purchased at the office.) Cross the wooden road bridge back over to the left bank of the Middle Saluda. A parking fee and trailhead registration are mandatory.

## THE TRAIL

After registering, leave the trailside kiosk and climb along Jones Gap Trail, Trail 1. To your right, the Middle Saluda froths and drops amid rocks, all shaded by a rich forest. Follow the wide, sandy track a short distance before reaching a trail junction. Reach Rim of the Gap Trail, Trail 6, and turn left. This yellow-blazed, narrow trail climbs away from the river,

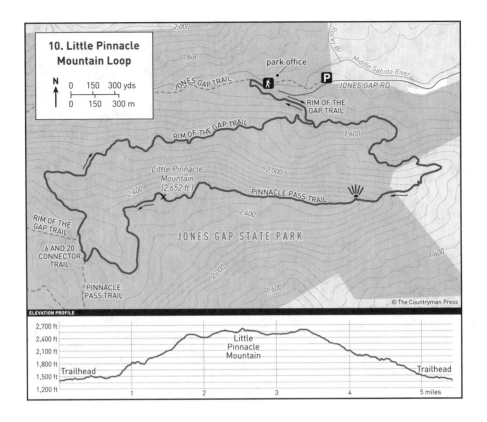

**10. Little Pinnacle Mountain Loop**

N

| 0 | 150 | 300 yds |
| 0 | 150 | 300 m |

JONES GAP TRAIL

park office

RIM OF THE GAP TRAIL

JONES GAP RD.

Rocky Br.

Middle Saluda River

1,600

RIM OF THE GAP TRAIL

Little Pinnacle Mountain (2,652 ft.)

2,000

PINNACLE PASS TRAIL

2,400

2,400

RIM OF THE GAP TRAIL

6 AND 20 CONNECTOR TRAIL

JONES GAP STATE PARK

PINNACLE PASS TRAIL

2,000

1,600

1,600

2,000

1,600

ELEVATION PROFILE

| 2,700 ft |
| 2,400 ft |
| 2,100 ft |
| 1,800 ft |
| 1,500 ft |
| 1,200 ft |

Little Pinnacle Mountain

Trailhead

Trailhead

1    2    3    4    5 miles

turning downstream. Head about 100 yards and pass a streamlet bordered by massive boulders. Just upstream is a huge boulder. Once you're beyond the stream, follow a faint track to your right leading to the biggest boulder. You can see that this boulder has fallen onto another smaller boulder to form an arch. Known as a rockfall arch, this isn't a true erosion-created feature. You can easily walk under this arch standing up.

Return to the main trail and continue climbing. At one point you'll need to use an installed steel cable to work up the slope. Continue ascending past boulders, crossing a second small stream to reach another junction at 0.4 mile. This is where you begin the loop portion of the hike. To your right Rim of the Gap Trail continues. This is

your return route. You, however, stay left, joining Pinnacle Pass Trail, Trail 20. The single-track path travels amid big boulders in rich woods of maple and oak. Pass along the lower edge of a sheer rock face, sometimes covered in moss, skirting the mountainside. The trail works up the north slope of Little Pinnacle Mountain, crossing some open rock faces. Look to your left for obscured views across the Middle Saluda Valley.

Appreciate the hard labor that must have been involved in making this trail as it works its way along the ultrasteep mountainside, cutting through laurel thickets. The trail reaches a steep creek, then turns suddenly right. Ascend abruptly along the branch, moderated by one switchback, which slides over a sheer rock face but is normally very

LIGHT POURS THROUGH A ROCKFALL ARCH

low flow. This is known as Walking Fern Falls. Huff and puff, then step across the streamlet at 0.9 mile and continue uphill to enter a mountain laurel-oak complex. Reach a large rock face, stepping across its lower reaches. You can climb up this face and gain views of the valley below. Scraggly pines and blackberries border the open slab. The trail makes a few more switchbacks to reach the crest of Little Pinnacle Mountain at 1.3 miles. The trail turns west here, among oak, laurel, blackberry, and other dry-situation species. The level walking offers brief respite as Pinnacle Pass Trail resumes ascending via switchbacks, only to level off again. The walking then becomes pure joy as the path rambles along the high ridgeline, which drops precipitously on both sides. Resume stair-stepping up the ridge, passing among some rocks. Locust, cane, dogwood, and more grow here. The trail dips to the north side of the mountain where Fraser magnolia, goosefoot-maple and tulip trees grow. Stop for a moment and listen for the Saluda River far below.

Descend to reach a prominent gap at 2.3 miles. Ascend from the gap in dry woods over a piney knob, with outcrops from which you can gain views. Descend again to join an old roadbed at 2.7 miles. The walking becomes easy and nearly level as the trail curves through a moist cove with tall trees, circling a high knob. Watch for dwarf-crested iris along the trail in spring. Cross two streams by a culvert, reaching another small stream and a trail junction at 3.2 miles. Here the hike turns right onto the 6 and 20 Connector Trail (Trail 22). Climb by switchbacks on a single-track path to reach a four-way junction. This loop turns right, rejoining the interestingly named Rim of the Gap Trail. Here Rim of the Gap Trail traces another roadbed, beginning a nearly continuous descent. The walking is easy, despite the sometimes muddy nature of the old roadbed.

The path curves downward to the west then angles back east, in rich woods of tulip trees, Carolina silverbells, and buckeyes, where vines dangle from the heights. Stinging nettles and ferns carpet the forest floor in summer. At 4.0 miles, you will reach a view. To your left, across the chasm of the Saluda, Cleveland Cliff is clearly visible. Standingstone Mountain is in the background. Rim of the Gap Trail keeps its downward track, winding into moist but steep and shallow creeks, shaded in rhododendron. The first stream you pass has a noisy but hard-to-see fall. Subtle, dry pine and laurel rib ridges divide the stream sheds.

On its lower reaches Rim of the Gap Trail becomes eroded, exposing clay soil. Be careful when it rains—the path will be slick. In other parts it will descend directly on potentially slick rock faces. Finally, at 4.8 miles, the path intersects Little Pinnacle Mountain Trail. You have now completed the loop. Backtrack, passing the rockfall arch again, before reaching the Middle Saluda River and Jones Gap Trail, heading downstream to finish the hike at 5.4 miles.

# 11

# Lower Whitewater Falls/Coon Den Natural Area

---

**TOTAL DISTANCE**: 6.0 miles round trip

---

**HIKING TIME**: 3.5 hours

---

**VERTICAL RISE**: 400 feet

---

**RATING**: Moderate

---

**MAPS**: USGS 7.5' Cashiers, Reid; Foothills Trail, Jim Timmerman Natural Resources Area at Jocassee Gorges

---

**TRAILHEAD GPS COORDINATES**: N35° 0.741', W82° 59.948'

---

**CONTACT INFORMATION**: Jocassee Gorges, 1344 Cleo Chapman Hwy, Sunset, SC 29685, (864) 868-0281, www.dnr.sc.gov

---

This trek actually incorporates two connected hikes into one, since they depart from the same trailhead. The two destinations are Lower Whitewater Falls, which is 4.2 miles round trip, and Coon Den Natural Area, 3.0 miles round trip. Each of those distances is considered a separate hike from the trailhead. If you do them at the same time, however, it's only 6.0 miles, since you won't have to return to the trailhead to do each hike. Lower Whitewater Falls is one of the most spectacular falls in the Southeast, which is saying a lot. I believe it's even more spectacular than its upstream cousin, Upper Whitewater Falls, also simply known as Whitewater Falls. Lower Whitewater Falls sees a tenth of the foot traffic of the upper. The side hike to Coon Den Natural Area travels up the right bank of the Whitewater River through a 300-acre, old-growth forest that is worth seeing.,

## GETTING THERE

From the junction of SC 11 and SC 130 just north of Salem, South Carolina, head north on SC 130, S. Bruce Rochester Memorial Highway. Keep north for 10.2 miles to the gated entrance to the Bad Creek Project. Drive up to the gate and it will open (from 6 am to 6 pm). Pass through the gate and keep downhill for 2.1 miles, turning left at the sign for Foothills Trail. Continue 0.3 mile to a large parking area. Bad Creek Access Trail starts in the far left-hand corner of the parking area.

## THE TRAIL

This hike runs in conjunction with Hike 21, "Whitewater Falls," for its first 0.6 mile. If you're feeling really aggressive, you could go for Whitewater Falls,

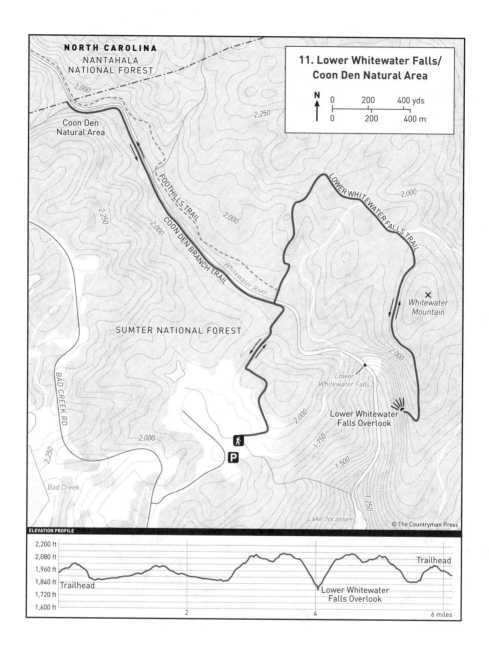

**11. Lower Whitewater Falls/
Coon Den Natural Area**

NORTH CAROLINA
NANTAHALA
NATIONAL FOREST

Coon Den
Natural Area

FOOTHILLS TRAIL

COON DEN BRANCH TRAIL

Whitewater River

LOWER WHITEWATER FALLS TRAIL

SUMTER NATIONAL FOREST

× Whitewater
Mountain

Lower
Whitewater Falls

Lower Whitewater
Falls Overlook

BAD CREEK RD

Bad Creek

Lake Jocassee

© The Countryman Press

ELEVATION PROFILE

2,200 ft
2,080 ft
1,960 ft
1,840 ft   Trailhead
1,720 ft
1,600 ft

Trailhead

Lower Whitewater
Falls Overlook

2        4        6 miles

Lower Whitewater Falls, and Coon Den Branch Natural Area in one big hike of 10.8 miles. Leave the large Bad Creek Access parking area, taking a graveled brushy path bordered by scrubby trees, grass, and regrowth over disturbed land. The open area does offer good views of Grassy Knob and other surrounding mountains. You can hear the Whitewater River flowing to your right, before it becomes part of Lake Jocassee. Keep east, then turn left, walking through more brush until the trail enters full-blown woods. Bad Creek Access Trail skirts the west side of a small knob then gently descends into a flat, where you

LOWER WHITEWATER FALLS

can hear the Whitewater River again. Drift across the wooded riverside flat to reach a trail junction and the first of two bridges over the Whitewater River at 0.6 mile. To your left, before the bridge, is the 1.0-mile Coon Den Branch Trail. This path shows much less use than any other trails in the area, but it's easily followed. Head upriver, with the Whitewater River to your left. Cross a small stream on a footbridge and officially enter the Coon Den Branch Natural Area. A thicket of rhododendron, doghobble, fern, and other typical Southern

Appalachian understory trees forms a greenbelt beneath a massive canopy of giant white pine and tulip trees. Pass more small creeklets before returning to the river near a contemplation bench.

Coon Den Branch Trail continues up the river, bridging another small sandy seep flowing through the woods. Span a third and fourth small branch to open to a second flat. Notice the black and yellow birch, which indicate a cool, moist environment. After 1.0 mile of Coon Den Branch Trail, you'll reach the North Carolina–South Carolina state line and the end of Duke Power's domain, returning to the river's edge. Around you, the mountainside has become an impenetrable thicket of greenery, with a large, inviting pool just upstream. Backtrack 1.0 mile to the two iron bridges over the Whitewater River to meet Foothills Trail. Here Foothills Trail leads left for 2.3 miles to Whitewater Falls Overlook.

This hike stays forward on Foothills Trail, heading toward the Lower Whitewater Falls Overlook. The blue-and-white-blazed trail shortly spans a small branch on a bridge, then leaves the riverside flat it has been crossing. Head up along a different trickling branch, only to switchback away and climb onto a ridgeline. The wide trail is rooty. The ridge steepens and Foothills Trail slips over to the right-hand side of the wooded ridge, joins an old roadbed, turns right, and makes a trail junction 1.1 miles from the Bad Creek trailhead. Lower Whitewater Falls Access Trail continues forward while Foothills Trail leaves left. From here to the falls overlook, the blazes skip off and on old dirt and gravel roads, so if you lose the blazes en route to Lower Whitewater Falls, backtrack. Still, the trail is well marked and well used.

Keep forward, traversing a small knob, then turn left to follow a red dirt track beyond a metal gate. At the gate, turn right, then make a quick left to join a bona fide gravel road, Musterground Road, open to public access in fall hunting season. The wide pea-gravel track makes for easy hiking, but you leave the road 0.3 mile distant from the Foothills Trail junction, a total of 1.4 miles from the trailhead. This is a right turn away from the gravel road.

Pine, sourwood, and cane border the trail as it gently climbs the west slope of Whitewater Mountain. You can't help but wonder where the trail is going as you climb without hearing any water. The trail reaches a high point, then begins a gentle downgrade to reach a double blaze at 1.9 miles. Drop right here as the descent steepens and joins yet another roadbed, where you turn right again. Keep descending. By now water is clearly audible. A final right turn and a narrowing to a single-track path heralds your arrival at the Lower Whitewater Falls Overlook at 2.1 miles. It's 300 feet down from the high point of Whitewater Mountain to the overlook.

But you will agree the trip was completely worth it. The overlook brings you face-on with Lower Whitewater Falls, which drops across a chasm. The river makes a few warm-up tumbles, just for kicks, then it makes a final practice drop before diving off a sheer ledge in a roaring sheet of white bordered in gray granite, framed in dense forest, with mountain ridges and sky beyond. The general claim is that the falls are 200 feet high, but they seem higher to me. Maybe it's just that last sheer drop being so impressive. Save some energy for the ups, and downs, and ups, and downs of the return trip.

# Miuka Falls/ Secret Falls via the Winding Stairs

**TOTAL DISTANCE**: 4.6 miles round trip

**HIKING TIME**: 3 hours

**VERTICAL RISE**: 800 feet

**RATING**: Moderate to difficult

**MAPS**: USGS 7.5' Tamassee; Sumter National Forest—Andrew Pickens District

**TRAILHEAD GPS COORDINATES**: N34° 56.478', W83° 5.382'

**CONTACT INFORMATION**: Sumter National Forest, 112 Andrew Pickens Circle, Mt. Rest, SC 29664, (864) 638-9568, www .fs.usda.gov/main/scnfs

This hike leaves the greater Cherry Hill Recreation Area of the Sumter National Forest and travels down the east slope of Chattooga Ridge along West Fork Townes Creek to reach 100-plus-foot Miuka Falls, then continues down to the big prize: 100-foot Secret Falls. Despite the name, Winding Stairs Trail isn't terribly steep, especially the part to Miuka Falls. This cascade makes a drop over a rock rim, descending in stages to continue down a rock slide into rhododendron and out of sight. Adventurous hikers will continue to Secret Falls, on Crane Creek. The end of this segment requires a bit of off-trail hiking down to the creek, then up to Secret Falls. Your return trip winds back up the stairs.

## GETTING THERE

From Walhalla, drive north on SC 28 for 8.5 miles to SC 107, then turn right. Follow SC 107 for 8.5 miles. The trailhead is on the gravel pull-off on your right, just before the right turn into Cherry Hill Campground. Winding Stairs Trail starts on the same side of the road as the gravel parking area.

## THE TRAIL

Leave the SC 107 trailhead, ascending into dry woods of maple, sourwood, and pine. An understory of blueberry and other low brush covers the forest floor. The single-track path shortly reaches a high point, then begins descending toward West Fork Townes Creek. You can see the Pells Cemetery through the woods on your right. Briefly level out in a flat and curve to reach a T-intersection. To your left, an old roadbed leads toward Cherry Hill Campground. Winding Stairs Trail turns right and begins descending along West

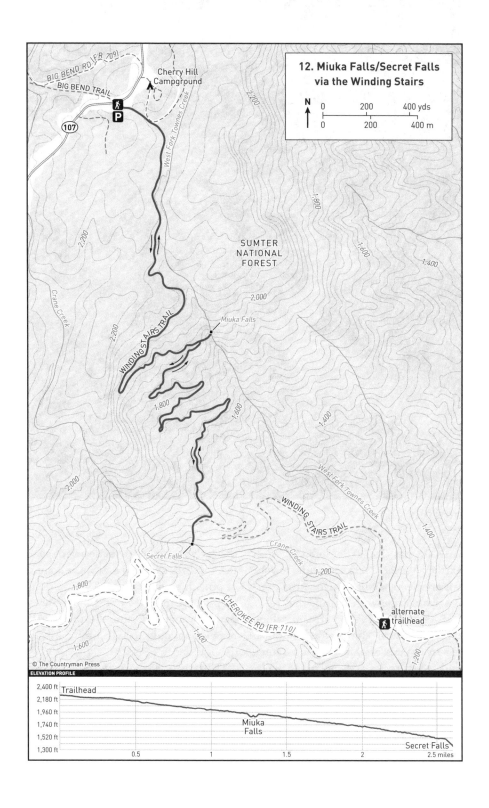

**12. Miuka Falls/Secret Falls via the Winding Stairs**

N

| 0 | 200 | 400 yds |
| 0 | 200 | 400 m |

BIG BEND RD (FR 709)

BIG BEND TRAIL

Cherry Hill Campground

107

West Fork Townes Creek

SUMTER NATIONAL FOREST

2,200

1,800

1,600

1,400

2,000

Crane Creek

2,200

WINDING STAIRS TRAIL

Miuka Falls

1,800

1,600

1,400

West Fork Townes Creek

2,000

WINDING STAIRS TRAIL

Crane Creek

1,200

1,400

Secret Falls

1,800

CHEROKEE RD (FR 710)

1,600

1,400

alternate trailhead

1,200

© The Countryman Press

**ELEVATION PROFILE**

| | | | | | |
|---|---|---|---|---|---|
| 2,400 ft | Trailhead | | | | |
| 2,180 ft | | | | | |
| 1,960 ft | | | | | |
| 1,740 ft | | | Miuka Falls | | |
| 1,520 ft | | | | | |
| 1,300 ft | | | | | Secret Falls |
| | 0.5 | 1 | 1.5 | 2 | 2.5 miles |

SECRET FALLS

Fork Townes Creek. Scramble over an earthen barrier. Cascades falling to your left are clearly audible beyond the evergreen brush between you and the creek.

Saddle alongside the stream, which displays South Carolina's mountain beauty in a mix of white frothing waters, dark mossy rocks, and cool green pools. Pass a rock overhang at 0.5 mile on your right. Turn away from the rock overhang and the stream, entering oak-and-pine woods. You will notice a second rock bluff along with the many standing and fallen tree trunks. These are relics of the pine beetle attack in the early 2000s. This beetle swept over the South, destroying many fine stands of pine, including these. The relationship between pines and the beetle is perfectly natural, and the pines will regenerate, only to fall prey again in generations to come.

The turn away from West Fork Townes Creek marks the beginning of the actual Winding Stairs. This trail was named for the way the trail curves back and forth, ever downhill along this steep east slope off Chattooga Ridge. The old forest road upon which the trail is laid could never have followed West

Fork Townes Creek—it's too steep. And after seeing Miuka Falls, you will understand why the "wind" is necessary in the Winding Stairs.

Reach the first sweeping 180-degree turn in the Winding Stairs at 0.8 mile. The vegetation changes a bit as increased shade on the slope allows for moister plants, such as tulip trees and vines, to grow. Pass another big boulder, exposed when the old forest road was blasted. The trail then crosses a small spring branch. West Fork Townes Creek becomes audible again. As Winding Stairs Trail makes a sharp curve to the right, at 1.1 miles, you can clearly hear Miuka Falls and can partially see the uppermost part of the fall through the trees, even in summer. At the exact point of the curve, two spur "trails" lead precipitously downward toward the falls. The lower trail leads to the slide part of the falls and offers the best viewing opportunities. Miuka Falls puts on a show, changing from small creek to towering cascade. Here West Fork Townes Creek makes a narrow drop, crashing three times, then widening and falling over a wide rock formation. The fall then joins together to slide 70 or more feet over a colorful rock slab, leaving the open sunny area and descending into a tunnel of rhododendron and out of sight. It's hard to say where these falls end, but I'd put them at 100-plus feet. If you want to explore the falls, stay on the land trails beside them. Do not get on the falls themselves or the rock slab part of the falls; it's too slippery and dangerous. These trails around the falls are not official trails and aren't maintained.

Return to Winding Stairs Trail, continuing downward. At the fourth turn past Miuka Falls, you are once again within earshot of West Fork Townes Creek. Here a spur trail leads down to slide falls that tunnel through rhododendrons, obscuring the greater view. The main trail then works its way southwest and downhill toward Crane Creek and Secret Falls.

Trace the old roadbed downhill, curving around a rib ridge, where a more faint bed keeps left, but the main trail curves right. The next major switchback, at 2.3 miles, curves left; the spur trail to Secret Falls leaves right. This has been marked with surveyor's tape in the past, and it may be again in the future.

Angle toward the creek on a well-trod yet narrow track. Crane Creek comes into view, and you can go left or right. Go right, heading upstream with the creek to your left. The slope is steep here, so be careful as you cross an intermittent streambed. Keep upstream and descend to Crane Creek. You should be across from a rock bluff, with Crane Creek shooting downstream in a crevice between you and the bluff. Just upstream, Secret Falls is sliding over a rock face after passing over a rock lip. No singular perfect viewing platform exists, but you get a good look. This is about a 15-minute trek from Winding Stairs Trail. For the more adventurous, a series of falls tumbles upstream of Secret Falls, called the Even More Secret Falls. Okay, I'm kidding about the name, but the upstream falls are there.

If you want to make this a downhill-only excursion, you can place one car at the bottom of Winding Stairs Trail, 1.2 miles beyond Secret Falls. The right turn to Forest Road 710, Cheohee Road, is 6.2 miles north on SC 107 from the point where 107 meets SC 28. Turn right and follow it to the rocked-in parking area near West Fork Townes Creek. (The trail does not come out on the narrow hairpin turn at Crane Creek, which you will reach first.)

# Opossum Creek Falls

**TOTAL DISTANCE**: 4.6 miles round trip

**HIKING TIME**: 2.5 hours

**VERTICAL RISE**: 700 feet

**RATING**: Moderate

**MAPS**: USGS 7.5' Rainy Mountain; Sumter National Forest—Andrew Pickens Ranger District, Chattooga Wild and Scenic River

**TRAILHEAD GPS COORDINATES**: N34° 46.401', W83° 18.219'

**CONTACT INFORMATION**: Sumter National Forest, 112 Andrew Pickens Circle, Mt. Rest, SC 29664, (864) 638-9568, www .fs.usda.gov/main/scnf

This is the westernmost marked and maintained trail in the state of South Carolina, located in the tip of Oconee County near the Georgia state line— hence it's also the westernmost hike in this entire guidebook. The trail is often overlooked because it isn't connected to others in the greater Chattooga River trail system. It offers a walk from a high to a low elevation on a well-maintained, nicely graded trail that leads to the Chattooga River. An alluring beach and swimming hole are located on the federally designated Wild and Scenic River. In the warmer season, you'll often see rafters and kayakers paddling the Chattooga. The trail then turns away from the river and up the cool, incised valley of Opossum Creek to reach a high waterfall that descends in a series of drops, saving its biggest splash for last.

## GETTING THERE

From Westminster, take US 76 west for 13.5 miles to near Long Creek. Turn left onto Damascus Church Road. (The Long Creek Volunteer Fire Department is here.) Follow Damascus Church Road for 0.9 mile to Battle Creek Road, Oconee County Road S-37-102. Turn right and follow Battle Creek Road for 1.9 miles to Turkey Ridge Road, gravel Forest Road 755. Follow Turkey Ridge Road for 2.1 miles; you will see Opossum Creek Trail on your left. However, continue up the road another 50 yards to a parking area on your left, near the point where FR 755F meets FR 755. Backtrack to the trail.

## THE TRAIL

You'll get some good views along the drive to the trailhead here, especially of Rabun Bald across the Georgia state line. Leave the trailhead, passing a

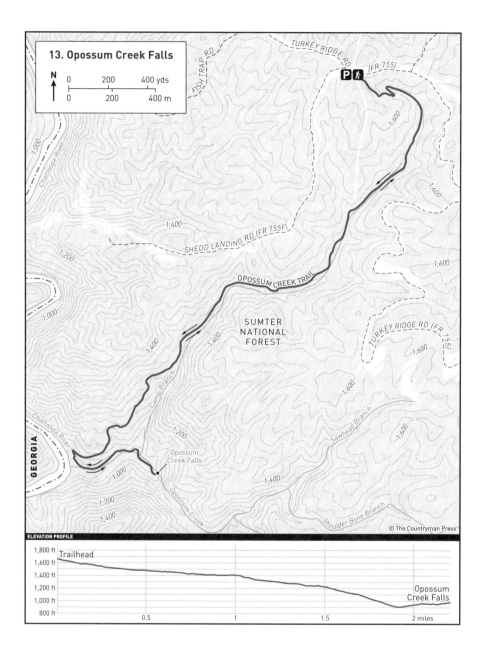

N

| 0 | 200 | 400 yds |
| 0 | 200 | 400 m |

FISH TRAP RD

TURKEY RIDGE RD

(FR 755)

1,600

Chattooga River

1,000

1,400

SHEDD LANDING RD (FR 755F)

1,200

1,600

OPOSSUM CREEK TRAIL

1,000

SUMTER
NATIONAL
FOREST

TURKEY RIDGE RD (FR 755)

1,600

1,400

1,600

1,400

Camp Branch

1,600

Sawhead Branch

1,600

Chattooga River

GEORGIA

1,200

Opossum
Creek Falls

1,000

1,400

1,200

Opossum Creek

1,400

Shoulder Bone Branch

© The Countryman Press

**ELEVATION PROFILE**

| | | | |
| --- | --- | --- | --- |
| 1,800 ft | Trailhead | | |
| 1,600 ft | | | |
| 1,400 ft | | | |
| 1,200 ft | | | Opossum |
| 1,000 ft | | | Creek Falls |
| 800 ft | | | |
| | 0.5 | 1 | 1.5 | 2 miles |

carsonite post marker and then a sign-board, in addition to a sign indicating your eventual entry into the Chattooga Wild and Scenic River corridor. Dry piney woods border the path, with water-bars and contouring to make the 700-foot descent as painless as possible in such mountainous terrain. Circle into the valley of Camp Branch, which feeds Opossum Creek. You will be in this val-ley for most of the hike. Hickories, oaks, and dogwood trees are prevalent along the upper part of this streambed, which is normally dry and only flows during times of high precipitation.

As the trail deepens into the valley,

Camp Branch begins flowing, and species such as holly, sycamore, and Fraser magnolia appear. A spur creek flows in from the left, and the valley widens. The going is easy in this perched vale that transitions into Southern Appalachian streamside forest, with black birch and rhododendron plentiful.

The graded track picks up an old roadbed, making the way wider and more open even as the valley narrows again, slicing through tight hills, forcing the stream to run narrow over rocky chutes under evergreens. At 1.0 mile, leave the old roadbed and resume the dug path, which is well above the creek. Camp Branch is now diving sharply for the Chattooga and making its own noisy waterfalls, in cascading stages, mostly unseen through the rhododendron and difficult to access due to the sheer slope between trail and water. The path works around the big drop to your left, circling into tiny feeder streamlets and even going uphill some, continuing its quest for the Chattooga River.

White pines tower overhead, and the valley widens further. You sense the width of the Chattooga Valley, maybe even feel warmer air on a summer day, and begin to hear the deeper roar of the rapids rather than the splashy drops of the stream you have been tracing. Reach the flat of the Chattooga at 1.9 miles. The wooded flat is sandy, and paths diverge: Previous hikers have been anxious to view the big waterway. Opossum Creek is coming in at an angle, flowing left to right, while the Chattooga is flowing right to left. Walk out to the river and you will see that the Chattooga is pooling up here as it makes a big bend to the west. A wonderful sand beach is located in front of the pool and would make for an ideal swimming and picnicking spot. If it's a warm day, especially on a week-

end, you'll see rafters plying the series of rapids upstream and jumping off a big rock well upriver. The immediate series of named upstream rapids are Class IV and V, and include Corkscrew Rapid, Crack-in-the-Rock, Jaw Bone, Sock 'em Dog, and Shoulder Bone. These, and the ones just below the bend you're at, are the lowermost rapids on the Chattooga before the river is dammed to make Tugaloo Lake.

River floaters will tell you the Chattooga River deserves its Wild and Scenic designation, and then some. Culled from South Carolina's Sumter National Forest, the Nantahala National Forest of North Carolina, and the Chattahoochee National Forest of Georgia, this river corridor protects one of the most significant free-flowing streams in the Southeast. The river itself is 50 miles long, starting in North Carolina; it then heads southwest for 40 miles, forming the Georgia–South Carolina border before meeting the Tallulah River and forming the Tugaloo. The Chattooga is perhaps best known for serving as the backdrop of the Burt Reynolds movie *Deliverance*. It was around this time, in 1974, that the Chattooga received its Wild and Scenic designation—a place where rafters, canoers, kayakers, and anglers enjoy a valley of massive boulders, clear trout- and bass-filled waters, and deep forests. Hikers have 36 miles of river corridor hiking, and more in adjacent national forest lands, which include Opossum Creek Trail.

Opossum Creek Trail turns left at the river, heading upstream along Opossum Creek. Pass through a small campsite, then slice between carved beech trees, now leaving the Chattooga to reenter the narrower valley down which you walked. At this point the trail is more heavily used, as boaters sometimes

OPOSSUM CREEK FALLS

access the falls. On a summer day you will undoubtedly notice the cooler air in this valley, as opposed to the wide-open warmer Chattooga Valley. Reach Camp Branch just above its confluence with Opossum Creek at 2.1 miles and step over this small stream. Turn up Opossum Creek. The trail becomes jumbled with boulders just before reaching Opossum Creek Falls. And before you it opens. Through the trees you can see the stream make an initial slide to the right, then come toward you in a drop. The creek splits and turns, always descending, before gathering one last time for a single sliding dramatic drop onto a stony bed, where it continues working its way toward the Chattooga. The area just below the falls is open to the sun, and you have some decent relaxing spots, including a shaded boulder or two. Below you, the stream makes a couple more falls, lesser-noticed in competition with dramatic Opossum Creek Falls.

# Pinnacle Mountain Loop

**TOTAL DISTANCE**: 7.6-mile loop

**HIKING TIME**: 4.5 hours

**VERTICAL RISE**: 2,250 feet

**RATING**: Difficult

**MAPS**: USGS 7.5' Table Rock; Table Rock State Park

**TRAILHEAD GPS COORDINATES**: N35° 1.918', W82° 42.009'

**CONTACT INFORMATION**: Table Rock State Park, 158 Ellison Lane, Pickens, SC 29671, (864) 878-9813, www.southcarolinaparks.com/tablerock

This outing features the greatest elevation change of any hike in this entire guidebook. A tough loop at Table Rock State Park, it also offers rewards aplenty, including waterfalls and views, as well as the chance to summit Pinnacle Mountain at 3,425 feet. Bring water with you—you'll travel many miles on high ridges before reaching any in the field. Start on the famed Table Rock Trail, passing waterfalls and a great view from the Civilian Conservation Corps (CCC) shelter before joining a wooded ridgeline traveling west. The trail trends ever upward, topping out at wooded Pinnacle Mountain. A sharp descent meets Foothills Trail, and your loop will follow South Carolina's master path and its final miles to its traditional ending. Along the way you'll pass my favorite rock view, Bald Rock, then descend the declivitous Mill Creek Gorge, passing numerous falls and cascades before curving around a steep mountain slope to join Carrick Creek, which offers more falls of its own.

## GETTING THERE

From Pickens, drive north on US 178 West for 9.0 miles. Turn right onto SC 11 and follow it for 4.4 miles to West Gate Road. Turn left onto West Gate Road, continuing to the park entrance. From the park entrance station, follow the main road for 0.7 mile to Carrick Creek Nature Center and trailhead. The hike starts behind the nature center. A parking fee and trailhead registration are mandatory.

## THE TRAIL

Leave the nature center breezeway, crossing Carrick Creek. Take the paved

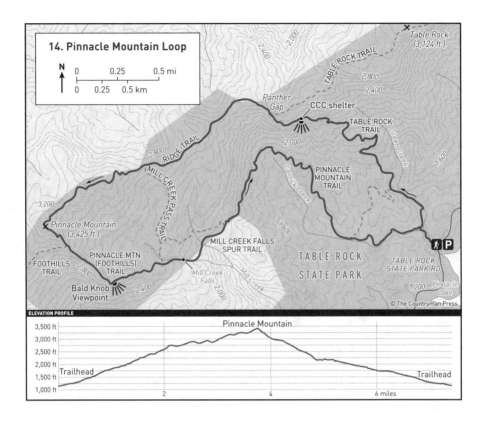

## 14. Pinnacle Mountain Loop

N

0      0.25      0.5 mi

0   0.25   0.5 km

Table Rock
(3,124 ft.)

TABLE ROCK TRAIL

2,800

2,400

Panther
Gap

CCC shelter

TABLE ROCK
TRAIL

Green Creek

1,600

2,000

RIDGE TRAIL

2,800

PINNACLE
MOUNTAIN
TRAIL

Carrick Creek

MILL CREEK PASS TRAIL

3,200

Pinnacle Mountain
(3,425 ft.)

1,600

PINNACLE MTN.
(FOOTHILLS)
TRAIL

FOOTHILLS
TRAIL

2,800

MILL CREEK FALLS
SPUR TRAIL

TABLE ROCK
STATE PARK

TABLE ROCK
STATE PARK RD

Mill Creek
Falls

Mill Creek

2,000

1,200

Pinnacle
Lake

Bald Knob
Viewpoint

2,400

© The Countryman Press

**ELEVATION PROFILE**

| 3,500 ft | Pinnacle Mountain |
| 3,000 ft | |
| 2,500 ft | |
| 2,000 ft | |
| 1,500 ft | Trailhead                                                     Trailhead |
| 1,000 ft | |

2                         4                    6 miles

path along the stream, passing a waterfall and plunge pool. The paved path continues up the valley, crossing Carrick Creek to a trail junction. Split right here, staying with Table Rock Trail. The wide dirt path joins shaded Green Creek, spanning the stream. Watch for a 4-foot ledge drop just above the crossing. Continue up the valley, passing a stair-step cascade of 40 feet. A second ledge cascade lies ahead. Cross Green Creek again to pass the green-blazed Carrick Creek Nature Trail at 0.5 mile.

Table Rock Trail ascends amid boulders and trickling branches. Keep working up a wash, weaving amid car-size stones. Pass two cabin-size boulders, one of which you climb using wooden

steps, at 1.2 miles. The ascent steepens, and partial views open from the mountainside. Reach the CCC shelter and overlook. The roofed wooden structure stands in the woods, just above a huge rock face that offers expansive views. Paris Mountain and Greenville are to your left. Below is the state park's Pinnacle Lake. Beyond, hills give way to the flatlands.

After the shelter, you'll reach Panther Gap and a trail junction at 2.1 miles. Here Ridge Trail leaves left for Pinnacle Mountain. If you're itching for a view, walk east on Table Rock Trail for 0.6 mile to Governors Rock. Otherwise, ascend west from Panther Gap on a narrow ridge nose. The trail is shaded by oak, birch, beech, and hickory. You

LOOKING OUT FROM BALD ROCK

will notice how much less this trail is used, compared with Table Rock Trail. Slip over to the south side of the ridge in thick woods, with many vines hanging from the trees.

Reach a gap, then climb again, only to work over to the north side of the ridge. Ridge Trail immediately enters rhododendron thickets, tunneling down to a gap and a trail junction at 3.0 miles. Mill Creek Pass Trail leaves left. If you're tired, you can shortcut your loop by taking this trail, but you'll miss two major highlights—Pinnacle Mountain and Bald Rock.

Work your way directly up the ridge-line on Ridge Trail, then pick up an old woods road. This grade weaves through heavy woods, gaining elevation. Top out on the pinnacle of Pinnacle Mountain at 3.8 miles, elevation 3,425 feet. The wooded summit is designated with a survey marker, but there are no views. A small clearing stands at the crest. Head left here, now on Pinnacle Trail, which nose-dives down the south face of the mountain to meet and join Foothills Trail at 4.0 miles. This route follows the traditional and original terminus of the FT, ending at Table Rock State Park.

Stay left again as the Foothills and Pinnacle Trails run in conjunction beneath tunnels of mountain laurel. Work down the rocky nose of a ridge, losing elevation fast (this is a 2,265-foot descent!), to open onto Bald Rock and a superlative view, my favorite in the Palmetto State, at 4.4 miles. To the northeast you can clearly see Table Rock; swinging east, as much land as the eye can behold. To the south lies yet more wooded country. Bald Rock has many vista points and exploration areas, so plan to linger here a while.

To continue your loop, keep heading downhill and east on the rock to find the blazed trail opening into the woods, dominated by pine and laurel on a rocky root-filled track to join sparkling Mill Creek amid rhododendron. Here Mill Creek Pass Trail has cut down from the ridge of Pinnacle Mountain. Mill Creek begins its precipitous descent to the foothills below. You descend, too, but not as fast, because the trail employs switchbacks to follow the steep stream gradient. Mill Creek drops nearly as one continuous fall; it's hard to figure out which is Mill Creek Falls. And it doesn't matter, really, for what you have is a small scenic stream slicing down the mountainside and a trail that offers nearly continual views of it.

Cross Mill Creek on a bridge. Here, a 60-or-so-foot drop falls upstream of you. Below the bridge, there are more slide-type water drops. Farther still, the stream plunges over a rim lip and out of sight. Wow! Turn away from Mill Creek and begin working around the steep slope of lower Pinnacle Mountain. Small feeder streams make more low-flow falls. Reach a distinctive overhanging bluff at 5.3 miles. Pinnacle Trail travels along and under this bluff for a while.

Pinnacle Creek Trail becomes more of a widely dug path as it winds in and out of small drainages. Look for huge boulders and boulder fields in the adjacent woods. Keep a moderate but steady descent. The sights aren't over yet: You meet the far end of Carrick Creek Nature Trail at 6.8 miles. Leave the solitude behind here to saddle alongside Carrick Creek—and enjoy the ride, as Carrick Creek makes its own fall-, chute-, and cascade-laden descent for the lowlands. Many of the drops here are rock slab slides. White pines grow tall over the rooty, beaten trail. Cross Carrick Creek a total of three times by rockhop and reach a final junction, meeting Table Rock Trail and then completing the loop portion of the hike. From here you'll backtrack the short distance to the nature center, finishing the hike at 7.6 miles.

# 15

# Raven Cliff Falls Loop

**TOTAL DISTANCE**: 7.9-mile loop

**HIKING TIME**: 5 hours

**VERTICAL RISE**: 1,250 feet

**RATING**: Difficult

**MAPS**: USGS 7.5' Table Rock; Mountain Bridge Wilderness Area, Foothills Trail

**TRAILHEAD GPS COORDINATES**: N35° 6.948', W82° 38.317'

**CONTACT INFORMATION**: Caesars Head State Park, 8155 Greer Highway, Cleveland, SC 29635, (864)836-6115, www.southcarolinaparks.com/caesarshead

This challenging loop hike takes you to a well-visited overlook of famed Raven Cliff Falls, then onward, looping to see the falls as few do. The trip is arduous, but it separates you from the rest of the crowd in the south end of the Mountain Bridge Wilderness.

Start in the high country, rambling above 3,000 feet, to enjoy a long-range view of the falls, then travel down to the cool mountain valley of Matthews Creek, its source. Climb away from the trout-teeming stream to an overlook astride Raven Cliff Falls, passing rockhouses and other stone features, before crossing upper Matthews Creek on a dramatic suspension bridge. Join South Carolina's main mountain track, Foothills Trail, for some more highland rambling, completing the loop. This hike is a strenuous one, thanks to the drop to Matthews Creek and subsequent climb out of it.

## GETTING THERE

From Pickens, take SC 8 north for 15 miles to SC 11. Veer right onto SC 11/ SC 8 and follow it to the point where SC 8 turns left. Stay with SC 8 for 1.3 more miles, then keep forward on US 276. Follow US 276 as it climbs, passing Caesars Head State Park Visitor Center at 6.4 miles (a Mountain Bridge Wilderness map can be purchased here). Continue on US 276 for 1 mile past the visitor center to reach the trailhead on your right. A parking fee and trailhead registration are mandatory. Raven Cliff Falls Trail starts on the opposite side of US 276 from the parking area.

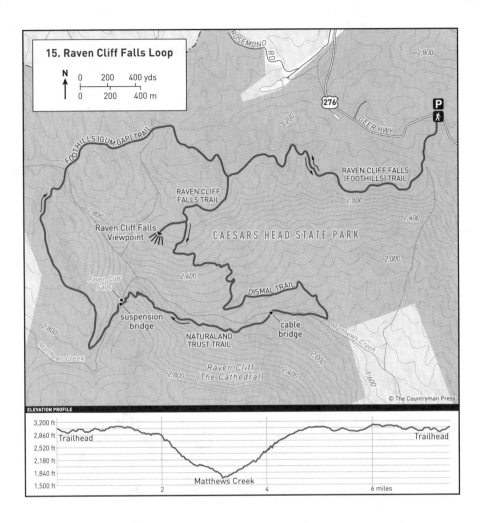

**15. Raven Cliff Falls Loop**

N
0   200   400 yds
0   200   400 m

ROSEMOND RD

2,800

276

GEER HWY

P

3,200

FOOTHILLS (GUM GAP) TRAIL

RAVEN CLIFF FALLS (FOOTHILLS) TRAIL

2,800

2,400

RAVEN CLIFF FALLS TRAIL

Raven Cliff Falls Viewpoint

CAESARS HEAD STATE PARK

2,000

2,800

Raven Cliff Falls

2,400

DISMAL TRAIL

Matthews Creek

2,800

suspension bridge

cable bridge

2,000

1,600

NATURALAND TRUST TRAIL

Matthews Creek

Raven Cliff (The Cathedral)

2,800       2,400

© The Countryman Press

**ELEVATION PROFILE**

3,200 ft
2,860 ft  Trailhead                                              Trailhead
2,520 ft
2,180 ft
1,840 ft
1,500 ft                 Matthews Creek
                    2                    4                    6 miles

## THE TRAIL

Leave the trailhead and registration area, descending on a gravel road. Foothills Trail runs in conjunction with Raven Cliff Falls Trail here. Pass a power-line clearing and outbuilding, then veer right onto a foot trail that follows an old roadbed. The wide dirt track meanders westerly on the cusp of a deep drop-off into Matthews Creek and features great winter views to the south. You can hear the stream and falls roaring below.

The nearly level track passes over some rock slabs in a pine-oak-laurel forest. Pass side trails leading left to slabs with few views at 0.9 mile. Descend into a rhododendron thicket, then rise back into dry wood to pick up a straight roadbed at 1.3 miles. Veer left here, keeping southwest to reach a junction at 1.5 miles. Here the Foothills and Raven Cliff Falls Trails part ways; Foothills Trail will be your return route.

Stay with the red-blazed Raven Cliff Falls Trail, descending via switchbacks, still on the edge of the drop-off. Watch for a rock bench at one switchback. Meet

RAGGED BLUFFLINE ABOVE MATTHEWS CREEK

Dismal Trail in a gap at 1.9 miles. Keep forward here, following Raven Cliff Falls Trail for 0.1 mile to reach a rock overlook and wooden viewing platform. Through a frame of trees, you get a long-range vista of the 400-foot falls dropping over a sheer rock face. Backtrack to the purple-blazed Dismal Trail and begin your big descent. This single-track footpath shows much less use. You'll soon pass an outcrop that offers a superior view of Raven Cliff Falls. The path continues a rough, curving, switchbacking track down a steep slope crowded with small trees. Come along a creek, then continue winding down to reach an old woods road, which (mercifully) has superior footing.

Keep aiming for Matthews Creek, loudly rushing below you, unseen but easily heard. The woods thicken with vegetation just before you meet Naturaland Trust Trail at 3.3 miles. This is the low point of your hike, below 1,800 feet. Turn right here, heading upstream among rhododendrons. Continue up the gorgeous remote valley to reach a crossing of Matthews Creek. You can see big rocks, frothing water, and pools in this mountain watercourse that cuts a huge gorge. At normal flows, the creek can be rock-hopped, but just in case, double steel cables are tightly strung across for high-water, high-wire-act crossings. The cable crossing is actually fun, and challenging. Before you cross, linger at the creek to check out the cabin-size boulder upstream.

Climb away from Matthews Creek, leaving the streamside environment. The boulder-strewn track makes an irregular ascent on a single-track footpath. You are way above the creek, ultimately reaching a cliff line. The second cliff line you reach is simply incredible.

The rock wall heads straight up for the sky, making mere mortal humans feel puny by comparison.

Beyond the bluff, the climbing remains relentless, using ladders and steps to gain ground. Emerge onto an outcrop at 4.2 miles. The view of the upper Matthews Creek and the moun-

SUSPENSION BRIDGE ABOVE RAVEN CLIFF FALLS

tains upon which you will shortly be walking is inspiring. Below you, and mostly out of sight, Raven Cliff Falls roars. Relax and take it all in. But be careful: The drop is a doozy.

Switchback uphill some more on a laurel-and-galax-lined path, soon coming across a rock shelter, left of the trail, which could come in handy during a rainstorm. Work your way forward on a narrow, rooty track, then meet Matthews Creek and a costly, impressive suspension bridge. It stands above the uppermost fall of Raven Cliffs Falls, which you can see. Downstream, the main drop of Raven Cliffs Falls disappears over a rock rim, with a sheer mountain as a backdrop. Upstream are more cascades of Matthews Creek, which continues to display superlative beauty.

Beyond the span, Naturaland Trust Trail continues up the perched valley of Matthews Creek before curving away from the creek to enter hickory-oak-pine woods, tracing an old roadbed. Meet Foothills Trail at 4.7 miles. To your left, it's 80-odd miles to Oconee State Park. Turn right here, heading uphill on the FT, on an eroded rocky and sandy track. Foothills Trail levels off, then offers easy highland cruising. It takes a little while for your ears to adjust to the quiet, as opposed to the continual rushing water roar of Matthews Creek Valley.

You are now back above 3,000 feet and feeling every inch of the climb. Take your time and enjoy the woods here, tramping in the high country, now atop the mountains you were looking at earlier from the outcrop beside Raven Cliff Falls.

Leave the high pinewoods for dark rhododendrons to cross a small stream by a culvert at 5.5 miles. Rise from the stream shed to make an abrupt right turn at 6.0 miles, soon climbing past a gate, most likely open, to meet Raven Cliff Falls Trail at 6.4 miles. Begin backtracking here, returning to the trailhead at 7.9 miles.

# 16

# Raven Rock Loop

**TOTAL DISTANCE**: 3.9-mile loop

**HIKING TIME**: 2 hours

**VERTICAL RISE**: 350 feet

**RATING**: Moderate to difficult

**MAPS**: USGS 7.5' Salem; Keowee-Toxaway State Park

**TRAILHEAD GPS COORDINATES**: N34° 55.922', W82° 53.151'

**CONTACT INFORMATION**: Keowee-Toxaway State Park, 108 Residence Drive, Sunset, SC 29685, (864)868-2605, www .southcarolinaparks.com/keoweetoxaway

This loop offers a natural bridge over which to walk, rocky views, a primitive campsite, a lake, and a surprisingly challenging hike, all occurring within Keowee-Toxaway State Park. Leave the trailhead—winding through thick forest—then dip to Poe Creek; you will hear it first, then cross it before you know it, because the crossing is on a natural bridge. The path winds through an interesting boulder field before rising to Raven Rock, where you will have nice views from a semi-wooded outcrop. From here, the trail takes a rugged up-and-down track along McKinney Mountain before diving to meet Lake Keowee. Pass another outcrop and view while leaving the lake. The trail then winds through lower Poe Creek, a classic mountain stream, before climbing again to complete the loop. Be apprised that the trail features some primitive campsites beside Lake Keowee.

## GETTING THERE

From Pickens, drive north on US 178 West for 9 miles to SC 11. Turn left onto SC 11 and continue for 7.9 miles to Keowee-Toxaway State Park. Turn right into the part of the state park with the campground, on the north side of SC 11. Drive just a short distance toward the campground and look to your right. You will see a narrow road leading up to a meetinghouse. The trailhead and a small parking area are up the road, behind the Meeting House.

## THE TRAIL

Leave the Meeting House parking area on Natural Bridge Trail, descending over some concrete before reaching a single-track path in mesic woods of oak, hickory, and pine trees, standing over

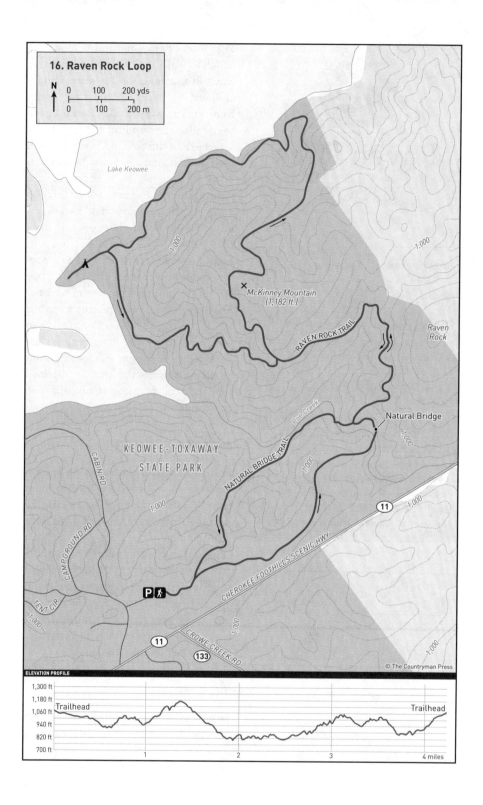

16. Raven Rock Loop

N
0    100    200 yds
0    100    200 m

Lake Keowee

1,000

McKinney Mountain
(1,182 ft.)

RAVEN ROCK TRAIL

Raven
Rock

1,000

Poe Creek

Natural Bridge

KEOWEE-TOXAWAY
STATE PARK

1,000

NATURAL BRIDGE TRAIL

1,000

1,000

CABIN RD

CAMPGROUND RD

TENT CIR

1,000

P

11

CHEROKEE FOOTHILLS SCENIC HWY

11

CROWE CREEK RD

133

1,000

1,000

© The Countryman Press

ELEVATION PROFILE

| | | | | |
|---|---|---|---|---|
| 1,300 ft | | | | |
| 1,180 ft | | | | |
| 1,060 ft | Trailhead | | | Trailhead |
| 940 ft | | | | |
| 820 ft | | | | |
| 700 ft | 1 | 2 | 3 | 4 miles |

LOOKING OUT ON LAKE KEOWEE AND BEYOND

scads of mountain laurel. You'll shortly reach a split; continue forward, still on Natural Bridge Trail, which joins an old roadbed. SC 11 is off to your right. Undulate along the old roadbed, eventually aiming for Poe Creek. The forest thickens as you begin to hear the creek. Then suddenly, at 0.5 mile, you are beyond Poe Creek, having bridged it on a wide stone slab so well integrated into the land (after all, it is perfectly natural) that it's virtually indiscernible. Stop here and explore the landscape. Just after the crossing, you can access Poe Creek to your left. Work your way up several feet, and you can peer under the Natural Bridge, hearing the stream's babblings echo off the rock slab.

Natural Bridge Trail climbs away and turns to parallel Poe Creek. More rock slabs lie below, along the stream. Reach a trail junction at 0.6 mile. Natural Bridge Trail keeps forward—you'll be rejoining it later. This is where you begin a little dry hiking, on Raven Rock Trail. Turn right and uphill, soon entering a world of rocks and boulders, passing small rockhouses and wide slabs and tall boulders that invite rock scrambles. Keep uphill, reentering full-fledged woodland before opening onto a wide rock slab at 1.0 mile. This is Raven Rock. Views open to the west amid the pines. This is a partially vegetated rock slab—the thin soils that accumulate support pines, lichens, and moss, among other limited species. The trailbed becomes faint across the slab. You are at 1,100 feet in elevation.

The trail drops from the slab rock hill, then goes down farther than you think it would, or should, as it dives into a sharp-sided ravine with an intermittent stream at its base. The trail takes this route to stay inside the park boundaries. It then ascends just as steeply, now joining McKinney Mountain. Head west along the mountain, sporting redbud and sassafras trees aplenty. Squirrels scatter as you trek on, reaching a trail junction at 1.8 miles. Stay right and downhill here, on a peninsular path that makes a subloop to the shores of Lake Keowee. Young trees crowd the trail. Begin dropping off McKinney Mountain and then loop to the right, on the steepest part of a steep hike. Glimpses of Lake Keowee open through the trees. In winter, the views will be more prevalent here. Water closes in on both sides of you, and you wonder where the trail will go. One thing you know: It will be going back up.

Finally you level off as the trail reaches the primitive campsites stretched out on the peninsula. These lake-view camps have metal fire rings and are mostly shaded by pines. The trail extends to the very point of the land, reaching its tip and the final primitive campsite at 2.1 miles. Look out on the lake, hills, and shoreline development across the water—this isn't a deep wilderness hike. The water remains clear and appealing, due to inflow from mountain streams such as Poe Creek. Backtrack and begin looping to your right, entering heavy woods along the shore, which will seem extra dark after the open lakeshore. The trail angles on a sharp slope and reaches an outcrop at 2.3 miles. You can look down on Lake Keowee and westward toward Georgia.

Keep climbing very steeply back up the slope of McKinney Mountain to rejoin the main loop at 2.5 miles. Stay forward here, enjoying some brief level walking before dropping precipitously on a dirt path. This descent could be treacherous if rain has fallen lately. Reach cool and dark Poe Creek Valley at 2.9 miles, where beech and tulip trees, rhododendrons, and ferns thrive. The valley is steep sided, and the trail remains rugged as it heads upstream. Poe Creek falls in noisy stair-step cascades over mossy rock ramparts. While walking upstream, you may notice a path across the creek—you will be on that path soon enough, as the trail skirts a flat, then comes to a trail junction and bouldery crossing of Poe Creek at 3.1 miles. Look for a small waterfall just upstream of the crossing. Rock-hop the watercourse and begin heading downstream, joining a steep slope and working around a bluffline. Meet a roadbed that turns up a side hollow, then veers onto a ridgeline to make the final steep climb of the trip. At 3.7 miles, you'll reach a trail junction: You have completed the loop portion of the hike. Backtrack 0.2 mile to reach the trailhead.

# Rim of the Gap Loop

| | |
|---|---|
| **TOTAL DISTANCE**: 9.1-mile loop | |

**TOTAL DISTANCE**: 9.1-mile loop

**HIKING TIME**: 6.5 hours

**VERTICAL RISE**: 1,500 feet

**RATING**: Difficult

**MAPS**: USGS 7.5' Cleveland, Standingstone Mountain, Table Rock; Mountain Bridge Wilderness Area

**TRAILHEAD GPS COORDINATES**: N35° 7.564', W82° 34.271'

**CONTACT INFORMATION**: Jones Gap State Park, 303 Jones Gap Road, Marietta, SC 29661, (864) 836-3647, www.southcarolinaparks/jonesgap

This challenging loop traverses the lower Middle Saluda River Valley at Jones Gap State Park. You'll begin by walking up the richly wooded river valley of a pure mountain stream to reach Jones Gap Falls, a side stream that makes a series of drops over a bare, jagged rock face. The hike continues up the watercourse, a state-designated scenic river, to meet one of its major feeders, Coldspring Branch. The loop ascends this rugged valley, ultimately rising to near 3,000 feet, whereupon the hike joins Rim of the Gap Trail. Here the hiking slows but becomes visually exciting as you travel for miles along a rugged bluffline replete with small falls and rugged hiking over rock formations and fallen boulders, around cliffs, and through a rockfall arch. The trail becomes more foot friendly atop a ridgeline before joining Ishi Trail—which, despite its mostly downhill trend, is about as tough as Rim of the Gap Trail. Pass a cave to come along the Middle Saluda River once again, completing the loop. This trek is strenuous and slow, thanks not only to its numerous elevation gains but also to the rocky, rugged nature of its paths.

## GETTING THERE

From Pickens, take SC 8 north for 15 miles to SC 11. Veer right onto SC 11 and follow it for 2.0 miles to US 276. Turn right and follow US 276 for 4.0 miles to River Falls Road. Turn left onto River Falls Road; continue for 5.5 miles as it turns into Jones Gap Road to dead-end at Jones Gap State Park. From the parking area, follow the path to bridge the Middle Saluda River. Continue beyond the park office on your right (a trail map can be purchased at the office). Cross

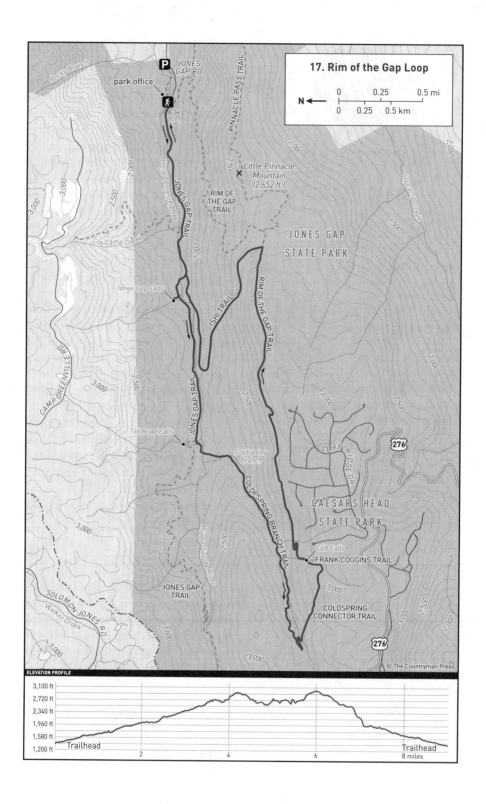

## 17. Rim of the Gap Loop

N ←

| 0 | 0.25 | 0.5 mi |
|---|------|--------|
| 0 | 0.25 | 0.5 km |

P
JONES
GAP RD

park office

Rocky Branch

PINNACLE PASS TRAIL

Little Pinnacle
Mountain
(2,652 ft.)

RIM OF
THE GAP
TRAIL

JONES GAP
STATE PARK

Oil Camp Creek

Cox Camp Creek

Middle Saluda River

JONES GAP TRAIL

Jones Gap Falls

ISHI TRAIL

RIM OF THE GAP TRAIL

CAMP GREENVILLE RD

Toll Road Falls

JONES GAP TRAIL

Coldspring
Branch

COLDSPRING BRANCH TRAIL

CLIFF RIDGE DR

276

CAESARS HEAD
STATE PARK

Cliff Falls

FRANK COGGINS TRAIL

Middle Saluda River

JONES GAP
TRAIL

COLDSPRING
CONNECTOR TRAIL

SOLOMON JONES RD

Walker Creek

276

© The Countryman Press

**ELEVATION PROFILE**

| 3,100 ft |
| 2,720 ft |
| 2,340 ft |
| 1,960 ft |
| 1,580 ft |
| 1,200 ft |

Trailhead                                                                 Trailhead

2        4        6        8 miles

the wooden road bridge back over to the left bank of the Middle Saluda. A parking fee and trailhead registration are mandatory.

## THE TRAIL

After registering, leave the trailside kiosk and climb along Jones Gap Trail, Trail 1. This wide, sandy track travels along the rolling and rambling Middle Saluda River, with its deep pools, large boulders, and trout, which lurk in the chilly waters. The path traces the old Jones Gap Turnpike, an historic hand-built road. Keep forward, soon passing Rim of the Gap Trail. Other side trails head off toward primitive campsites. Overhead, a rich forest of beech and maple, bordered by rhododendron, surrounds the sandy, rocky track. Ferns, sweet birch, and brushy doghobble are also abundant. At .5 mile, pass Rainbow Falls Trail, leading right to Rainbow Falls, which tumbles over a cliff along Cox Camp Creek. Briefly turn away from the river, and climb, only to return to the stream. At 0.8 mile, reach a bridge spanning the Middle Saluda River. Ishi Trail leaves left—this will be your return route. Span the Middle Saluda, passing more primitive campsites, to reach the side trail to Jones Gap Falls at 1.1 miles. This spur trail leads 60 yards up to a cascade, spilling 60 feet over a widening rock face, bordered by thick woods. The low-flow tributary can be but a dripping trickle during drier times.

Continue up Jones Gap Trail, passing a huge rock slab open to the sky that would make a good river-hanging-out spot. Just past this slab, at 2.1 miles, meet the orange-blazed Coldspring Branch Trail, Trail 3. Turn left here, descending to a small stream then meeting the (now smaller) Middle

Saluda River. There has been a bridge here in the past, and high water could make this crossing difficult. If you are concerned about the potential for high water, check with Jones Gap State Park at (864) 836-3647 for the latest conditions at this crossing before undertaking the hike.

Enter Coldspring Branch Valley, a good wildflower destination, reaching another intersection. Signboards at key trail junctions here make getting lost unlikely. Coldspring Branch Trail meets Bill Kimball Trail, Trail 5, near a primitive campsite. Keep forward, up Coldspring Branch Trail, which soon climbs steeply up the declivitous valley, only to level off and cross the stream three times. You'll notice mossy boulders and fallen timber in the creek. These crossings can be rock-hopped in times of normal flow. Coldspring Branch has its own feeders, which you will also cross. The next three crossings are spread apart, but after the sixth, the trail turns away from the creek and climbs through fern fields. Intersect the Coldspring Connector, Trail 7, at 3.7 miles. Turn left here, dropping very steeply to step over Coldspring Branch one last time, before climbing out just as steeply to meet Frank Coggins Trail, Trail 15, at 4.0 miles. You are nearly at 3,000 feet but have many ups and downs ahead. Caesars Head State Park Visitor Center lies but a short distance to your right; this loop, however, turns left, dropping along the purple-blazed trail to meet another intersection where Frank Coggins Trail makes a loop. Stay left again to reach Cliff Falls at 4.2 miles. You are atop the falls and at yet another junction just on the far side of a bridge over Cliff Falls. Turn left, now on the rugged portion of the yellow-blazed Rim of the Gap Trail. Ahead, a rough track heads to the

JONES GAP FALLS

bottom of the waterfall on top of which you just walked. It offers a good view of the 50-foot cascade. At the bottom is a small, cavelike shelter.

Thus begins the portion of this hike that boasts numerous rock features, from open rock slabs to boulders and outcrops. The trail cuts a very rugged path along the rim. Travel is slow; take your time. Ladders and cables are necessary in places. Keep working down the waterfall stream, then turn east, traveling along rock walls and places where water skims over open rock and reflects the sun.

At points, you will have to scramble amid the boulders on all fours. Watch for a mini-cave to the right of the trail at 5.0 miles. Also watch for intermittent views across the Middle Saluda Valley. Unfortunately, dying or dead hemlocks will be in the foreground of the views. The path has some ups and downs but generally runs between 2,600 and 2,800 feet as it keeps east, passing too many dripping rock slabs to mention. At 5.7 miles, the path goes under a rockfall arch, which necessitates a "Fat Man's Squeeze." The official name is Weight Watchers Rock. Either way, it's a crawl.

From the rockfall arch, the trail climbs around a huge crevasse below to reach the crest of a ridge and wooded easy walking. Start descending, then intersect John Sloan Trail, Trail 21, at 6.2 miles. Continue your downward course. Enjoy the easy walking and reach a four-way intersection at 6.7 miles. Turn left here, joining the white-blazed Ishi Trail, Trail 8. If you're tired, you can keep forward on Rim of the Gap Trail and reach the trailhead in 2.2 miles. To complete this hike, though, stick it out on Ishi Trail, wondering if "Ishi" is Cherokee for "rough path." (In fact, it's the name of the California woman who donated the money for the trail.)

Ishi Trail starts out innocently enough, winding through rich steep coves on an old roadbed before dropping sharply and irregularly. Look for Rainbow Falls across the gorge in winter. The dirt path is often sloped downhill as it angles through the woods. It also goes over downed timber aplenty. Pick up a logging grade at 7.2 miles. You think the going is getting easier, but the grade travels uphill. Eventually the path leaves the roadbed and finds a break in the bluffline, using a ladder to descend. Pass an incredible sheer bluff to the right of the trail. Just beyond, look to your left for a faint path leading to an overhanging rock shelter known as Misty Caverns. This shelter has housed a few people over the years.

Come ever closer to the singing Middle Saluda. The rough trail mercifully picks up an old roadbed and keeps downhill, paralleling the Middle Saluda to reach Jones Gap Trail at 8.3 miles. You have been here before. Enjoy more of the Middle Saluda scenery, completing your loop at 9.1 miles.

# Station Cove Falls via Historic Oconee Station

This hike begins at one of South Carolina's first mountain frontier outposts, Oconee Station, which is worth an exploratory ramble before you take off to circle a pond at Oconee Station State Historic Site. The trek then enters Sumter National Forest, heading up Station Creek. Beavers have dammed the lower reaches of the stream in a large, wide cove, and streamlets trickle toward Station Creek beneath lush woodlands, rife with wildflowers in spring. The valley narrows, and the trail enters the declivitous valley that harbors Station Cove Falls. On your return trip you can circle the other side of the pond. Consider bringing a picnic lunch, as Oconee Station has an excellent picnic ground.

**TOTAL DISTANCE**: 2.3 miles round trip

**HIKING TIME**: 1 hour

**VERTICAL RISE**: 240 feet

**RATING**: Easy

**MAPS**: USGS 7.5' Walhalla; Oconee Station Historic Site, Palmetto Trail—Oconee Passage

**TRAILHEAD GPS COORDINATES**: N34° 50.763', W83° 4.254'

**CONTACT INFORMATION**: Oconee Station State Historic Site, 500 Oconee Station Road, Walhalla, SC 29691, (864) 638-0079, www.southcarolinaparks.com /oconeestation

## GETTING THERE

From the intersection of SC 28 and SC 11 in Walhalla, head north on SC 11 for 6.3 miles to Oconee Station Road. Turn left and follow Oconee Station Road for 2.1 miles to the park entrance on your right. Follow the park road to its dead end at a parking area, adjacent to the picnic ground and a small park office. The trail starts a little way back on the park road.

## THE TRAIL

Just up the hill from the trailhead are Oconee Station and the William Richards house. Take the time to see the buildings before or after your hike. Guided tours are held on Saturday and Sunday between 1 and 5 pm. Oconee Station is closed in January and February. Oconee Station was erected first, probably in 1792. It was built as one in a series of fortifications to protect white settlers from Indian attacks as they moved into

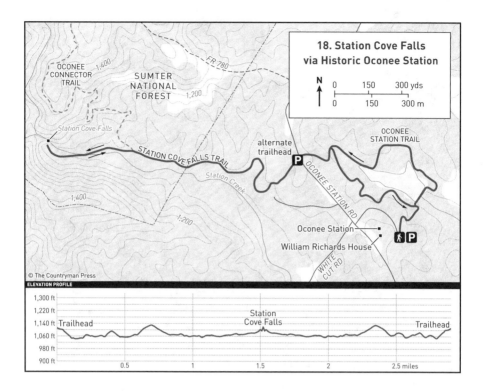

18. Station Cove Falls
via Historic Oconee Station

N

| 0 | 150 | 300 yds |
| 0 | 150 | 300 m |

OCONEE
CONNECTOR
TRAIL

SUMTER
NATIONAL
FOREST

FR 780

1,400

1,200

Station Cove Falls

STATION COVE FALLS TRAIL

Station Creek

1,400

1,200

alternate
trailhead

P

OCONEE
STATION TRAIL

OCONEE STATION RD

Oconee Station

William Richards House

WHITE CUT RD

P

© The Countryman Press

ELEVATION PROFILE

1,300 ft
1,220 ft
1,140 ft  Trailhead
1,060 ft
980 ft
900 ft

Station
Cove Falls

Trailhead

0.5     1     1.5     2     2.5 miles

what was then the western frontier. Tensions had mounted as white settlers moved into the Cherokee Foothills, leading to run-ins between the settlers and the Cherokee. The government response was to build seven outposts, such as Oconee Station, in the Upstate. The brick structure housed soldiers over an 8-year period, by which point the local Indians were subdued and settlements were well established, making further attacks unlikely. During this period, the outpost also became a trading center. Troops were removed for good by 1799.

William Richards was the lead trader at the outpost, and in 1805, he built the brick house up the hill from Oconee Station. At this time, deerskins were in high demand across the Atlantic. Local Indians hunted deer and brought them to the trading post to exchange for goods ranging from iron pots to guns, whiskey, and cotton clothing. The guns were the most highly prized: Natives used them to gain tactical advantages over their foes as well as for hunting deer. Over time, they brought thousands of deerskins to the station. Imagine all the interactions here more than two centuries ago. Alas, the American frontier moved westward, and with the death of William Richards, Oconee Station became a backwater. Now the 210-acre site, listed on the National Register of Historic Places, is part of the South Carolina State Park system.

At the trailhead a path leads just a few yards uphill to Oconee Station. The main trail leads in the opposite direction, downhill past a sign that reads NATURE TRAIL, FALLS. Wind through thick woods to reach a trail junction shortly.

HISTORIC OCONEE STATION

To your left, a sign indicates the falls; you continue forward and downhill, first circling the park pond. Pass over the dam, open to the sun overhead. This lake can be popular with bank fishermen going after bream and other species. The trail then curves to the right, away from where you think it should go. Give it time: Eventually it curves back to the left to circle the pond amid pine, sweetgum, and sourwood forest about 30 feet above the water. Step over a couple of dry streambeds, which lead to quiet coves in the pond.

Join an old roadbed along the pond, circling to its head, then reaching a trail junction at 0.4 mile. Turn right here, now on the one-way track to Station Cove Falls, climbing to reach a second roadbed. The path curves right to shortly reach Oconee Station Road and a second trailhead, with a parking area and kiosk. Dip back into woodland on a wide track. The path is blazed in yellow as part of Palmetto Trail, South Carolina's master path, which traverses the length of the state, from the Upstate to the Lowcountry.

Dip into white-oak-dominated woods and reach the first of several small feeder branches of Station Creek. Span the stream on a wooden footbridge. This forested cove has many wildflowers in spring. To your left is Station Creek, but you can't hear it flowing. That's because beavers have dammed up the creek, forming a mountain wetland. Beavers were once common all over the Palmetto

State, save for the coast, but they were trapped to such an extent that many naturalists believed the rodent had disappeared from South Carolina. In 1940, six beavers from Georgia were reintroduced to Sandhills National Wildlife Refuge in Chesterfield County. Around that same time, beavers from the Savannah River Basin in Georgia came over the border on their own. From these two populations, beavers have spread throughout the state and are now found in all 46 counties. Beaver dams create shallow ponds such as this, which attract other wildlife, especially waterfowl, and are in general a boon to any ecosystem. The dams slow watercourses, settling sediment and filtering waters to make them cleaner.

After you pass the beaver dam area and the hollow narrows, Station Creek begins to flow anew. Bridge more side streams. You have now entered Sumter National Forest. Reach a trail junction and stile at 1.1 miles. The Oconee Passage of the Palmetto Trail leaves right and uphill to reach Oconee State Park via Station Mountain. The stile here allows only hikers to continue to the falls. The hollow narrows further and then steepens. Rock-hop clear Station Creek on a wide rock slab to reach the falls at 1.2 miles. Station Cove Falls drops over a rock lip then descends in stages, flowing level for a brief period only to widen over a final stage, completing a 60-foot drop. The rock cathedral around the cascade is the catch point for many fallen logs.

From here, backtrack along Station Creek, crossing Oconee Station Road to reach the trail junction near the pond. This time, take the right fork, circling the south side of the lake and crossing intermittent branches to finally climb back to Oconee Station and the end of your hike.

STATION COVE FALLS

# 19

# Sulphur Springs Loop

**TOTAL DISTANCE**: 3.8-mile loop

**HIKING TIME**: 2.5 hours

**VERTICAL RISE**: 700 feet

**RATING**: Moderate

**MAPS**: USGS 7.5' Paris Mountain; Paris Mountain State Park

**TRAILHEAD GPS COORDINATES**: N34° 55.921', W82° 22.997'

**CONTACT INFORMATION**: Paris Mountain State Park, 2401 State Park Road, Greenville, SC 29609, (864) 244-5565, www .southcarolinaparks.com/parismountain

This loop exemplifies the myriad hiking opportunities available at Paris Mountain State Park, just outside Greenville. The trail traces a stream flowing from the uppermost slopes of Paris Mountain to reach Mountain Lake, a small impoundment. From this quiet body of water, it resumes its climb past slide cascades to the upper shoulder of Paris Mountain, making a 700-foot ascent. Though views are limited on the peak, you can see the fire tower keeper's cabin site before working your way back down through piney woods. This trek will undoubtedly make you more curious about the rest of the trails here.

Note that the dual-use trails at Paris Mountain State Park are open to hiking and biking Sunday through Friday, but are hiking-only on Saturday. The trailhead is in an attractive setting, with two stone picnic shelters bordering either side of a mountain stream.

## GETTING THERE

From downtown Greenville, drive north on US 25/276 and turn right onto SC 253. At the traffic light, bear left to continue on SC 253. Drive for 2.5 miles and turn left onto State Park Road. The park entrance is on your left. Enter the park, drive for 0.8 mile, and stay right, heading for Shelters 5 and 6. Continue forward another mile, turning into Sulphur Springs Picnic Area (Shelters 5 and 6) on your left. There is a park entrance fee.

## THE TRAIL

Sulphur Springs Trail starts on the right bank of the stream, disappearing into lush streamside forest. The clear creek gurgles to your left as it flows clear over rocks, shaded by rhododendron. You'll

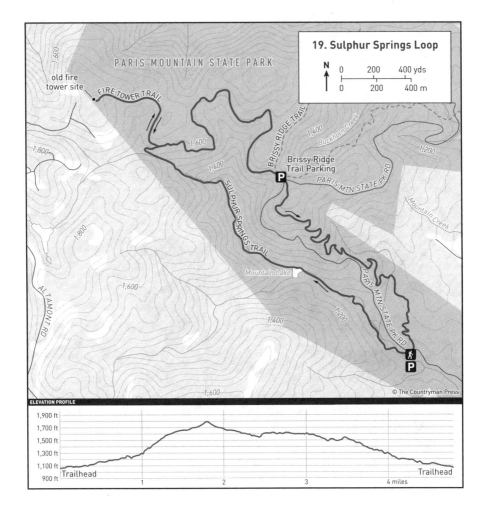

**ELEVATION PROFILE**

soon bridge the watercourse; continue up the sandy track. Sweetgum, pine, and hickory tower overhead. Bridge the stream a second time and continue up the right bank, passing a gazebo where a trail leads right. Here another track parallels Sulphur Springs Trail up the hill to your right.

The valley tightens, and rock outcrops appear. Listen for a loud falls. When you approach it, however, you'll realize that it's the spillway of the dam for Mountain Lake, an impoundment of but a few acres. Stone steps lead past the rustic stone dam. You now walk along the lakeshore on red clay. This section of trail is always hikers-only.

Leave the lake at 0.7 mile and continue ascending into a closed hollow. You become one with the creek, pinched in by the dense vegetation, while the stream noisily spills toward Mountain Lake. Fallen trees form light gaps in the forest. Step over the creek, climbing sharply past a low-flow slide cascade on your right at 1.0 mile. Keep ascending as the low-flow falls become nearly continuous, rolling over open rock slabs. Cross over to the right bank in front of one last drop, this one 8 or 10 feet, and make your way

REMAINS OF FIRE TOWER KEEPER'S CABIN

uphill into dry woods and a trail junction at 1.5 miles. Fire Tower Trail leads down and to your right; you, however, should continue forward and uphill to reach the high eastern shoulder of Paris Mountain and the foundation of the old fire tower keeper's residence. Woods now surround two brick chimneys and steps. The tower foundation is nearby. In the old days, towers such as these were manned by full-time, on-site residents, often using cisterns from roof runoff for water. Nowadays, fire watching is done by plane at times of high fire danger.

Views are limited up here by thick vegetation, save for winter, when the leaves have fallen off the trees. Reach a high point of nearly 1,800 feet. The actual peak of Paris Mountain is to the west and is more than 2,000 feet in elevation. Beyond the trail's high point, the path curves east. Enjoy the gentle cruise. Dip to a low point, then rise to the companion knob of Paris Mountain and its high point at 2.3 miles. The downhill begins in earnest as the trail drops to meet the other end of Fire Tower Trail at 2.6 miles. Sulphur Springs Loop stays left here, joining the old fire tower access road as it works around fallen pine trunks scattered on the old roadbed. Intersect the Brissy Ridge Trail parking area at 2.9 miles.

Keep forward across the parking lot to continue on Sulphur Springs Loop. The now narrower path climbs a small knob, then resumes a downgrade on a rocky, rooty track. Bridge a small branch three times while descending. You'll pass a side trail leading to the Archery Range trailhead on your right at 3.3 miles. Continue descending through piney woods as the valley flattens. Intersect Mountain Creek Trail at 3.7 miles. Turn right here, as Mountain Creek Trail continues forward, to shortly reach the trailhead, completing your loop.

Paris Mountain State Park was developed by the Civilian Conservation Corps (CCC) in the 1930s and is one of South Carolina's oldest state parks. The many wood and stone structures, such as the picnic shelters at the trailhead, offer rustic man-made beauty complementing the natural scenery increasingly seen as an urban getaway for Greater Greenville. The park trail system is growing in popularity, too, with hikers and mountain bikers both plying the paths. Other popular outings include Brissy Ridge Trail, which makes a 2.4-mile loop circling both Brissy Ridge and Buckhorn Creek; Fire Tower Trail, a trail within Sulphur Springs Loop; Mountain Creek Trail; North Lake Loop; and Pipsissewa Trail. Check with the park on the status of the latest trails. In addition to Mountain Lake, which also runs along Sulphur Springs Loop, the park has other impoundments. Paris Mountain was once used as the watershed to provide water for Greater Greenville. A camping area with water and electric sites caters primarily to RVs, but tents are welcome.

QUIET MOUNTAIN LAKE

# 20

# Upper Saluda River Loop

**TOTAL DISTANCE**: 5.5-mile loop

**HIKING TIME**: 3.2 hours

**VERTICAL RISE**: 1,100 feet

**RATING**: Difficult

**MAPS**: USGS 7.5' Cleveland, Table Rock, Standingstone Mountain; Mountain Bridge Wilderness Area

**TRAILHEAD GPS COORDINATES**: N35° 6.948', W82° 38.317'

**CONTACT INFORMATION**: Jones Gap State Park, 303 Jones Gap Road, Marietta, SC 29661, (864) 836-3647, www .southcarolinaparks/jonesgap

This classic loop hike takes in both the low and the high of the Mountain Bridge Wilderness at Jones Gap State Park. You'll leave the trailhead at 3,000 feet and make a ridge ramble to a gap, where you'll join the remote and little-used Bill Kimball Trail. The ridge running remains glorious and pleasant, but all good things must end, in this case for the better, as Bill Kimball Trail dives into the Middle Saluda Valley, passing some incredible bluffs. From here the path straddles the Middle Saluda in the deep, dark world of a high mountain valley. Cross the river, then turn upstream on the upper Jones Gap Trail, which traces the old Jones Gap Toll Road, a masterpiece of primitive engineering that makes a steady but moderate uptick past rockhouses and waterfalls. Travel through "The Winds"—as in "wind" a clock—to enter the highest part of the valley, where the cool climate is demonstrated by the presence of the yellow birch tree, a northern species rarely seen in the Palmetto State. Finally you'll make a huffing and puffing climb back to the trailhead via Tom Miller Trail.

## GETTING THERE

Veer right onto SC 11/SC 8 and follow it to the point where SC 8 turns left. Stay with SC 8 for 1.3 more miles, then keep forward on US 276. Follow US 276 as it climbs, passing Caesars Head State Park Visitor Center at 6.4 miles, where a Mountain Bridge Wilderness map can be purchased. Continue on US 276 for 1.0 mile to reach the trailhead, on your right. A parking fee and trailhead registration are mandatory. Coldspring Branch Trail starts on the left side of the parking area as you face US 276.

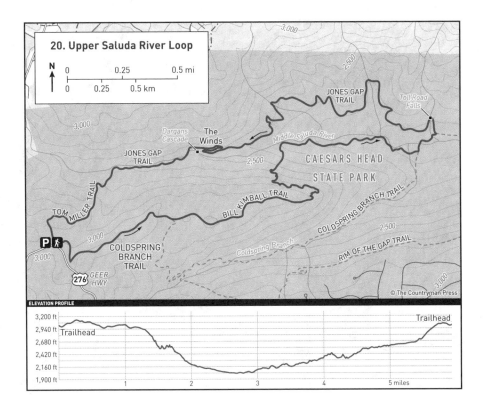

20. Upper Saluda River Loop

N

| 0 | 0.25 | 0.5 mi |
| 0 | 0.25 | 0.5 km |

JONES GAP
TRAIL

Toll Road
Falls

Dargans
Cascade

The
Winds

Middle Saluda River

JONES GAP
TRAIL

2,500

CAESARS HEAD

STATE PARK

BILL KIMBALL TRAIL

COLDSPRING BRANCH TRAIL

TOM MILLER TRAIL

3,000

COLDSPRING
BRANCH
TRAIL

Coldspring Branch

2,500

RIM OF THE GAP TRAIL

276 GEER
HWY

© The Countryman Press

ELEVATION PROFILE

3,200 ft
2,940 ft  Trailhead
2,680 ft
2,420 ft
2,160 ft
1,900 ft

Trailhead

1    2    3    4    5 miles

## THE TRAIL

Leave the trailhead on Coldspring Gap Trail, immediately entering a highland cove with Carolina silverbell and tulip trees rising above a fern-covered forest floor. Climb a bit to come near US 276. Turn left here, joining an old woods track leading away from the paved road. Tunnel through rhododendron, then head northeasterly into a mixed forest of dry species such as oak, as well as moist species like Fraser magnolia and sweet birch. The shaded track curves right and descends to a ferny gap and a trail junction at 0.6 mile. Leave Coldspring Branch Trail, keeping forward on the pink-blazed Bill Kimball Trail, Trail 5. Ascend from the gap, staying on the ridgeline, which levels off. Continue your

pleasant forest cruise on a path often bordered by galax, the shiny-leaved ground plant. Its tall stalk of tiny white flowers blooms in June here. Blueberries also find their place.

The ridgeline narrows as the trail makes a sharp left, leaving the ridgecrest to enter the Middle Saluda Valley. Winter views open across the valley as the path makes hard-core downhill switchbacks through tightly wound trunks and limbs of rhododendron. Meet a bluffline where the trail is so steep that chains have been installed to help you descend. Look up at the bluff and notice the laurel and rhododendron clinging to crevices in the rock.

Continue tunneling through dense greenery. Surprisingly, after the outcrop the trail turns up and climbs, but

for a reason you will soon see. Here, at 1.7 miles, is a three-tiered bluff so tall it curves beyond the sight of hikers. It tempts a scramble . . . but you may want to leave that to the pros.

Pass along the edge of the bluff, drifting in and out of woods before leaving the bluff for good on a diving descent. The single-track dirt path enters thickening woods, leading to a fern flat. The Middle Saluda is ricocheting down, gathering in pools, then following the rules of gravity to make the next pool. The trail drops, too, paralleling the beautiful watercourse, beneath the shade of Southern Appalachian splendor. Doghobble crowds the trailside. Keep downhill, eventually joining a woods track staying within earshot of the river.

In one spot the trail is undercut by the river and is in danger of being eroded away. This location, however, affords a fine upstream look at the watercourse between mossy boulders.

Reach Campsite B and Coldspring Branch Trail at 2.7 miles. Turn left here onto Coldspring Branch Trail, dipping to the Middle Saluda. A bridge has been here in the past and may well be in the future. In possible times of high water, check with the Jones Gap State Park office at (864) 836-3647 between 11 am and noon to learn the condition of this bridge. However, the stream can usually be crossed via logs or rocks unless it is really high.

Pass a small stream on a flat bridge before reaching Jones Gap Trail at 2.8

miles. Turn left here, now enjoying a graded path that heads up the Middle Saluda Valley. Jones Gap Trail traces a toll road built in the nineteenth century. The toll-road-cum-trail works its way westward into hollows then back out along rib ridges. This valley will be cool even on the hottest day. The moderate upgrade makes ascending a breeze. Pass Primitive Campsite 14, then the spur rail to Campsite 15 on your left at 3.7 miles. Ahead, look for a rock shelter to the right of the trail at 4.0 miles.

At 4.2 miles, make a 180-degree switchback to your right. Watch at the turn for a waterfall dead ahead, Dargans Cascade. The upper fall makes a wide 15-foot drop. The lower drop, just before the big turn in the trail, slides over a smooth rock face. Now Jones Gap Trail enters "The Winds," named for the winding nature of the climbing track. These wide and moderate switchbacks are a fine example of engineering, done before the era of heavy machinery. Below you the Saluda drops steeply in several more falls.

At 4.5 miles the trail passes just above a slide cascade. The stream settles down, quietly flowing to the right of the trail. Begin searching for yellow birch here. These trees are rare in South Carolina but plentiful here. Look for yellowish gold peeling bark with horizontal stripes. Larger yellow birches feature bark peeling on their upper branches but not on their lower trunks. Yellow birches grow along a few cool high-elevation streams in South Carolina.

Reach a trail junction at 4.8 miles. The Middle Saluda is but a small creek now, losing its force. Jones Creek Trail crosses the river, but you turn left, now on Bill Miller Trail, which passes a primitive campsite then wastes no time in climbing steeply in lung-busting fashion. The ascent continues in fits and starts as it joins a slender spur ridge. It reaches a high point and, seemingly for good measure, mocks all your efforts by dropping into ferny woods before making a slight uptick to complete the loop at 5.5 miles.

# Whitewater Falls There-and-Back

**TOTAL DISTANCE**: 5.8 miles round trip

**HIKING TIME**: 3.3 hours

**VERTICAL RISE**: 700 feet

**RATING**: Moderate to difficult

**MAPS**: USGS 7.5' Cashiers, Reid, Foothills Trail, National Geographic Trails Illustrated #785 Nantahala & Cullasaja Gorges

**TRAILHEAD GPS COORDINATES**: N35° 0.741', W82° 59.948'

**CONTACT INFORMATION**: Jocassee Gorges, 1344 Cleo Chapman Hwy, Sunset, SC 29685, (864) 868-0281, www.dnr.sc.gov

This trail heads to one of the most noteworthy destinations in the Carolinas, Whitewater Falls, also known as Upper Whitewater Falls. Crossing the line between North and South Carolina, the Whitewater River makes a stunning drop of 400-plus feet over a rocky face. Your hike will take you to a platform with a fantastic view of the falls. However, that's not the only highlight on this hike, which leaves the Bad Creek Project (run by Duke Power) and drops into the beautiful Whitewater River Valley. You'll pass through a former farming flat known as "The Hemlocks," then head up a clear trout stream, enveloped by lush woods, with beauty everywhere you look, only to bridge the river amid massive boulders. A series of challenging switchbacks brings you to the overlook. Bring your camera.

## GETTING THERE

From the junction of SC 11 and SC 130 just north of Salem, South Carolina, head north on SC 130, S. Bruce Rochester Memorial Highway. Keep north for 10.2 miles to the gated entrance to the Bad Creek Project. Drive up to the gate and it will open (from 6 a.m. to 6 p.m.). Pass through the gate, keep downhill for 2.1 miles, and turn left at the sign for Foothills Trail, driving 0.3 mile to a large parking area. Bad Creek Access Trail starts in the far left-hand corner of the parking area.

## THE TRAIL

Leave the large Bad Creek Access parking area, taking a graveled, brushy path bordered by scrubby trees, grass, and regrowth over disturbed land. The open area does offer good views of Grassy Knob and other surround-

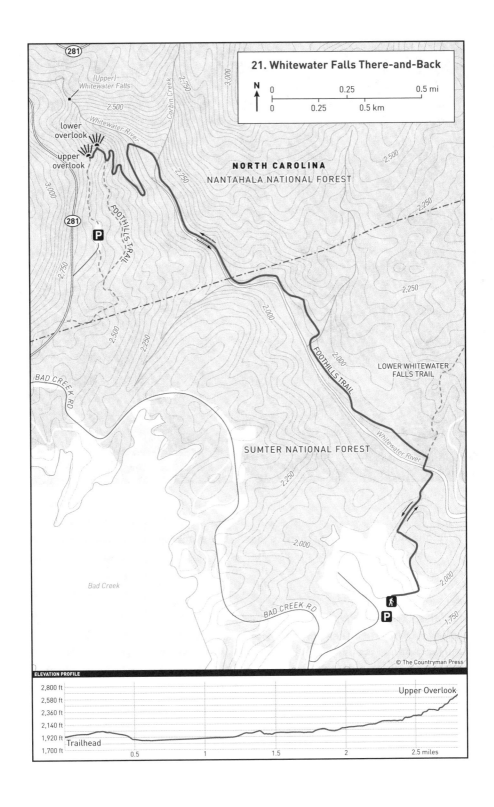

21. **Whitewater Falls There-and-Back**

N

| 0 | | 0.25 | | 0.5 mi |
| 0 | 0.25 | | 0.5 km | |

(Upper) Whitewater Falls

2,500

Whitewater River

Corbin Creek

2,750

3,000

lower overlook

upper overlook

281

3,000

FOOTHILLS TRAIL

281

P

2,750

2,500

NORTH CAROLINA
NANTAHALA NATIONAL FOREST

2,500

2,250

2,250

2,250

2,250

2,000

2,000

FOOTHILLS TRAIL

LOWER WHITEWATER
FALLS TRAIL

BAD CREEK RD

2,500

2,250

SUMTER NATIONAL FOREST

Whitewater River

2,250

Bad Creek

2,000

2,000

2,000

BAD CREEK RD

1,750

P

© The Countryman Press

**ELEVATION PROFILE**

| | | | | Upper Overlook |
| 2,800 ft | | | | |
| 2,580 ft | | | | |
| 2,360 ft | | | | |
| 2,140 ft | | | | |
| 1,920 ft | | | | |
| 1,700 ft | Trailhead | 0.5 | 1 | 1.5 | 2 | 2.5 miles |

BRIDGE OVER WHITEWATER RIVER

ing mountains. Keep east, then turn left, walking through more brush until the trail enters full-blown woods. Bad Creek Access Trail skirts the west side of a knob then gently descends into a flat, where you can hear the Whitewater River. Drift across the flat to reach a trail junction and the first of two bridges over the Whitewater River at 0.6 mile. To your left, before the bridge, is Coon Den Branch Trail, which heads up the left bank of the Whitewater River, passing through a 300-acre grove of old-growth trees to dead-end at the North Carolina–South Carolina border. (See Hike 11.)

Cross the two iron bridges over the Whitewater River and reach Foothills Trail. This trail continues forward toward Table Rock State Park and Lower Whitewater Falls Overlook. Your hike, however, heads left, up through one of the most beautiful yet imperiled slices of South Carolina, entering an area known as "The Hemlocks." This mountainside flat, formerly a farm, has now grown up into a gorgeous forest of hemlock, maple, pine, and tulip trees. Look for piled rocks indicating fields back in the woods. The hemlocks are under attack from the hemlock woolly adelgid, which means the name of this spot may have to be changed. Bridge a few streamlets

WHITEWATER FALLS

before turning up along Pam's Creek to bridge that stream at 1.3 miles. The trail steepens and works up a slope around a rock outcrop.

Reach the state line in a flat at 1.7 miles. A sign indicating the end of the Duke Power maintenance of Foothills Trail marks this spot. Enter North Carolina and Nantahala National Forest. The valley pinches in and the trail angles up a steep slope, using steps working over a wet outcrop. The trail continues upriver, well above the crashing stream. You begin to hear a falls. But it isn't Whitewater Falls. Instead you have come to Corbin Creek and a bridge at 2.3 miles. Look upstream beyond boulders and you can enjoy a preview cascade, spilling over a rock face bordered in verdant woodland. Leave Corbin Creek and return to the Whitewater River. Cross the watercourse on an iron bridge, using massive boulders to join and leave the span. Look around from the bridge: The Whitewater River is coursing between huge rocks and boulders, and it offers a large pool just upstream.

Beyond the bridge, Foothills Trail leaves the river and begins switchbacking up the side of the now incredibly steep valley. First you'll turn downstream for a long period, then begin winding back and forth. Avoid cutting across the switchbacks—the erosion problems they cause are evident here. Rocks, roots, and ragged wooden steps offer footholds as you climb, working your way amid outcrops and tall tulip trees, as well as fallen trees. This path must've been tough to construct. Reach a trail junction at 2.8 miles. Here Foothills Trail stays left to cross NC 281 and points beyond on its way to Grassy Knob. To reach Whitewater Falls, keep right at this trailhead, still climbing, to open onto a well-developed overlook that will be a surprise after the rough trail. Before you, the falls—dropping from 400 to 600 feet, depending upon whom you listen to—form an impressive sight as they spill over a rim, then tumble over rocks before making a second sheer drop, only to tumble down and regroup as they make their scenic way through the gorge through which you just walked. You may also see other falls admirers, who have come the easy way, 0.2 mile from a parking area off NC 281. The fine steps beyond the developed overlook lead to an upper overlook then to the parking area. You could make this an end-to-end hike with two cars: Leave one at the Nantahala National Forest parking area just mentioned, the other at Bad Creek Access. However, I believe the falls are best appreciated when they're well earned. You get the added benefit of all the scenery on the way. Furthermore, taking the Bad Creek Access lets you enjoy Coon Den Branch Natural Area and even bag Lower Whitewater Falls before returning to the parking area.

II.

MIDLANDS

# 22

# Aiken State Natural Area Loop

**TOTAL DISTANCE**: 2.6-mile loop

**HIKING TIME**: 1 hour

**VERTICAL RISE**: 30 feet

**RATING**: Easy

**MAPS**: USGS 7.5' Kitchings Mill; Aiken State Natural Area

**TRAILHEAD GPS COORDINATES**: N33° 33.074', W81° 29.815'

**CONTACT INFORMATION**: Aiken State Park, 1145 State Park Road, Windsor, SC 29856, (803) 649-2857, www.southcarolinaparks .com/aiken

The name of this path—Jungle Nature Trail—accurately represents this botanically rich area. Aiken State Natural Area is a preserve on the banks of the South Edisto River. The area also protects spring-fed ponds and a variety of flora. First developed by the Civilian Conservation Corps (CCC), the historic state park overlays fine facilities upon an even finer natural setting that will surprise those who come to this part of the Midlands. The hike makes an easy loop through South Edisto River Valley, exploring the banks of the river and a bubbling spring as well as one of the park ponds.

## GETTING THERE

From Aiken, take US 78 east to Windsor. Turn left onto Oak Road at the sign for "Aiken State Natural Area." Follow Oak Road just a short distance to State Park Road. Turn left onto State Park Road and continue for 4.7 miles to Old Tory Road. Turn left and follow Old Tory Trail just a short distance to the right turn into the state park. Jungle Nature Trail begins shortly after you enter the state park's one-way loop road. The trailhead is on your right. Look for the sign indicating "Nature Trail."

## THE TRAIL

The trailhead, like the rest of this park, is a scenic spot. Large trees shade a picnic area with pavilions, all overlooking a lake. Notice the big cedars, too. This would be a fine place for a pre- or post-hike picnic. Leave the trailhead to enter rich, thick woods immediately. Pines form a superstory over smaller hardwoods, holly, wax myrtle, sweet bay magnolia, and cane, the latter two of which conspire to produce the junglelike woods

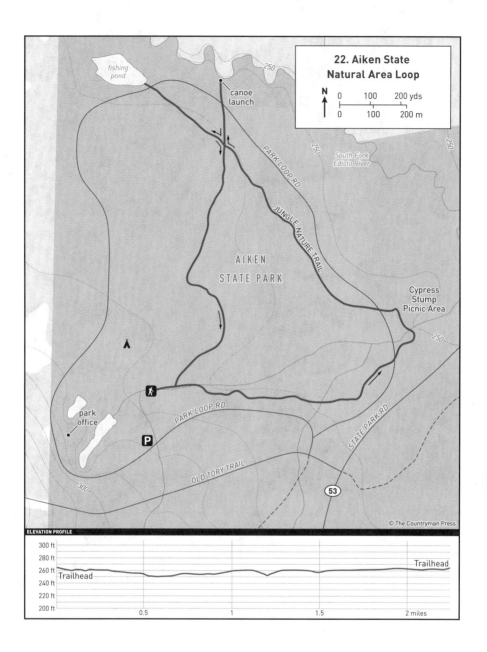

© The Countryman Press

that give the trail its name. Sweet bay is a slow-growing small- to medium-size tree found on wet, often acidic soils of coastal swamps and lowlands farther inland, such as here at Aiken. South Carolina is one of four states where it grows most abundantly, and it is common in the lower half of the state to the coast.

Look for the long elliptical evergreen leaf with the shiny upside.

Walk just a few feet and stay right at a junction—the campground is ahead on the other path. Soon you'll pass a second trail junction—this will be your return route. Stay right again and cross the first of many boardwalks, this one over

ARTESIAN SPRING FOUNTAIN BESIDE THE SOUTH EDISTO RIVER

a stream. Ferns galore cover the lowland floor, especially around the small creeks such as this that flow into the South Edisto River across the nearly level terrain. These clear, appealing streams would go unseen beneath the thickets if it weren't for the park cutting the trail across them.

Notice how many of these boardwalks twist in their course, where dry and wet terrain are intermingled. The elevated walkways give hikers a chance to explore swampland without ever getting their feet wet! At 0.6 mile, cross the park road and cut through Cypress Stump Picnic Area. The trail bisects more thick terrain before crossing back over to the inside of the park loop road. Bracken ferns grow in the drier ground here. At 1.3 miles, reach a four-way trail junction. Turn right here and take the spur trail to the South Edisto River, which is back across the park road. A boardwalk leads to the river's edge. This is known as the River-side Area. Here you can see the swamp stream that is the South Edisto silently pushing along under a canopy of cypress and other trees. Canoes are for rent at the park. Visitors can arrange a shuttle with the ranger and take a 1.7-mile trip down the river to come out at the park landing downstream. The park keeps the canoe trail clear. Bream, bass, and catfish are sought for by paddling anglers.

The South Fork Edisto River watershed drains more than 137,000 acres of sandhills and upper coastal plain, 60 percent of which is forested, such as here at Aiken State Natural Area. The South Fork joins with the North Fork Edisto to form the main stem of the Edisto, which is said to be the largest free-flowing blackwater stream in the world. Over-all, the river basin is in good health and can be kept that way. The greater Edisto basin even has a group started on its behalf called Friends of the Edisto that encourages good stewardship of the river and the lands it drains.

You will notice the splashing artesian spring bubbling up at the water's edge as much as you notice the river. Here, an artistic stone fountain was built around the spring, forcing it to well up from the fountain! The water is good for those of you who dare to taste nature's unspoiled offerings.

Backtrack to the four-way junction, this time going right from the junction to cross the one-way road and check out a spring-fed pond. Now that you have seen the spring, you can see how these ponds are kept full. This one is open to fishing for catfish, bass, and bream. A picnic shelter stands on the far side of the dam. Return to the junction and resume your loop, entering the swampiest terrain yet. Several long board-walks span the wettest terrain. Pass a spur trail to the campground before returning to where you started, completing your loop at 2.6 miles.

If you haven't already, drive the one-way loop road through the state park. The CCC did some fine work on park structures that add to the atmosphere. Most of the buildings are still in use. Stop in at the park office, sit under the breezeway, and just look out toward one of the four lakes here. The campground is nice and well maintained. It's in tall pinewoods, very level, with a pine needle understory. All the sites have electrical hookups. Between hiking, canoeing, picnicking, and camping, this state park is worth a day—and a night—of your life.

# Blackstock Battlefield Passage of the Palmetto Trail

**TOTAL DISTANCE**: 1.7-mile loop

**HIKING TIME**: 1 hour

**VERTICAL RISE**: 110 feet

**RATING**: Easy

**MAPS**: USGS 7.5′ Cross Anchor; Blackstock Battlefield Passage of the Palmetto Trail

**TRAILHEAD GPS COORDINATES**: N34° 40.740′, W81° 48.985′

**CONTACT INFORMATION**: Palmetto Conservation, 722 King Street, Columbia, SC 29205, (803) 771-0870, www.palmettoconservation.org

This hike loops along the Tyger River and onto Blackstock Battlefield, a Revolutionary War site where the British were defeated in 1780 by Thomas Sumter, South Carolina Revolutionary War hero, for whom the town of Sumter, Sumter National Forest, and the famed flashpoint of the Civil War—Fort Sumter—are named. The preserved battlefield, on the banks of the scenic Tyger River, has a hilltop monument overlooking the place where Sumter engaged Banastre Tarleton, a British colonel and sworn enemy of Sumter. This trail is part of the greater Palmetto Trail, which is slated to run the length of the state. Leave the trailhead, then cruise down to Hackers Creek, a clear stream feeding the Tyger River. Here Palmetto Trail saddles alongside the Tyger, offering views of the riffles and sandbars of the stream. The path then climbs a hill to the battlefield site. A spur trip to a spring offers more watery scenery before the path returns to the trailhead.

## GETTING THERE

From Exit 44 off I-26, take SC 49 east for 2 miles to Cross Anchor. Continue east on SC 49, entering Union County 1.1 miles east of Cross Anchor. At 2.3 miles east of Cross Anchor, turn left onto Blackstock Road. Follow Blackstock Road for 1.1 miles, then turn right onto Battlefield Road. Continue for 0.3 mile, then turn left onto Monument Road and reach the trailhead at 1.1 miles, on your left. All the turns, starting with Blackstock Road, are signed.

## THE TRAIL

This 107-acre preserved battlefield was dedicated November 19, 2005, 225 years and 1 day after the Battle of Blackstock,

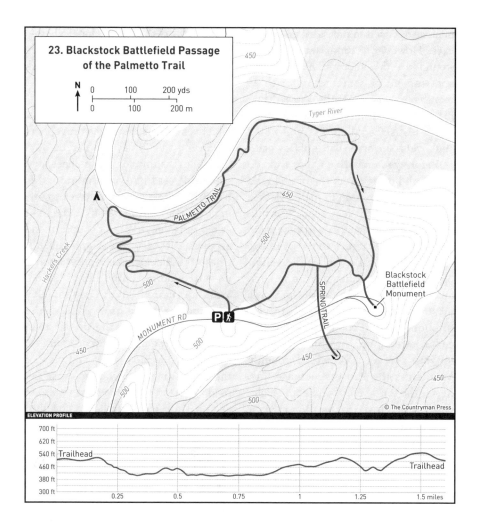

N
0      100      200 yds
0      100      200 m

Tyger River

PALMETTO TRAIL

450

500

Hackers Creek

500

Blackstock
Battlefield
Monument

SPRING TRAIL

MONUMENT RD

P

500

450

450

500

450

500

© The Countryman Press

ELEVATION PROFILE

700 ft
620 ft
540 ft Trailhead
460 ft
380 ft
300 ft

0.25      0.5      0.75      1      1.25      Trailhead
1.5 miles

also known as the Battle of Blackstocks Plantation. On that day, ol' Thomas Sumter, the "Fighting Gamecock," from whom USC got its nickname, led a band of Patriots against Banastre "Bloody" Tarleton. Sumter and Tarleton didn't like each other too much and had been battling off and on in the Palmetto State. Tarleton got Sumter's ire after he decided to burn Sumter's house during one of his sweeps through the state. Sumter then rallied backwoods Patriots to fight Tarleton in the Midlands and Upstate, just when many Americans were losing faith in the viability of an American revolution. Sumter's harassment of Tarleton was the inspiration for his nickname. Tarleton got the better of Sumter at Fishing Creek. Sumter was planning to attack a British force near the Little River, then he got wind that Tarleton was coming after him. Sumter immediately retreated to muster his force of 1,000 at Blackstocks Plantation, on high ground, a good place for a defensive stand, with the Tyger River below and some five log houses and a wooden fence from which Patriot sharpshooters could fire. Here Tarleton's force of 400 British soldiers split and attacked Sumter but lost 50 men, as opposed to the Patriots' 3 fatalities. However, Sumter was severely wounded with a shot into his shoulder, and was out of commission for three months. Nevertheless, he showed that his ragtag militiamen could stand up to the British regulars. Tarleton would suffer yet again at the Battle of Cowpens.

Before you embark on your trek, go ahead and drive on up the gravel road past the parking area to the battlefield monument and the loop road. This hilltop position gives you a good view of the battlefield. Now return to the trailhead and begin the hike. Follow the yellow blazes leading left beyond the wooden fence into the woods. South Carolina's master path, Palmetto Trail, travels through piney woods mixed with oak, cedar, sweetgum, and hickory. Keep forward past an old roadbed, roughly paralleling the Patriots' defense line. Reach the top of a hill and angle right, descending toward the Tyger River on switchbacks. Angle downhill on a surprisingly steep slope to reach rich flatwoods in the greater Tyger River floodplain. Come alongside Hackers Creek and travel downstream along this surprisingly clear tributary of the Tyger amid tall tulip trees and river birch bordered with cane. At 0.4 mile the trail reaches the confluence of Hackers Creek with the Tyger, where there is a Palmetto Trail campsite. A short spur trail leads left, down to a spot where you can access the Tyger. Here the river is in its typical form, one high bank with a gravel bar on the inside bend, flowing shallowly toward the lowlands.

Palmetto Trail turns downstream along the Tyger, running the bluffline, where ironwood and beech thrive in the moist valley. Gain glimpses of the river through the woods. Unfortunately ATVs have marred some of the setting and made paths of their own. Hopefully this will be stopped in the future. Palmetto Trail ascends a high bluff then dips back to the left. Note the mountain laurels, white oaks, and cedars on the bluff.

Work back down to the river's edge. Hikers can access riverside gravel bars bordering the Tyger, and maybe do a little bank fishing for bream, bass, and catfish. Peeled bark on the ground is from the ample sycamore trees towering overhead. Turn away from the river at 0.9 mile, leaving the floodplain and ascending to dry forest and the hill where the Blackstocks Plantation and its surrounding outbuildings stood. Walk up the red South Carolina clay and open onto the grassy hill of the battlefield, reaching the gravel road that circles the monument at 1.2 miles. Check out the monument and view of the Tyger River Valley, then cross the road and head down the mown path on Spring Trail. This path heads downhill

MONUMENT ATOP BATTLEFIELD HILL

SUNLIT SANDBAR ON THE TYGER RIVER

back into woods to bridge a small creek in a deep hollow. Walk amid ferns to dead-end at the point where the spring emerges. Backtrack to the main trail and continue west on a brushy path, paralleling the gravel road. Just before reaching the trailhead, the path rejoins the gravel road, ending the hike.

# 24

# Buncombe Loop

**TOTAL DISTANCE**: 28.9-mile loop

**HIKING TIME**: 14 hours

**VERTICAL RISE**: 170 feet

**RATING**: Difficult

**MAPS**: USGS 7.5' Newberry NW; Sumter National Forest—Enoree Ranger District; Buncombe Trail

**TRAILHEAD GPS COORDINATES**: N34° 27.014', W81° 42.320'

**CONTACT INFORMATION**: Sumter National Forest, Enoree Ranger District, 20 Work Center Road, Whitmire, SC 29178, (803) 276-4810, www.fs.usda.gov/main/scnf

Buncombe Trail (BT)—actually a system of trails—is situated in Sumter National Forest. The BT offers hikers and backpackers a chance for extended loops in the upper Midlands and is the best backpacking destination in the heart of South Carolina. The outermost loop alone is a full 28.9 miles. It alternates between piney ridges and rich creek valleys that offer great places to camp overnight. The Buncombe is a good initiation trail for a multi-night backpack. The trails are wide and well maintained, the terrain isn't too steep, campsites are prevalent, and the loop can be shortcut should problems arise, or if you simply want a shorter trek. Be apprised that bikers and especially equestrians share the trails, but there is room for everyone here. The best times to visit are spring, when wildflowers are blooming in the hollows, and fall, when the trails are dry and the hardwoods are showing off their colors. I have hiked it in both seasons, and you simply can't go wrong here. Trail maps are posted at the major intersections. Watch for plastic post markers indicating mileages. They are marking the trail mileage in the opposite direction, so you will be seeing them in descending order. Some markers are missing.

Note: A free backcountry camping permit is required from Sumter National Forest; it can be obtained ahead of time by calling (803) 276-4810. In addition, Brick House Campground is within walking distance of the trailhead, so you could use the campground as a base camp for day-hiking parts of the Buncombe. The Sumter National Forest—Enoree District map will prove very useful should you hike the trail in sections.

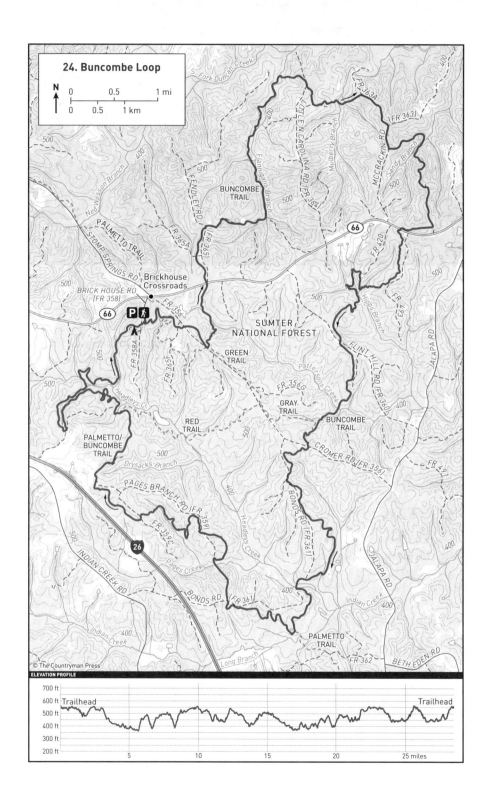

# 24. Buncombe Loop

N

0        0.5        1 mi
0    0.5    1 km

S. Fork Duncan Creek

FR 363A

FR 363

BUNCOMBE TRAIL

Ned Wesson Branch

PALMETTO TRAIL

STOMP SPRINGS RD

FEANDLEY RD

FR 365A

FR 365

Flannigans Branch

LITTLE N CAROLINA RD (FR 394)

Mulberry Branch

Sandy Branch

MCCRACKIN RD

66

FR 420

FR 423

Brickhouse Crossroads

BRICK HOUSE RD (FR 358)

66

FR 356

FR 358A

FR 365F

Headleys Cr.

GREEN TRAIL

SUMTER NATIONAL FOREST

Hipps Branch

FLINT HILL RD (FR 360)

JALAPA RD

Pattersons Creek

FR 356G

GRAY TRAIL

BUNCOMBE TRAIL

RED TRAIL

PALMETTO/ BUNCOMBE TRAIL

Drysacks Branch

PAGES BRANCH RD (FR 359)

FR 359C

26

INDIAN CREEK RD

Pages Creek

Headleys Creek

CROMER RD (FR 356)

FR 49

BONDS RD (FR 361)

JALAPA RD

FR 400

BONDS RD (FR 361)

Indian Creek

Indian Creek

Long Branch

PALMETTO TRAIL

FR 362

BETH EDEN RD

© The Countryman Press

**ELEVATION PROFILE**

700 ft
600 ft   Trailhead                                          Trailhead
500 ft
400 ft
300 ft
200 ft
        5        10        15        20        25 miles

TINY TRAILSIDE WILDFLOWERS

## GETTING THERE

From Exit 60 off I-26 near Clinton, take SC 66 east for 3.6 miles to Brick House Road. Turn right onto Brick House Road, or Forest Road 358, and follow it for 0.3 mile to reach the trailhead on your left. Two short connector trails start at the far end of the field, away from the trailhead entrance. There is a parking fee.

## THE TRAIL

The trail starts on the far side of the field from the kiosk. Brick House Campground, located nearby, makes for a good base camp. You can see two trails heading into the woods. Both meet the actual blue-blazed Buncombe Trail soon. Take a left here, following the Buncombe in oak woods through undulating hills on a wide track.

Immediately turn around the head of a desiccated hollow in a pine forest accompanied by sweetgum, oak, and maple. Horses will have punched into the red clay in particularly wet spots. At 0.5 mile the BT passes a huge white oak. The wide limbs of this tree reveal

that these woods were once open. Late-arriving backpackers can use the flats to the left of the trail for a campsite. Cross two gravel roads in succession: Forest Road 356F, then FR 356. The trailway is often open to the sun overhead in these pinewoods. Reach your first trail junction at 1 mile. Green Trail continues forward for 1.2 miles to bisect the loop. The main Buncombe Trail, however, veers left, now following white blazes, and winds into its first drainage, Patterson Creek, which has a bridge. Notice the Youth Corps monument from 1977. Span the bridge, then head upstream, ascending to cross SC 66 at 1.7 miles. The path enters younger pines. Roads often divide forest areas, and these areas are managed with different techniques. Watch for blackberries and honeysuckle growing tall on the open edges of the trail. Cross FR 365F, then FR 365 at 2.5 miles. Pass around a wooden gate to follow a seeded grassy road before veering right off the roadbed, descending into Flannigan Creek Valley. The bottom is pleasingly wooded with beech, tulip, and ironwood trees, and bisected by the watercourse where moss and ferns grow by slabs of rock. Watch for a particularly wide rock slab at 3.7 miles—Flannigan Creek is open to the sky overhead. The bottomland widens as the trail circles feeder branches. Cross the creek in a sandy ford, a dry-shod proposition in fall, at 5.3 miles. Leave the creek to ascend to pine-dominated woods and reach FR 364 at 5.6 miles. Trace the forest road a short distance, nearing private land.

Dip to Mulberry Creek at 6.3 miles, and reach a camping flat. Climb away to follow FR 363A to meet FR 363. Turn right and follow FR 363. Leave FR 363 at 7.6 miles. The trail dips to Sandy Branch at 8.2 miles, an appealing rocky stream with potential camping. Notice yuccas in the valley. Ascend from this steep-sided valley back into pinewoods mixed with sourwood and sweetgum. Cross SC 66 again at 10 miles. The track remains level, followed by a gradual downtick to a small creek. The BT traces the creek downstream into a flat, turns away from the flat, and swings around, passing another stream flowing over a big rock slab open to the sun. The trail is circling large level land created by Hipps Branch. Gradually dip back into the valley. Campsites are prevalent. Notice the undercut eroded rocks in the streambeds. Span an iron truss bridge at 11.6 miles, then reach Hipps Branch proper, only to ascend a feeder branch.

The BT crosses FR 360 in ridgetop pines, only to dip into Patterson Creek at 13.6 miles, dominated by a grassy bottomland. The trail ascends away from the stream in a wildlife clearing, reenters woods, and crosses another stream, much smaller. Climb to reach a trail junction at 14.1 miles. Here Gray Trail leads right for 0.75 mile to meet Green Trail and shortcut the loop. Beyond, the BT follows the purple-blazed path.

This part of the BT is much less used; solitude is almost certain. You're also more likely to find blowdowns and brush along the path. Immediately cross FR 356. Roughly parallel FR 361, coming alongside it now and then as the BT shares the south-running ridge. The BT comes near posted private land at 16.1 miles. Dip into a dry tributary and end up alongside a field. Reach FR 361 and follow it down to span Headleys Creek at 17 miles. The BT turns left back into woods. Climb to pass through a small clearing and reach an intersection at 18 miles. The southbound Sumter Passage of the Palmetto Trail continues forward on yellow blazes while the BT turns right, briefly following a gas-line clearing to turn back right into woods. The BT and the northbound portion of Palmetto Trail run in conjunction for the rest of the loop.

Stay in the high pines as the path angles northwesterly. I-26 is clearly audible. The trail is often open overhead. Cross FR 361 and begin following Pages Branch Road, FR 359, at 19.5 miles. The BT follows this forest road down to span Pages Branch, also known as Peges Branch. The area is swampy, but a campsite could be found here. Turn right, back into the forest, ascending on red clay to level pines. Stay on high, dry land to cross FR 359 at 20.7 miles. The path circles on the edge of a drainage to parallel a small creek at 21.9 miles. This area has camping flats, but the water could run dry in late summer or early fall. Climb sharply from the drainage to reach an old homesite at 22.2 miles. Look for stone and metal relics. Just beyond, cross FR 359 for the last time. You can glimpse the interstate here. The BT veers right before the interstate and keeps northwest, passing a site of tragedy at 22.7 miles. Here, on July 13,

2004, a medical ambulance helicopter went down; all aboard perished. A cross, among other items, marks the spot.

Wind through woods to reach an open area and metal gate. Stay right here and turn toward a wooden Forest Service gate on grassy track to reach another trail junction at 23.6 miles. Red Trail leads right 2.5 miles to meet Green Trail. You proceed forward, now following the blue blazes away from I-26. Soon you'll drop to a grassy bottom on a track, which is once again well used. The trail goes over the swampy branch on a culvert at 24.4 miles. Despite the wetness, a persistent camper could find an acceptable site. The valley is mostly shielded from interstate noise. The BT quickly climbs from the bottom on a grassed-over gravel track. Reach a clearing, then turn right again into woods near private property. Dive to a gorgeous hardwood hollow, created by upper Headleys Creek. Maples, tulip trees, beeches, oaks, and dogwoods grow here, along with tall loblolly pines. The hollow widens to cross the sandy Headleys Creek at 26.5 miles. If the water is up, you'll get your feet wet here. Climb into the big pines on a red clay ridge only to drop once again to span another Mulberry branch on a bridge at 25.5 miles. Note another Youth Conservation Corps monument here and just ahead. Reach the rear of Brick House Campground, then circle behind the camp to cross FR 358. Keep forward a short distance to turn left on the spur trail leading back to the parking area, completing your loop at 28.7 miles.

Brick House Campground is laid out in a classic loop. Tall pines form the forest superstory. Elms, dogwoods, sweetgums, and other hardwoods are below the tall evergreens. The forest floor is littered with pine needles and pointy

MAJESTIC PINES REACH FOR THE SKY

sweetgum balls. Gravel auto pull-ins spur from the main loop. There is little brush between campsites, but campsite privacy isn't as much of an issue as you would think. You likely won't have a neighbor next to you. This 23-site campground, open year-round, rarely if ever fills. Campsites 1 and 2 are situated together, and they act as one double site. The site offers vault toilets. Bring your own water.

# 25

# Cheraw State Park Loop

**TOTAL DISTANCE**: 4.2-mile loop

**HIKING TIME**: 2 hours

**VERTICAL RISE**: 115 feet

**RATING**: Moderate

**MAPS**: USGS 7.5' Cheraw, Cash; Cheraw State Park

**TRAILHEAD GPS COORDINATES**: N34° 38.424', W79° 55.548'

**CONTACT INFORMATION**: Cheraw State Park, 100 State Park Road, Cheraw, SC 29520, (843) 537-9656, www .southcarolinaparks.com/cheraw

Cheraw State Park seemingly offers something for everyone, including two interconnected loop trails that are underutilized. The first loop is more of a nature trail that offers interpretive information and passes through restored red-cockaded woodpecker habitat. The second loop enters a remote area of the park, dipping into the valley of Juniper Creek before arriving at a scenic lake overlook where Atlantic white cedars—an uncommon tree in the Palmetto State—border Lake Juniper, an impoundment of Juniper Creek. The path then winds its way back on old sand roads to complete its loop. Fall, winter, and spring are the best times to enjoy this path—summer can be excessively hot, especially since some of the trail canopy is open overhead.

## GETTING THERE

From Cheraw, take US 1 South/US 52 East to where they split. At the road split, stay left on US 52 East and follow it for 1.0 mile to the park entrance on your right. Turn right into the entrance and follow the entrance road for 0.9 mile to reach a T-intersection. Turn right and continue for 1.4 miles to the trailhead parking area on your left. There is a parking fee.

## THE TRAIL

Cheraw Nature Trail and the Turkey Oak leave as one from the parking area. Enter pine woods that have been restored to their natural state. At one time the park suppressed fires here, resulting in a heavy undergrowth of turkey and blackjack oaks. Eventually many of the small oaks were cut, opening the longleaf pine woods to their natural habitat, with a primary understory of wiregrass.

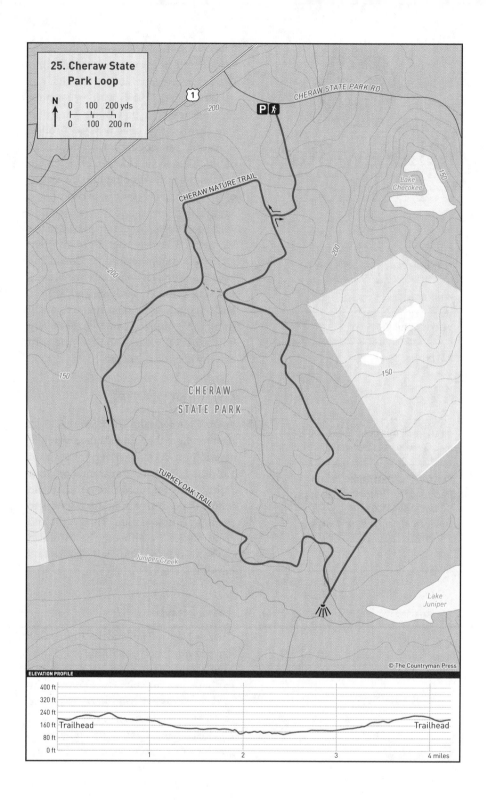

## 25. Cheraw State Park Loop

N

0  100  200 yds
0  100  200 m

1

200

CHERAW STATE PARK RD

P

Lake
Cherokee

150

CHERAW NATURE TRAIL

200

CHERAW
STATE PARK

150

200

150

TURKEY OAK TRAIL

Juniper Creek

Lake
Juniper

© The Countryman Press

**ELEVATION PROFILE**

400 ft
320 ft
240 ft
160 ft  Trailhead
80 ft
0 ft

1       2       3       4 miles

Trailhead

ATLANTIC WHITE CEDARS STAND GUARD OVER LAKE JUNIPER

The longleaf-wiregrass ecosystem covered much of the South at one time, but was cut over and converted to agriculture and other uses. It is important that Cheraw State Park restore and preserve this habitat. The purposes of state parks are many—preservation, recreation, and wildlife habitat are just a few. Here at Cheraw, a large state park at more than 7,300 acres, not only are there hiking trails, but you'll also find a campground, a fishing, swimming, and boating lake, a golf course, and trails for mountain bikes and equestrians. The park also has rental cabins.

The needle-covered sand track dips to cross a low drainage on a boardwalk. The forest here isn't all pine. Other trees such as hickory, turkey oak, and blackjack oak add variety to the woodland. Reach the loop portion of the nature trail at 0.3 mile. Turn right here, heading north, and look for interpretive signs, about the size of your hand, nailed onto trees along the path. Cheraw Nature Trail curves west and descends into more lush woods, where a swale between piney hills gathers enough moisture to change the forest somewhat.

Ahead, a sign indicates that the trail is entering a red-cockaded woodpecker nesting area. As this forest was being restored to its natural state, park personnel actually created artificial nesting cavities in the longleaf pines and brought woodpeckers to the area. The birds stayed, and the reintroduction has been successful. Reach a trail junction here, at 0.9 mile. Cheraw Nature Trail continues left, but Turkey Oak Trail turns right. Stay right, following the red blazes over piney sandhills, which contrast with the wetter lowlands around them.

The wet lowlands grow thick with bay trees and ferns and are as thick as the longleaf-wiregrass forest is open. But the longleaf forest offers its own beauty—the green needles of the tree contrast with the brown trunk and bronze needles, which fall onto lime-green, lichen-covered ground. Young longleaf pines have a spindly "trunk" coming up from the ground and are topped with a single bulblike expanse of needles emerging from the top of the plant. These pines are using all their energy to grow their trunk high enough to be able to withstand a low-intensity, lightning-caused ground fire, like those that often swept through forests before fire suppression. Once they are tall enough, longleafs begin to branch out and gain height. The longleaf-wiregrass ecosystem once covered more than 50 million acres in the Southeast and now grows in less than 3 million. These pine flatwoods are easy to develop or alter and thus have been cut over, changed, or allowed to evolve into other forest types due to fire suppression. Cheraw State Park is doing its part in restoring the longleaf pine.

The path begins dipping into Juniper Creek Valley—a moister environment but not quite a wetland. With the change come different trees: loblolly pines, dogwoods, and more mature oaks. The trail acts as if it is going to completely dip to Juniper Creek but never quite does, always turning away. However, at 2.3 miles, it does bridge a moving tributary of Juniper Creek, along which cane grows.

The path turns away then, back toward Juniper Creek, to reach a trail junction on an old roadbed at 2.6 miles. Here, walk right along the old roadbed to shortly reach an overlook of Lake Juniper, where a bench offers a resting and reflection spot. Look over the lake—Atlantic white cedars thrive here. Known to early locals as juniper trees, hence the name Juniper Creek, Atlantic white cedars grow in an irregular coastal belt from Mississippi all the way to Maine. They thrive in wet soils along sluggish streams and in swamps. The cedars may have been misnamed by the locals, who settled Cheraw, but they knew a useful tree when they saw one. Atlantic white cedars are coveted as a long-lasting wood for log cabins, from the floors up to the shingles. Undoubtedly some of these "junipers" provided shelter for Cheraw residents. Atlantic white cedars resemble cypress trees and enjoy the same habitat. Their brownish gray bark grows in vertical strips, and you won't find "knees" rising around the trunks as in cypress trees. Cypresses also lose their needlelike leaves in winter, whereas the Atlantic white cedar is evergreen. Both grow in this vicinity.

Turkey Oak Trail now heads away from the lake on the old roadbed, gently rising from Lake Juniper. At 3.1 miles the path abruptly turns right, leaving the old roadbed to ramble through mixed woods, with cane bottomland off to your right. Continue climbing away from the lake to cross a wide, sandy old road at 3.6 miles. Pine woods dominate beyond the sand road. You are in very open country, pocked with tall longleafs. Before you know it Cheraw Nature Trail and Turkey Oak Trail meet; keep right, making your way on the shorter loop. Continue in longleaf woods to complete the loop part of the nature trail. Reach the final trail intersection. You have been here before. Backtrack to the trailhead, completing your loop at 4.2 miles.

# 26

# Dreher Island State Park Hike

| | |
|---|---|
| **TOTAL DISTANCE**: 2.4-mile loop | |

**HIKING TIME**: 1.3 hours

**VERTICAL RISE**: 55 feet

**RATING**: Easy

**MAPS**: USGS 7.5' Lake Murray West; Dreher Island State Park

**TRAILHEAD GPS COORDINATES**: N34° 4.933', W81° 24.139'

**CONTACT INFORMATION**: Dreher Island State Park, 3677 State Park Road, Prosperity, SC 29127, (803) 364-4152, www.southcarolinaparks.com

This hike takes place at popular Dreher Island State Park, located in the heart of Lake Murray. Despite the overwhelming presence of water, Dreher Island has enough land to lay out a fine walk along hills and shorelines with aquatic panoramas that last for the entire trek, or most of it. Start at one of the many picnic shelters, then trace a single-track trail to a vista point. Next, head out to the edge of a peninsula, where a loop circles you around a wooded hill with a little detour to one of the best views on Lake Murray. Since the hike is relatively short, plan to engage in other activities at this enticing state park.

## GETTING THERE

From Exit 91 on I-26 northwest of Columbia, take Columbia Avenue west for 2.1 miles. Cross railroad tracks, then turn right onto Chapin Road, which you follow for 0.2 mile, then turn left on St. Peters Church Road. Follow St. Peters Church Road for 3.2 miles, then turn left on Dreher Island Road, which you follow for 2.9 miles, then turn left onto Park Road. Enter Dreher Island State Park after 2.5 miles. Continue straight on the main park road, passing the visitor center to stay right on the loop. At 1.5 miles from the park entrance, turn left on Red Maple Drive, toward picnic shelters #7 and #8. Little Gap Trail starts at the parking area for these shelters.

## THE TRAIL

Water, water everywhere but enough land for a hike and other recreation amenities here at Dreher Island State Park. Despite the name, this preserve is actually comprised of three separate islands linked by bridges with a total land coverage of 348 acres and miles of

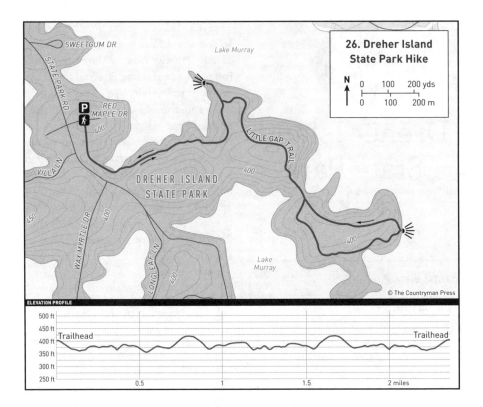

shoreline. Of course these islands were not always islands, but came to be after the Saluda River was dammed in the late 1920s by what became South Carolina Electric and Gas, in order to generate electricity.

Creating Lake Murray was quite an undertaking. Nearly 100,000 acres of land were purchased from nearly 5,000 different property owners. Entire communities with names like Savilla, Boylston, and Pine Ridge were abandoned. Schools were closed, churches were moved, and many bodies interred at graveyards were dug up and reinterred. Families had to leave homes handed down over generations to make way for progress.

The soon-to-be-underwater land was stripped of its timber while the dam was being built. The Lake Murray Dam stretched 1.5 miles long; it was more than 375 feet thick and 208 feet high. Upon completion, Lake Murray was the world's largest power-generating reservoir. Since that time, to further prevent floods and to be strengthened from earthquakes, the dam has been raised and reinforced twice.

Today we have a power-generating reservoir covering more than 50,000 acres with around 600 miles of shoreline. The lake, as well as Dreher Island State Park, is a major recreation destination for capital city residents and is also the site of some major bass fishing tournaments.

Most visitors come to the state park for fishing, swimming or boating—and camping. However, the preserve has a fine hiking path as well, called Little Gap Trail. It heads out to an undeveloped peninsula of Dreher Island. Solitude seekers and those wanting quiet will come here during winter, when the boats are few. Furthermore, when the leaves are off the trees, the lake views are nearly constant. On weekends, expect to see boats out on the lake, especially during the warm season.

Leave the trailhead kiosk near shelter #7. The single-track, hiker-only footpath starts atop a hill, then it descends through hardwoods and pines. The main park road is off to your right. Water is almost always visible. Descend to a lake cove and a low point. Little Gap Trail then curves left and heads out toward the undeveloped peninsula of Dreher Island.

Come near a power line at .3 mile on a surprisingly steep hillside. White quartz outcrops brighten the forest floor. By .5 mile, you reach a junction. Take the spur left, descending to a point overlooking Lake Murray. Enjoy a view of a small island in the foreground and an expanse of water ringed in shoreline in the distance. You are looking up the Camping Creek arm of the lake. When the impoundment is drawn down to winter levels, a gravel beach connects the mainland to the small island here.

Backtrack to the main path and con-

TRAILSIDE VIEW OF LAKE MURRAY

tinue out the peninsula. Little Gap Trail climbs a big wooded hill, which you top at .8 mile. It is enough to get you huffing and puffing. What goes up must come down, though, and you drop to a little gap with water on both sides of the trail. Come to the loop portion of the hike at 0.9 mile. Keep straight, making a counterclockwise circuit. Reach peninsula's end at 1.2 miles. A big sign advertising Dreher Island State Park extends toward the main part of the lake.

A few steps off the trail leads to the shoreline and a fantastic view, near a lighted boat marker. Here, hikers can gain an appreciation for just how large this reservoir is, and how much land was flooded when the Saluda River was dammed. A century back, this damming changed life for the residents of the valley. However, today we appreciate the power-generating capabilities of the dam as well as its ability to mitigate floods.

From this vista, turn back and complete the loop portion of the hike at 1.4 miles. From this point, it is a .9 mile backtrack to the trailhead. The hike starts near one of the 14 picnic shelters at the park. Bring a little lunch while you are at it. While you are here, consider engaging in other activities at Dreher Island. Campers can spend the night at one of the 97 RV campsites or at one of the 15 designated tent sites. Each camp has a picnic table and electricity. Hot showers are available. If you want to live a little higher on the hog, stay at one of the five lakeside villas available for rent. Boaters can tool around the lake, fishing for largemouth bass, stripers, catfish, or bream.

The park even has a fishing tackle loaner program. If you don't have a boat, you can fish from the shoreline anywhere in the park, and you can also swim along the shoreline anywhere except at the boat ramps, bridges, or boat docks. Just remember, despite being a water-oriented park, it does have a fun little hiking trail worth your time.

# Horn Creek/ Lick Fork Lake Double Loop

This hike begins at Sumter National Forest's Lick Fork Lake Recreation Area, where you can camp, fish, mountain bike, and swim in addition to hiking. The loop leaves the recreation area in pine woods, descends to the hardwood hollows of Horn Creek and its tributaries in undulating terrain, and then heads back to Lick Fork Lake. After passing along the attractive lake, it circles the steep and scenic terrain along Lick Fork Creek before returning to the trailhead. This very well-maintained path receives a lot of use, keeping the walking open and mostly free of brush.

**TOTAL DISTANCE**: 6.6-mile loop

**HIKING TIME**: 3 hours

**VERTICAL RISE**: 30 feet

**RATING**: Easy

**MAPS**: USGS 7.5' Colliers; Sumter National Forest—Long Cane District Lick Fork Lake Recreation Area

**TRAILHEAD GPS COORDINATES**: N33° 43.597', W82° 2.423'

**CONTACT INFORMATION**: Sumter National Forest, Long Cane Ranger District, 810 Buncombe Street, Edgefield, SC 29824, (803) 637-5396, www.fs.usda.gov/scnf

## GETTING THERE

From the town square in Edgefield, take SC 23 south for 8.3 miles to SC 230. Veer left onto SC 230 and follow it for 0.4 mile to Lick Fork Road. Turn left onto Lick Fork Road and follow it for 2.0 miles, then turn right into Lick Fork Recreation Area. Stay left here and follow a road through the campground to dead-end at a boat ramp and picnic area. The trail starts in the back of the picnic area.

## THE TRAIL

From the trailhead, you can either go left or right. Go left. The single-track dirt-and-rock path ascends to cross Lick Fork Road at 0.3 mile, then begins working mostly downhill into Horn Creek Valley, still in pines. Trail mileages are posted in 0.5-mile increments along the Horn Creek part of the loop, which is popular with mountain bikers as well as hikers. Bottomland hardwoods begin to dominate as you get deeper into the valley. Ferns grow extensively near the stream you are beginning to trace at this point. The trail stays in the margin between the hillside to your right and a

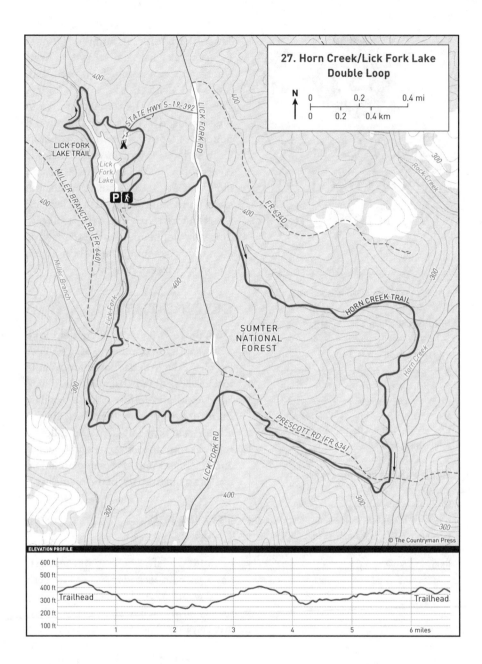

## 27. Horn Creek/Lick Fork Lake Double Loop

ELEVATION PROFILE

creekside flat to your left. Small bridges span intermittent streambeds. These bridges are covered with chicken wire to prevent hikers from slipping when the bridge is wet.

Cross the main stream leading into Horn Creek at 1.1 miles. The valley tight-

ens, and you work alongside the rocky rill. Span the branch a second time and keep aiming toward Horn Creek, reaching its valley at 1.7 miles. Horn Creek flows to your left, barely visible through the rich bottomland of hardwoods and thick underbrush. The path soon turns

LICK FORK LAKE

away from Horn Creek, aiming for hill-sides where it undulates between dry streambeds and small ridges. In places, tunnel-like brush borders the trail.

Reach FR 634 at 2.5 miles. Horn Creek is to your left. You can get your best look at the creek by walking FR 634 over to the low-water bridge cross-ing the stream. The path snakes uphill away from Horn Creek, working up a feeder branch. This time, however, the trail stays in pines well above the water. In places, the pines are younger. You are heading west on a shoulder of the valley. Keep uphill to cross Lick Fork Road again at 3.5 miles. Enter an area of much larger pines. The regal giants stand tall overhead. Keep an eye peeled to the south, where green ridges are

occasionally visible in the distance. The trail is overlaid upon an old road-bed for a while, until it begins working down into Lick Fork, where it takes a less erosive winding route. Leave the pines behind, once again entering hardwoods. Tulip trees are king down here. Bridge a feeder branch at 4.3 miles, just before turning right, upstream, into Lick Fork Valley proper. Take your time in this scenic area. The clear stream tumbles over rocks between long pools. A wide flat is home to tall trees that scream Big Woods. The path stays along the edge of the Lick Fork. Loblolly pines add an evergreen component to the large trees. Sycamores reach upward from the water's edge. A reroute leads above the stream. You can still discern the old track below. Bridge another side branch just before crossing FR 640 at 4.6 miles. Resume the walk in bottomland where ferns and beard cane hold sway over the forest floor.

Reach a trail junction at 5.2 miles. If you want to cut off your loop, stay to your right here and climb a short piece back to the trailhead. I recommend continuing the hike, however, so keep left, immediately hopping over Lick Fork on some big boulders. Climb away from Lick Fork, trying to reach the same elevation as the lake dam, which is visible through the woods to your right. Reach the lake, curving along its shore. The campground, swim beach, fishing pier, and picnic area are visible across the water. The track bridges intermittent streambeds dropping steeply from the hillside above. In some drainages, look for little "dams" made from concrete bags. These were placed here to prevent the steep drainages from silting Lick Fork Lake. Keep working up the lake as it narrows. Pass under a power line to enter a deeply incised drainage where beech trees grow tall. Turn back to the uppermost reaches of the lake before coming to Lick Fork Creek at 5.9 miles. This spot is also pretty, with the water forming small cascades over wide rocks beneath a tree canopy. Rock-hop the stream.

Ahead the trail splits, so you'll want to stay toward the lake. The lower path works back down to the lake's edge and circles a point where anglers gather, and from which you can get a good view of the lake. Circle around one last feeder stream before emerging onto the grassy lawn at the swim beach. Stay along the lake's edge, passing a pavilion to cross a bridge over a small lake embayment.

Now the path stays along the lake's edge beside the campground. Finally, trace the asphalt path from the fishing pier to return to the trailhead, completing your loop.

Consider extending your stay at this recreation area. Lick Fork Lake is a mere 12 acres, small in size compared with most impounds, but the recreation area campground only has 10 campsites, which is just about the right size to handle this lake. The area exudes a closed-in, intimate feel, as if you're in the middle of nowhere. The "no-gas-motors" rule on Lick Fork Lake and the widespread campsites mean that chirping birds and maybe the sounds of some kids swimming in the clear water will be your background noise.

The campsites are spacious and incorporated into a hilly setting; leveling and stonework make them both attractive and "campable," as do the oaks and pines shading the campsites.

The small number of campsites does mean that this park fills quickly at times, especially on weekends during late spring and early summer. When the heat kicks in, business dies off. The campground is open year-round. A newer restroom with warm showers overlooks the swim and picnic area. A picnic shelter here is a nice place to hang out during a summertime thunderstorm. Parts of the picnic area have been leveled with extensive stonework; the spot overlooks a grassy lawn adjacent to the roped-off swimming area. The swimming area has a sandy bottom for clean-footed entry into and exit from the pretty lake. Anglers vie primarily for catfish, but they also seek largemouth bass and bream.

# Kings Mountain Loop

**TOTAL DISTANCE**: 15.1-mile loop

**HIKING TIME**: 8 hours

**VERTICAL RISE**: 380 feet

**RATING**: Difficult

**MAPS**: USGS 7.5' Kings Mountain, Grover, King Creek, Filbert; Kings Mountain State Park; Kings Mountain Loop

**TRAILHEAD GPS COORDINATES**: N35° 8.928', W81° 20.846'

**CONTACT INFORMATION**: Kings Mountain State Park, 1277 Park Road, Blacksburg, SC 29702, (803) 222-3209; Kings Mountain National Military Park, 2625 Park Road, Blacksburg, SC 29702, (864) 936-7921, www.nps.gov/kimo

This is one long loop, and it can be done as a very long day hike or as an overnight backpack. Add another mile if you include the side trip to Browns Mountain, where you can get many nice views. The large area west of Rock Hill is preserved as both Kings Mountain State Park and Kings Mountain National Military Park. It was here that what is considered the turning point of the Revolutionary War took place. On October 7, 1780, British General Cornwallis clashed with the Overmountain Men of what would become Tennessee and other areas of what was then the western frontier, ending Loyalist support in the colonies and sending Cornwallis toward his ultimate surrender at Yorktown and the end of the war a year later. Though this loop doesn't directly travel over significant parts of the battlefield, you can tie a trip to the battlefield and visitor center, along with camping at the state park, into your hike.

The hike leaves the state park campground near Lake Crawford and up Long Branch to enter the national battlefield. Reach a spur trail leading to the main area where the American frontiersmen and British clashed. The primary loop climbs toward Browns Mountain, another spur trail where you can gain a piedmont view. Pass through former farmland to reach Garner Creek Campsite, then make your way down a tributary of Clark Creek. Travel through a mix of woods and hills and streams, finally making your way back up Long Branch to complete the loop. Deer are plentiful here—you should see one or two somewhere along the loop. If you are interested in backpacking, contact the national park at (864) 936-7921 for the latest overnighting regulations. Kings Mountain State Park offers more than just this hike.

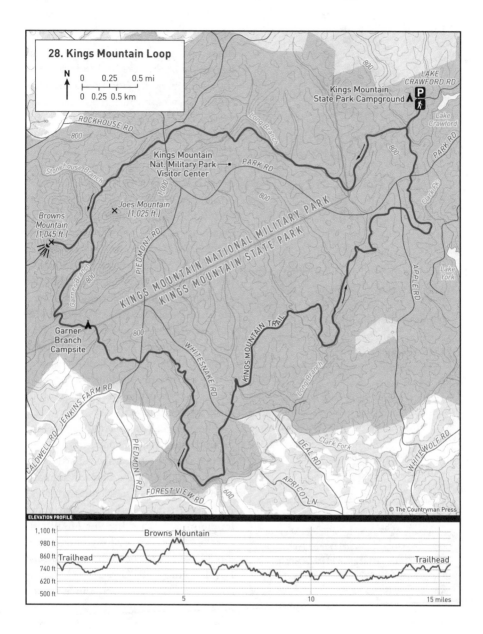

**28. Kings Mountain Loop**

N

| 0 | 0.25 | 0.5 mi |
| 0 | 0.25 | 0.5 km |

ELEVATION PROFILE

## GETTING THERE

From Exit 8, Kings Mountain, off I-85 just north of the North Carolina–South Carolina border, take NC 161 south for 5 miles, leaving North Carolina en route. Turn right onto Park Road and follow it into the state park. Follow the signs to the state park campground, picnic area, and Lake Crawford. Continue to the back of the picnic area, taking the gravel road past Picnic Shelter 1 to a gravel parking area. The trail starts near Picnic Shelter 3. A water spigot and restrooms are available at the parking area. There is a state park entrance fee.

## THE TRAIL

The blue-blazed trail leaves the picnic area behind a kiosk and descends to bridge a clear feeder stream of Clark Creek. Begin the loop portion of the hike, turning right toward the national battlefield visitor center. Climb into pine-oak-hickory woods on a wide trailbed, passing through the primitive group camping area, where a spigot stands beside the trail. Kings Mountain Trail rolls through hilly country among ferny swales to enter Kings Mountain National Military Park at 1.1 miles. Shortly drop into Long Branch and begin walking upstream along its headwaters, where rock shelves cross the watercourse, shaded by beech and birch trees, along with cane. The surprisingly rocky and mountainous valley occasionally opens into flats.

Bridge Long Branch, then climb to open woods. The national park and, to a lesser extent, the state park have conducted prescribed burns to reduce exotic vegetation and to return the forest to a more natural state. You will see scarred trunks, open understory, or even aged understory brush, along with leafless trees. It may not look too pretty now, but down the line, these prescribed burns will create a forest Palmetto State residents will enjoy.

Reach a trail junction at 2.3 miles. The battlefield visitor center, 0.2 mile forward, offers drinking water and restrooms in addition to informational displays and the Battlefield Loop, which circles the actual locale where the tide of the Revolution turned. The main loop turns right on a now narrower,

lesser-used path, descending over a clear branch then rising to cross Park Road, SC 216, at 3.1 miles. The path then travels a rocky ridge, rife with chestnut oaks, before dipping into the Stonehouse Branch drainage. Step over the stream three times, leaving it to climb a hill at 4.1 miles. Top out on another ridge, then reach the Browns Mountain Trail junction at 4.5 miles. Here a spur trail leads right for 0.5 mile over a knob to a higher knob to the site of a fire tower, now dismantled. However, views can be had from the mountaintop, elevation 1,045 feet. Your best looks are to the south and west.

Return to the main trail, heading southwesterly along a ridgeline above Garner Branch. Look for piled rocks here: This forest was once tilled, and farmers cleared rocks from the fields. Quartz is plentiful. Drop to bridge Garner Branch in a deep hollow. The trail climbs back into hills to reach Garner Branch Campsite at 5.8 miles. The oak-shaded campsite has a bench and fire ring.

Soon you'll leave the national battlefield and reenter Kings Mountain State Park on a narrower path. Cross gravelly Piedmont Road at 6.5 miles, then enter dogwood-rich woods, dipping to a laurel-lined scenic creek, winding south along the steep-sided valley and its tiny tributaries. Umbrella magnolia grows profusely here. This is a gorgeous trail segment where beech trees grow tall. At 8.6 miles the trail curves left and begins a gentle ascent, leaving the creek and heading north into drier woods. At 9.2 miles cross a horse trail making its own loop through the parks. The trail dips to circle a branch in brushy woods. At this point, horses sometimes illegally use the trail. Roll through piney woods,

PIEDMONT VISTA FROM BROWNS MOUNTAIN

dropping to occasional streamlets, with the trail not always going where you think it should or will go. Finally, make Long Creek at 11.5 miles. This creek is quite scenic here, with long, slow pools divided by rock shoals. Cross the horse trail again at 12.2 miles, then immediately step over an ultraclear tributary. Proceed up Long Creek, crossing it at a stream-wide rock shelf. The trail then circles a hollow to pass under a power line at 12.8 miles. Cross the horse trail connecting the equestrian camping area to the main horse loop, then immediately bisect Apple Road at 13.3 miles. The equestrian camping area is to your left.

From Apple Road, the trail makes a deeply incised U, again traveling where you think it won't or shouldn't. The woods are mostly dry here in rolling hills. Cross Park Road at 14.3 miles, then work down through oak woods to reach the creek you crossed miles back. This part of the stream is pretty, with large outcrops amid thickets of laurel. Reach the end of the loop portion of the hike at 15.0 miles; backtrack uphill to the trailhead to complete your hike.

Kings Mountain State Park has 116 sites at its campground, including 10 tent-only campsites, widespread among pines and oaks. Numerous bathhouses are evenly sited among the loops, including one near the tent campers' parking area. A recreation building makes rainy days more livable. The campground sees its most traffic during spring and fall, but only fills on major summer holidays and Pioneer Days in September. Pioneer Days is centered on a historic homestead at the state park that replicates an 1840s farm. The festival features crafts, music, and a muzzleloaders' competition. A trail connects the campground to the living history farm.

The state park offers 7,000 acres, which—combined with the 3,000 acres of the military park—makes for a lot of roaming space. Two lakes add to the attractive terrain. Lake Crawford covers 15 acres and has a swimming area for hot days. Lake York is larger at 65 acres and offers johnboats for rent, so anglers can vie for bass and bream. Basketball courts, volleyball courts, and a carpet golf course all lie near the campground.

# Long Cane Loop

**TOTAL DISTANCE**: 22.9-mile loop

**HIKING TIME**: 12.5 hours

**VERTICAL RISE**: 200 feet

**RATING**: Difficult

**MAPS**: USGS 7.5' Verdery, Abbeville East, Long Cane Horse Trail

**TRAILHEAD GPS COORDINATES**: N34° 5.817', W82° 21.274'

**CONTACT INFORMATION**: Sumter National Forest, Long Cane Ranger District, 810 Buncombe Street, Edgefield, SC 29824, (803) 637-5396, www.fs.usda.gov/scnf

This trail is your best opportunity for backpacking in the Savannah River Valley. It starts at Parsons Mountain Recreation Area, in the Long Cane District of Sumter National Forest, and circles the Long Cane Creek Valley, undulating among piney ridges and hardwood bottomlands. Of special note is the Long Cane Creek Scenic Area, home to wildflowers and South Carolina's champion shagbark hickory, among other noteworthy trees, relics of the Appalachian Mountains. Hikers, bikers, and equestrians all share the trail. There is a 5.3-mile trail that divides your route in half, should you want to shorten your outing. Note: Parsons Mountain Loop also starts here. See Hike 33 for this loop and more information about the recreation area.

## GETTING THERE

From Abbeville, take SC 72 west for 2.0 miles to reach SC 28. Turn left and take SC 28 south for 2.1 miles to Parsons Mountain Road. Turn left and follow Parsons Mountain Road for 1.5 miles to Parsons Mountain Recreation Area. Turn right and follow the forest road into the recreation area, then turn left and continue to the picnic area on your left before crossing the Parsons Mountain Lake Dam. The trail begins in the back of the picnic area.

## THE TRAIL

Begin the hike at the back of the picnic area, turning left onto a pine-lined former roadbed, passing behind the recreation area campground to cross SC 251 at 0.4 mile. Reenter woods and make a slow descent to bottomland and paved SC 33 at 1.1 miles. Turn right on the road, then left into the woods, to enter gray-trunked bottomland heavy with

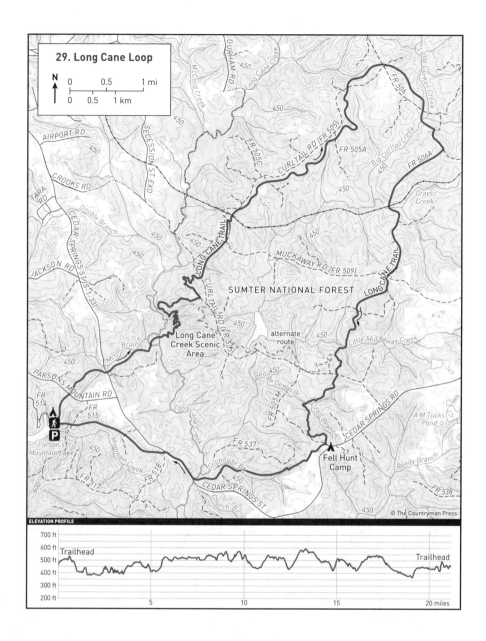

## 29. Long Cane Loop

N

| 0 | 0.5 | 1 mi |
| 0 | 0.5 | 1 km |

**ELEVATION PROFILE**

straight-trunked tulip trees, laurel oaks, ferns, and wildflowers in the McGill Branch watershed. Follow the drainage downstream as the valley widens, staying on the edge of the wetlands. Beard cane grows in profusion here.

Reach Long Cane Creek at 2.2 miles. To your right a trail leads uphill a short distance to FR 530. Long Cane Trail turns left here to reach a narrow sagging iron bridge and enter the official scenic area soon. The bridge, built in 1939 by the Forest Service, can be crossed. However, if the water is too high, it will be submerged. Campsites can be found on the far side of the crossing. Join a

STATE-RECORD SHAGBARK HICKORY

ridgeline above the stream before dipping back into bottomland. Significant work has been done to keep the trail in drier edges of the wetland; it now winds around more than a coiled-up snake. Look for wildflowers in the valley during spring.

At 3.5 miles, pass a sign describing the big trees of the scenic area. Just ahead, on your left, another sign indicates the state-record shagbark hickory—it's also the world's second largest shagbark hickory. It's downhill to your left, exceeding 11 feet in circumference. This forest is part of what makes Long Cane Creek scenic. The path winds more amid big trees to reach a trail junction at 4.3 miles. A trail leads right for 5.3 miles to shortcut the loop at Little Muckaway Creek. The main loop turns left here, passing an informative sign about the cotton-farming days. Imagine the past as you walk through this pine hardwood forest, once a cotton field. More reroutes lead to FR 505 at 5.2 miles. Cross 505 and leave the scenic area, undulating between shallow valleys and pineland to cross FR 505 again at 5.8 miles.

Enter spindly pine woods, cross a gas-line clearing, then reach a railroad crossing and potentially confusing area. Cross the railroad tracks at 6.2 miles and keep forward on the forest road, ignoring the blue-blazed ATV trails near the railroad tracks. The forest road you are following traces Old Charleston Road, the historic route between Charleston and the Upcountry. At 6.5 miles, veer right back into woods and begin an extended northeasterly ridgeline walk, roughly paralleling FR 505, staying mostly in pines but also dipping to shallow hardwood hollows to invariably rise again to the ridgeline, sometimes within sight of the forest road. The trail is often open overhead, giving room for honeysuckle and blackberries to grow. Cross a seeded and closed forest road at 8.6 miles.

At 9.5 miles you'll cross FR 505 again. The trail enters another very scenic area as it descends along hardwood slopes where outcrops and rocky rills cut steep valleys. Watch for the curved concrete bridge over a small stream. Campsites can be found here, but you must search for them. Look downhill and downstream for the best possibilities.

Keep on the valley edge, passing a trailside kiosk before emerging onto the intersection of FR 505 and FR 506 at 10.2 miles. Long Cane Trail continues forward here, crossing 506 to enter a kudzu-covered area that gives way to woods. Cross FR 506 again at mile 11.1 and pass through green bottomland to rock-hop Big Curltail Creek on a wet-footed crossing. Proceed on an old roadbed before turning away, staying southeast.

The trail can be overgrown and hard to follow here. At 12.0 miles it makes a hard right. A forest road is just to your left. Straddle the ridge between Grays Creek and Big Curltail Creek, passing through a wildlife clearing at 12.3 miles.

Reach the roundabout of another forest road, then turn right onto an open track heading down to reach the railroad line and Grays Creek. Pass under the trestle and through bottomland before reaching the crossing for Grays Creek at 12.9 miles. This one could also be wet if the water is high. As you climb away from the creek, note the rock piles in the woods. Farmers once piled stones while moving them out of their fields to make plowing easier. It's all forest now, of course. Emerge onto FR 509-C and turn right, climbing to T-intersect FR 509 at 14 miles. The trail is following the road while skirting between areas of private property. Turn right here, then make a quick left, passing around a metal forest gate to trace a seeded road, then veer right back into woods. Long Cane Trail makes a pleasant forest cruise in mixed woods, joining another seeded roadbed only to dip into pretty Little Muckaway Creek, bordered by sycamores. There is good camping on both sides of the creek. The rerouted trail makes a less erosive track to a trail junction at 15.2 miles. Here the other end of the loop shortcut heads right, while the main trail veers left. Cross FR 505 at 15.7 miles. A real mix of pines, hardwoods, and clearings is ahead, and the trail passes the gas-line clearing again.

The trail dips to reach George Devlin Branch, another alluring hollow with big beech trees, at 16.4 miles. Step over the branch and ascend to a particularly deep wooded gully. At 17.2 miles you'll reach a junction. A spur trail leaves left to reach Fell Hunt Camp, a favorite equestrian jumping-off point. The main loop stays right here, passing along the edge of a field before reentering woods. Begin working downward toward a drainage. Note the ravinelike edges of some watercourses. Many of these are relics from farming days, when cotton was king here and poor farming practices led to massive erosion problems. When acquired by the USDA Forest Service, these lands were planted over with trees, stabilizing the soil and desilting streams.

The trail begins descending into the Stillhouse Branch Valley, entering fern-heavy bottomland. Cross the stream at 18.9 miles. There's no bridge here, but there is a concrete ford. This bottom is suitable for camping. Keep downstream to reach SC 33 and span Long Cane Creek on a road bridge at 19.7 miles. The

THE AUTHOR ADMIRES THE BIGGEST SHAGBARK HICKORY IN SOUTH CAROLINA

sluggish creek is home to many a frog. Listen for its song. Climb the hill then veer left into woods on a rocky track. The walking is easy on a level pine-bordered track that may prove muddy after rains. Cross FR 518 at 20.2 miles. The woods are piney beyond the FR 518. Note the burn-scarred trunks on the trees here. Foresters are using prescribed fire to maintain a healthy ecosystem and the biggest pines. Dip into hardwood bottoms as the terrain steepens. Cross FR 515 at 21.9 miles. Finally, keep forward to reach the picnic area, completing your loop at 22.9 miles.

# Oakridge Loop at Congaree National Park

**TOTAL DISTANCE**: 6.5-mile loop

**HIKING TIME**: 3.5 hours

**VERTICAL RISE**: 15 feet

**RATING**: Moderate

**MAPS**: USGS 7.5' Gadsden, Congaree National Park Trail Guide

**TRAILHEAD GPS COORDINATES**: N33° 49.978', W80° 49.607'

**CONTACT INFORMATION**: Congaree National Park, 100 National Park Road, Hopkins, SC 29061, (803) 776-4396, www .nps.gov/cong

This is one of South Carolina's "can't-miss" hikes. It takes place in the Palmetto State's only national park, Congaree National Park, which is a land of superlatives. Formerly known as Congaree Swamp National Monument, it's also known as the "Redwood Forest of the East" for its number of huge trees. Among other things, it purportedly has the highest continuous forest canopy on earth, at 130 feet. Located within easy driving distance of Columbia, Congaree National Park has an extensive trail system, including a very long (and presumably costly) boardwalk that itself makes a 2.4-mile loop! This hike travels much of the boardwalk, which offers views above the forest floor on its elevated segment, as well as through sensitive wetlands where you are one with the environment. It leaves the boardwalk for Cedar Creek, a clear, canoeable tributary of the Congaree, then travels a "ridge" where some of the largest oaks you will ever see can be found. Return passing Weston Lake before rejoining the boardwalk for a national-park-standards hike. Note: Backpacking is also allowed here; consult the national park for specific rules and regulations.

## GETTING THERE

From Exit 116 off I-26 on the south side of Columbia, take I-77 at mile 0, heading north to Exit 5, Bluff Road, SC 48. Turn right and take SC 48 east for 12 miles to Mount View Road. Follow Mount View for 0.8 mile to Old Bluff Road. Turn right and take Old Bluff Road for 0.5 mile, then turn left into the national park, following the entrance road to the visitor center. The hike starts at the visitor center breezeway. Be apprised that after 5 p.m. all cars must be parked in

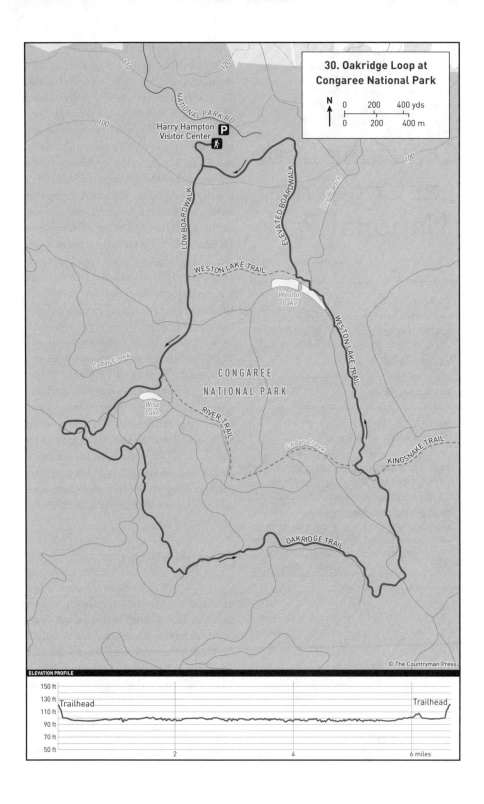

**30. Oakridge Loop at Congaree National Park**

N

| 0 | 200 | 400 yds |
| 0 | 200 | 400 m |

NATIONAL PARK RD

Harry Hampton
Visitor Center

LOW BOARDWALK

ELEVATED BOARDWALK

Dry Branch

WESTON LAKE TRAIL

Weston
Lake

WESTON LAKE TRAIL

CONGAREE
NATIONAL PARK

Cedar Creek

Wise
Lake

RIVER TRAIL

Cedar Creek

KINGSNAKE TRAIL

OAKRIDGE TRAIL

© The Countryman Press

ELEVATION PROFILE

| 150 ft | | | |
| 130 ft | Trailhead | | Trailhead |
| 110 ft | | | |
| 90 ft | | | |
| 70 ft | | | |
| 50 ft | 2 | 4 | 6 miles |

MASSIVE OAK TREES LIKE THIS ARE WHY CONGAREE IS NOW A NATIONAL PARK

the "after hours" parking lot 0.6 mile from the center.

## THE TRAIL

The hike leaves the visitor center breezeway to join a boardwalk, which may be slippery after rains. The boardwalk splits at 0.2 mile; stay right and begin the loop portion of the hike. Take the "Low Boardwalk," walking eye-level with wide, buttressed, moss-covered cypress and tupelo trees. These trees and others like them thrive in this wetland that becomes inundated by the overflowing Congaree River up to 10 times per year. Contemplation benches are placed along the boardwalk. Don't be surprised if you see birders looking for feathered creatures fluttering in the ultrahigh canopy.

Continue south along the Low Boardwalk and reach an intersection. The Boardwalk Loop leaves left; you continue forward, still on a boardwalk, shortly to be walking a natural surface on Weston Lake Trail. Notice piles of debris banked against trees. This occurs when the floodplain is inundated and leaves, brush, and other fodder flows and gathers. The trail moves forward in the land of the giants to bridge a strand connecting to Cedar Creek, the primary stream of the trail area.

Shortly come along gorgeous Cedar Creek, a dark-water stream draining from west to east. Cedar Creek is canoeable, and the national park has two paddle accesses for exploring the Congaree area by water. If you undertake this watery exploration, contact the park for water-level information. Also, expect to pull over some blowdowns over the creek. Open to a field, then Weston Lake Trail reaches a junction at 1.1 miles. Oakridge Trail leaves right, crossing Cedar Creek, while Sims Trail heads back toward the visitor center. Cross Cedar Creek on an iron bridge, reaching another junction. A short spur trail leads to Wise Lake, ringed in cypress, while you stay with the red-blazed Oakridge Trail, which begins to circle Wise Lake. The dirt footpath continues meandering through the back of beyond, crossing a pair of sloughs. Notice how the trees in and around the slough are more buttressed than the relatively higher and drier ground upon which you walk.

At 1.4 miles reach another junction. Here the remote River Trail heads to the Congaree River on its separate 6.3-mile loop. Oakridge Trail curves to the east in more giant trees—even the hollies are massive. When one of these vine-draped behemoths falls it takes other trees down with it, creating a light gap that stands out distinctly in these primordial woods. Nature can't stand a void, however, and new trees start racing upward to patch the "hole" in the canopy. The narrow footpath winds along a slough, bridging it at 2.8 miles. Keeping east,

WALKING THE LOW BOARDWALK

the path makes more twists and turns, always seeking the highest ground or curving around a fallen giant. The Congaree was established in 1976 after a successful grassroots campaign to preserve this floodplain. The area had been owned by one family for a long time. Timbering operations were under way, breaking the hearts of many South Carolinians. Eventually this special swath of the Palmetto State was preserved, including the critters that roam here. Don't be surprised if you see wild boar or deer—both are common here, though the boars aren't native. The trail bridges another major slough at 3.8 miles. To help keep you apprised of your position, the slough bridges are marked on the park map with letters, and the corresponding letters are cut into the bridge boards on either side of the span. This last bridge mentioned, for instance, is marked with an "H" on the span and the park trail map.

Oakridge Trail turns north, now among some of the biggest of the big trees, especially white oaks and loblolly pines. This is my favorite area. Meet Kingsnake Trail at 4.3 miles, just before bridging Cedar Creek for the second time. Peer from the bridge into the shaded dark waters, silently flowing to feed the Congaree. The hike now makes a junction on the north side of Cedar Creek, leaving Oakridge Trail to rejoin Weston Lake Trail, which has a more beaten-down trailbed than the lightly used Oakridge Trail. Big pines become more commonplace. Bridge a slough, which spreads into a wide floodplain, evolving into Weston Lake, which comes into view at 5.2 miles. Cypress

TRAILSIDE OWL

trees, their knees rising upward from the uneven wetland floor, stand as sentinels over Weston Lake.

Just ahead, you will meet the Elevated Boardwalk. Don't bypass the overlook of Weston Lake before continuing away from the lake on the high boardwalk, as opposed to the lower one also heading to the visitor center. Head north, looking out from a 10-or-so-foot perch into the forest. Pass Bluff Trail, Sims Trail, and Dog Trail in a short span before completing the loop portion of the hike at 6.3 miles. Backtrack and return to the park visitor center.

# Parsons Mountain Loop

**TOTAL DISTANCE**: 4.2-mile loop

**HIKING TIME**: 2.5 hours

**VERTICAL RISE**: 340 feet

**RATING**: Moderate

**MAPS**: USGS 7.5' Verdery; Parsons Mountain Recreation Area

**TRAILHEAD GPS COORDINATES**: N34° 5.817', W82° 21.274'

**CONTACT INFORMATION**: Sumter National Forest, Long Cane Ranger District, 810 Buncombe Street, Edgefield, SC 29824, (803) 637-5396, www.fs.usda.gov/scnf

This hike takes place at Parsons Mountain Recreation Area, a fine destination in the Long Cane District of Sumter National Forest. Consider combining your hike with camping, fishing, or swimming. The Parsons Mountain Loop travels both the high and the low. First, it skirts along steep-sided and scenic Parsons Mountain Lake; it then passes a dammed spring pond before climbing toward Parsons Mountain. Along the way you'll see some abandoned gold mines from 100 or more years ago before reaching the top of Parsons Mountain, which has limited views, as the fire tower there is now off limits. Backtrack down the mountain to resume your loop around the scenic 28-acre lake, crossing several streams that feed the impoundment. A spur trail leads to a bridge that goes to the center of the lake, where there is a grassy wildlife-viewing area. Finally the trail circles through the swim beach, campground, and a lakeside picnic area to cross the lake dam and complete the loop. The ascents and descents are not limited to the climb atop the mountain on this surprisingly challenging loop. The many hardwoods along the path would make it an ideal fall color hike.

## GETTING THERE

From Abbeville, take SC 72 west for 2.0 miles to reach SC 28. Turn left and take SC 28 south for 2.1 miles to Parsons Mountain Road. Turn left onto Parsons Mountain Road and follow it for 1.5 miles to Parsons Mountain Recreation Area. Turn right here and follow the forest road into the recreation area, then turn left to dead-end at the boat ramp, across the lake dam.

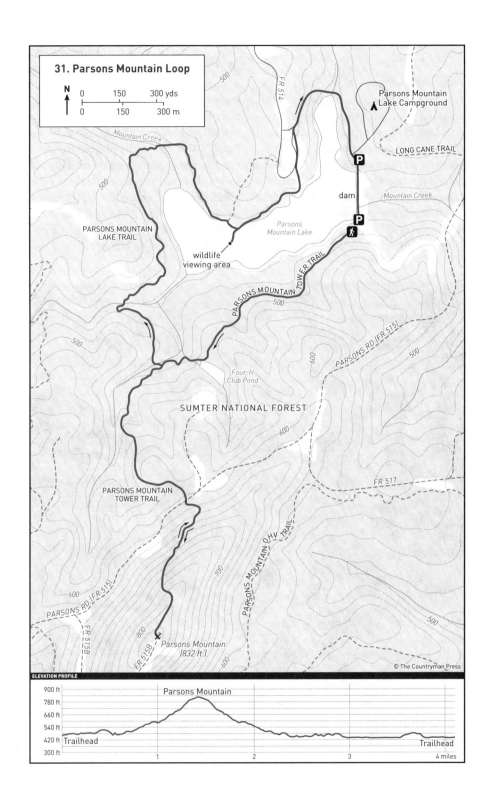

**31. Parsons Mountain Loop**

N

| 0 | 150 | 300 yds |
| 0 | 150 | 300 m |

Mountain Creek

FR 514

Parsons Mountain
Lake Campground

LONG CANE TRAIL

P

dam

Mountain Creek

P

PARSONS MOUNTAIN
LAKE TRAIL

wildlife
viewing area

Parsons
Mountain Lake

PARSONS MOUNTAIN TOWER TRAIL

500

PARSONS RD (FR 515)

500

Four-H
Club Pond

600

SUMTER NATIONAL FOREST

600

FR 517

PARSONS MOUNTAIN
TOWER TRAIL

PARSONS MOUNTAIN O.H.V. TRAIL

700

500

PARSONS RD (FR 515)

600

FR 515B

800

FR 515B

Parsons Mountain
(832 ft.)

600

© The Countryman Press

**ELEVATION PROFILE**

| | Parsons Mountain |
| 900 ft | |
| 780 ft | |
| 660 ft | |
| 540 ft | |
| 420 ft Trailhead | Trailhead |
| 300 ft | |
| | 1  2  3  4 miles |

## THE TRAIL

Parsons Mountain Trail leaves the boat-ramp area and makes a single-track dirt path rising along a steep slope. Pass a trail map kiosk showing an overview of the hike. Parsons Mountain Lake is visible through the trees to your right. Level off in an attractive hardwood forest of oak and beech. Note the especially large white oaks. The path loses sight of the lake as it turns into a hollow.

At 0.5 mile, the trail reaches a junc-tion. To your left, a path crosses the dam of a small pond, Four-H Club Pond, which is forested around its perime-ter and hard to access. This is not the spur trail to the top of Parsons Moun-tain. An old map I found calls this the Four-H Club Dam, but I couldn't find the history behind the name. Continue forward at the junction and not over the pond dam. Just ahead, the trail crosses the outflow of the pond and reaches a rocked-in spring. Stop and take a look. Note the clear water emerging from the

HIKER OVERLOOKS PARSONS MOUNTAIN LAKE

submerged reaches of the hole. This recreation area was developed by the Civilian Conservation Corps (CCC) in the 1930s, and the spring was likely rocked in by them. The roots of the recreation area were planted decades ago, when the CCC dammed Mountain Creek and developed the ensuing shoreline, including the campground. The historic part of the recreation area, stonework such as this spring, was left intact even after the area was modernized during recent years.

Just ahead, reach another junction. Here the trail to the mountaintop begins. Head left following the white blazes, still in bottomland. The path becomes rocky as it turns upward away from the valley. Gain a ridgeline that undulates to cross Forest Road 515. The climbing really begins. Stay left here, working up the mountain to reach the four shafts that make up the old gold mines. These shafts, dug around 1900, resulted from the success of the Dorn Mine, near McCormick, South Carolina. You can walk to the edge, but they're bordered by fences. The shafts extend vertically downward, though some have partially caved in. Entering abandoned mines, especially fenced-in ones, is a stupid proposition.

Keep working uphill in oak-dominated woods to reach the top of Parsons Mountain at 1.5 miles. This type of mountain is called a monadnock, which is geologist terminology for the mound of hard rock left over after all the land around it has succumbed to erosion. The crest is 832 feet high, named for James Parsons, who obtained this land in a grant from the King of England in 1772. The tower was once manned by rangers during the spring and fall fire seasons, but it's now closed and fenced

off. Fire-watching today is done from planes during high fire season. Despite the tower's closure, you can gain summer glimpses of the lands below through the trees. Winter offers better views. A mountaintop cedar provides shade near the tower.

Backtrack down Parsons Mountain and return to the lakeshore part of the loop. This time turn left and span a branch on a wooden bridge. Climb a knoll then dip into the next feeder stream, this once much larger. This bridged crossing is at 2.5 miles.

Begin the pattern of climbing a ridge, then dipping to branches flowing into the lake. This is where the hike earns its hilly reputation. A contemplation bench offers a long look at the lake. The next stream, Mountain Creek, is crossed at 3.0 miles and is the largest yet.

Keep the lake to your right and reach another trail junction at 3.3 miles. Take this side trail to reach the center of the lake and a grassy wildlife-viewing area. Parsons Mountain Lake covers 28 acres. The shoreline is pretty everywhere you look, whether that be the grassy picnic areas shaded by tall pines or the trees growing directly to the shoreline. No gas motors are allowed. Boaters will be pleased to know the lake does have a boat ramp. This makes boating or fishing easy. Largemouth bass, bream, and catfish are the most sought-after fishes. Picnic benches call out to you to sit down and look out on the lake. A long wooden bridge crosses to land. This is a popular bank-fishing area.

Return to the main trail and keep looping to reach the swim area at 3.5 miles. Here a grassy slope leads down to a roped-off swimming area. Shaded picnic tables and a large pavilion are also found here. Keep along the shore

WILDFLOWERS ADD TRAILSIDE BEAUTY

and pick up the trail again as it skirts the impoundment. Reach pavement and follow the road past the campground, then past an attractive picnic area, before crossing the lake dam and completing your loop at 4.2 miles. After you make this hike, you might wish you were camping here. The small campground offers a rustic atmosphere with only 23 sites—a desirable number for a campground. The size keeps the premises generally quiet, but the park isn't so small that it fills too quickly. Parsons Mountain does fill on ideal spring and early-summer weekends. The campground is a first-come, first-served prospect and is open from April through mid-December.

# Peachtree Rock Nature Preserve Loop

> **TOTAL DISTANCE**: 2.2-mile loop
>
> **HIKING TIME**: 11 hours
>
> **VERTICAL RISE**: 110 feet
>
> **RATING**: Moderate
>
> **MAPS**: USGS 7.5' Pelion East; Peachtree Rock
>
> **TRAILHEAD GPS COORDINATES**: N33° 49.702', W81° 12.139'

The Nature Conservancy deserves credit for preserving this fascinating parcel of land, a stone's throw southwest of Columbia. Amid this hilly country is the only naturally occurring waterfall in the Midlands, along with interesting rock formations including now-fallen Peachtree Rock, a strange eroded boulder that resembles an inverted pyramid. Yet other eroded rocks are standing. Also enjoy vistas from rock outcrops, clear creeks, and blinding white sand-hills dotted with green pines.

## GETTING THERE

From Exit 113 off I-26 south of Columbia, take SC 302 west for 11 miles to reach SC 6 as it heads for Swansea. (You will first intersect SC 6, 1.4 miles back, where SC 6 and SC 302 run in conjunction.) Veer left onto SC 6 and follow it for 0.9 mile to reach the trailhead in a sand parking area on your left at the intersection of SC 6 and Peachtree Rock Road. Alternate directions: From Exit 55 off I-20 west of Columbia, take SC 6 south for 8.0 miles until it reaches SC 302. Stay right with SC 6/SC 302 for 1.4 miles; then SC 6 veers left toward Swansea. Stay with SC 6 for 0.9 mile to reach the trailhead on your left.

## THE TRAIL

You will be surprised at the amount of scenery packed into this 306-acre Lexington County preserve with two loops. Leave busy SC 6 and enter a green world. Pines sway overhead, while oaks, sparkleberry, and other young trees grow thick. Drop off the piney ridge and enter a cooler, moister forest that includes bay trees, along with titi and sand myrtle. Step over a tiny streamlet. Even on the

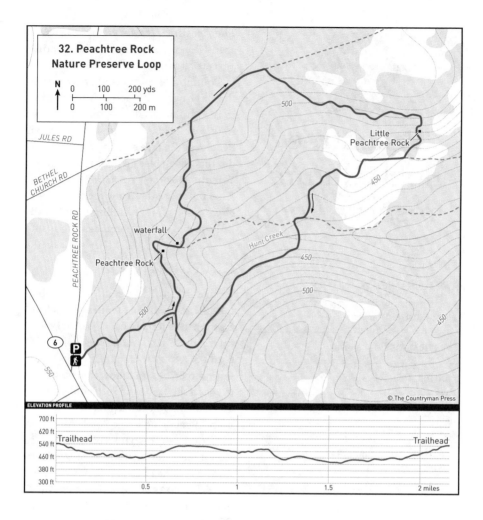

## 32. Peachtree Rock Nature Preserve Loop

N

| 0 | 100 | 200 yds |
| 0 | 100 | 200 m |

JULES RD

BETHEL CHURCH RD

PEACHTREE ROCK RD

Little Peachtree Rock

500

450

450

waterfall

Hunt Creek

450

Peachtree Rock

500

500

6

P

550

450

© The Countryman Press

ELEVATION PROFILE

| 700 ft |
| 620 ft |
| 540 ft | Trailhead | | | Trailhead |
| 460 ft |
| 380 ft |
| 300 ft | 0.5 | 1 | 1.5 | 2 miles |

hottest Midland summer day, this valley will be a little cooler.

At 0.2 mile reach a trail junction. Stay left here; the other way will be your return route. The loops are blazed in blue and red. Stay with the blue loop, rising a bit back into pines before dropping yet again to reach Peachtree Rock. This fascinating rock formation has fallen. Visitors were formerly asked to stay back 25 feet from the rock, which was so eroded at its base that it fell over. Despite the warning, numerous people carved their initials into it. Peachtree Rock is capped by a layer of hard sand-stone; softer layers beneath have eroded faster, creating the upside-down pyra-mid. Little paths run all over this area, as there are other rocks to visit that are interesting in their own right. Also, the waterfall is nearby. As you walk over to it, you will see an overhanging rock bluff about 15 to 20 feet high over which a nar-row strip of water flows, splashing to the ground below, then flowing on to meet Hunt Creek. Get near the falls to feel the cooler air and to see ferns that enjoy the moist microclimate. Early Columbians must've come here for a little solace from the summer heat. After heavy rains

PEACHTREE ROCK AS IT ONCE STOOD

this fall would be impressive. In late summer it can nearly run dry. The rock ridge over which the creek has carved its path extends outward, and visitors have clambered all over these rocks, creating trails. The area can be confusing, but feel free to explore all those interesting rock formations, and visit now-fallen Peachtree Rock, gaining perspective from different angles. While looking, you wonder how the thing ever stood up. Finally, on December 7, 2013 gravity and time tipped it over. Nevertheless, long after we are gone, gravity and time will carve another rock in these parts into an equally remarkable sight.

The blue-blazed trail works along a rock ridge, then veers left and climbs into pinewoods. Pass some old barrels that are relics of a former moonshine still. Deduce how these were part of the operation. This area was probably a remote locale back when whiskey was made from corn and sold without a government stamp. Climb away from the still to reach the preserve boundary. Stay right and walk along a sandy firebreak road. Stay with the blazes as old routes and paths spur off. The trail undulates in pinewoods on the sandy trail. Views open to the south and east—you'll be surprised at their extent. Where the firebreak road keeps straight to reach a second rocky area, drop off the ridgeline. Notice the mountain laurel, which blooms in spring. You certainly won't miss Little Peachtree Rock, another eroded specimen in this rocky area: It's a taller yet slimmer outcrop. Other outcrops are all over this vicinity; take your time and see how many spires and other formations you can find. The official path stays with the blue blazes. Stay right at the intersection after descending from Little Peachtree Rock.

The main path enters blinding sun-bleached sand, bordered by pines that seem impossibly green in contrast, along with turkey oaks. These smaller oak trees have leaves that resemble the tracks of a turkey, hence the name. Dip into cooler tall pinewoods and make a trail junction. A trail goes left heading downstream along Hunt Creek. Keep straight and reach another intersection. Here, a trail leaves right along Hunt Creek. You, however, stay left here to make the widest loop possible. Step over Hunt Creek then climb away, passing other rock formations. Short trails lead to these stone formations in the woods.

At 2.0 miles reach a trail junction. You have been here before. To your left it is 0.2 mile back to the parking area, or you can turn right to see Peachtree Rock again and take the middle connector trail along Hunt Creek. Either way, you will see the Midlands in a new light after visiting this gem of a place, bought for and maintained by The Nature Conservancy. Interestingly, the site was once owned by the University of South Carolina, used by its Biology Department as a research station before being bought and preserved by the Conservancy, whose mission is "to preserve the plants, animals and natural communities that

ANOTHER STRANGE ROCK FORMATION AT THE PRESERVE

represent the diversity of life on Earth by protecting the lands and waters they need to survive." This group set about acquiring these important lands using a "strategic, science-based planning process, called conservation by design." In this way it has found the places that hold the most promise for long-term biodiversity, saving the "last great places," like Peachtree Rock. For more information visit www.nature.org.

# Palmetto Trail near the Broad River

| |
|---|
| **TOTAL DISTANCE**: 7.2-mile there-and-back |
| **HIKING TIME**: 3.5 hours |
| **VERTICAL RISE**: 30 feet |
| **RATING**: Moderate |
| **MAPS**: USGS 7.5′ Chapin, Jenkinsville; Palmetto Trail—Peak to Prosperity Passage |
| **TRAILHEAD GPS COORDINATES**: N34° 14.626′, W81° 19.067′ |
| **CONTACT INFORMATION**: Palmetto Conservation, 722 King Street, Columbia, SC 29205, (803) 771-0870, www.palmettoconservation.org |

This is one of the Midland's finest stretches of Palmetto Trail, South Carolina's master path. Here, hikers start on the east side of the Broad River at Alston. The hike immediately crosses a 1,100-foot-long span over the Broad River. Here, hikers can enjoy exhilarating views from this former railroad trestle turned hiker-bridge. The hike continues past the hamlet of Peak, then it heads up the Crims Creek valley in wooded rural splendor. Cross other shorter trestles on a nearly level rail trail before reaching Hope Station, a former rail stop, now an alternate trailhead. Your return trip will yield more sylvan scenery before once more enjoying the view from above the Broad River.

## GETTING THERE

From Exit 97 on I-26 north of Columbia, take US 176 west 11 miles, then turn right on SC 213/Parr Road. Follow Parr Road for 3.1 miles, bridging the Broad River. Turn right onto Alston Road, the first road after Broad River and follow it, staying right at a fork, then cross a railroad track and go under a trestle, then reach the parking area on your left.

## THE TRAIL

The Palmetto Trail continues to be extended. The original goal remains the same—a continuous path extending from mountains of the Upstate through the Midlands into the Lowcountry and to the Atlantic Ocean, around 500 miles of trail. This particular stretch of Palmetto Trail is known as the Peak to Prosperity Passage. Segments of Palmetto Trail are divided into passages. This segment came to be when Palmetto Conservation—the organization

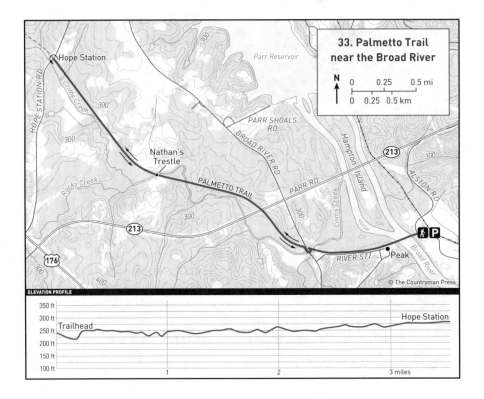

overseeing Palmetto Trail—purchased an 11-mile-long, 200-foot-wide right-of-way on an abandoned section of railroad line from the Norfolk Southern Railway.

In 2009, the decking of the bridge over the Broad River and the additional trestles were repaired and made safe for hikers and bicyclers. A total of 20 trestles stand along Peak to Prosperity Passage. These trestles add to the trail and offer elevated views of the waters they span.

This particular hike extends between Alston at the passage's eastern terminus and Hope Station, a former stop for the rail line that once connected Columbia and Greenville. You will cross a total of six trestles between Alston and Hope Station. The Alston trailhead has a covered picnic shelter and primitive camp-site, as well as a picnic area and canoe/kayak launch beside the river.

The hike starts off with a bang and you immediately join the long trestle over the Broad River. The line connecting Columbia to Greenville was originally laid out in 1850 but the first Broad River bridge was destroyed by flood in 1852. After a few years, the bridge was rebuilt and by the time Civil War began, two trains were running daily between Columbia and Greenville. However, during General Sherman's merciless March to the Sea he destroyed this bridge. At lower water levels, you can still see the stone abutments from that bridge destroyed by Sherman. Enjoy views up and down the Broad. Looking upstream, you can see where the river splits around Hampton Island.

Once across the river, the Palmetto Trail passes beside the small community of Peak, named after an early railroad superintendent. A spur leads left up to River Street. Continuing down the trail you will pass by old buildings as well as newer structures. Since you are traveling on a former railroad grade, it was kept as level as possible, therefore some segments of the passage are atop elevated berms while still other segments cut through small hills. Hikers will be pleasantly surprised at the extent of the forestlands along the trail. However, a few segments of the path go near meadows.

Enjoy the second trestle at 0.8 mile. This trestle and the others that follow are significantly shorter than the span over the Broad River. Cross Crims Creek, then the trail cuts left, passing below Broad River Road, then return to rejoin the railroad grade on the west side of the road. Note the picnic tables below the trestle. At 1.4 miles, Palmetto Trail passes under Parr Road. You are

HIKER LOOKS OVER THE BROAD RIVER AT HAMPTON ISLAND

heading up the Crims Creek valley, originally settled in the 1730s by German immigrants.

At 1.8 miles, a tributary of Crims Creek flows under the trail. Look for

HIKER LOOKS DOWNSTREAM FROM BRIDGE OVER THE BROAD RIVER

a wooded swamp ahead on your right. The water here is pinned between a hill to the right and the elevated berm of the rail line. At 2.1 miles, bridge Crims Creek again. While hiking ahead, look beside the trail for metal relics and old rail ties. At 2.3 miles, reach another trestle spanning the rapids of Crims Creek. This is known as Nathan's Trestle. Note the stone abutments from the original laying of the rail line. The original trestle was also burned in the Civil War. Today, stairs lead down from the trestle to the rapids of Crims Creek.

Beyond this trestle, the trail passes through a menagerie of woods, fields, and quiet countryside. Look for the old railroad mile markers, as well as other evidence of the path's former use. Ahead, you go down a long straightaway and can see the trail gate at Hope Station Road. Then, at 3.6 miles, you emerge at Hope Station Road. This was once a rail stop, but all you can see in the immediate vicinity is a small parking area. This is a good place to turn around. However, ambitious trail trekkers can continue on the path and cross six more trestles between Hope Station and Pomeria, another trailhead located off US 176. This segment also features a designated backcountry campsite about a mile-and-a-half from Hope Station.

# Poinsett State Park Loop

**TOTAL DISTANCE**: 1.7-mile loop

**HIKING TIME**: 1 hour

**VERTICAL RISE**: 90 feet

**RATING**: Easy

**MAPS**: USGS 7.5' Poinsett State Park; Poinsett State Park, Palmetto Trail—High Hills of Santee Passage

**TRAILHEAD GPS COORDINATES**: N33° 48.284', W80° 32.893'

**CONTACT INFORMATION**: Poinsett State Park, 6660 Poinsett Park Road, Wedgefield, SC 29168, (803) 494-8177, www.southcarolinaparks.com/poinsett

This is an overlooked gem in the South Carolina state park system. Located in what's known as the High Hills of Santee, an outlier of the Carolina Sandhills, Poinsett is where the vegetation of the Lowcountry meets that of the Upcountry, resulting in the overlapping of ecosystems, a place where Spanish moss hangs in trees that stand over blooming mountain laurel bushes amid surprisingly steep terrain. It's also a historic area. The park itself—developed in the 1930s by the Civilian Conservation Corps (CCC)—had an interesting past and a great location where spring-fed Old Levi Mill Lake, 10 acres in size, powered an old gristmill. The hike itself loops the lake, bordering the lower banks as well as the hills around the lake.

## GETTING THERE

From Exit 9 off I-77 in Columbia, take US 378 East, Garners Ferry Road, for 26 miles to SC 261. Turn right onto SC 261 South and follow it for 10.1 miles, passing through Wedgefield, to reach Poinsett Road. Turn right at the sign and continue for 1.7 miles to enter the state park. Continue beyond the park entrance, following signs on the main road to reach the lake and the trailhead. The hike starts near the park dam, on the far side of the buildings beside the lake.

## THE TRAIL

Leave the parking area, which has a large picnic area nearby, including picnic shelters. Head toward the park offices, located in historic CCC buildings. Poinsett formerly had a swim beach, with changing rooms in the old wood-and-stone structures, but it was closed in 1999. Circle behind the historic buildings to a reach a stone-

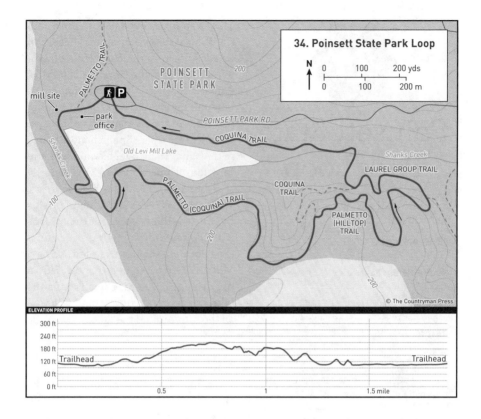

**34. Poinsett State Park Loop**

ELEVATION PROFILE

lined water raceway flowing from the lake. This was the original route of the raceway when it fed a mill here, but the wood was replaced with stone by the CCC in the late 1930s. Poinsett was one of South Carolina's first state parks. Long before it became a park, however, the area was appreciated for much more than its beauty. The Singleton family saw the valley of spring-fed Shanks Creek as a great place for a mill to grind corn, for Shanks Creek flowed year-round, giving them an endless power supply, whereas other local streams would cease to flow in late summer and fall. They dammed what you see as Old Levi Mill Lake, then built the raceway to the mill. Walk down along this raceway now to reach a pretty little spot where the water flows

over tiers amid more rock landscaping. Notice the stone walls standing below the outflow. These are relics of the mill, which changed hands over time but remains to this day one of the most beautiful spots in the Midlands.

Return to cross the raceway on a little stone bridge, flowing over crystalline Shanks Creek. You have now joined the state's master path, Palmetto Trail. This part of the Palmetto is known as the High Hills of Santee Passage. Palmetto Trail came in from the far side of the picnic area, traveling 6 miles from the Wateree River over a restored railroad grade via eight boarded bridges bisecting wetlands of the Wateree River then wandering through surprisingly hilly country to emerge here at the state park.

Reach Levi Mill Dam. The open

HERON ALONG OLD LEVI MILL LAKE

grassy barrier offers a good view of the lake, which is home to alligators. The presence of these gators is one more example of a way that Poinsett is a meeting ground for ecosystems representative of the entire state. A second outflow of the lake, beyond that of the millrace, is located on the other side of the dam. This outflow was added by the CCC to prevent the dam from bursting. Turn below the dam and span the outflow on a small bridge. You may notice a sign for Coquina Trail. This is the original name of the path. Palmetto Trail runs in con-

WATER SPILLS OVER THE OLD MILL RACEWAY

junction with Coquina Trail, which was laid out by the CCC as well. Coquina rock is found in abundance here; while laying out the trail the CCC likely hit a few outcrops and decided that Coquina would be the trail's name.

Ascend through a rich forest draped in Spanish moss, passing by the lake before climbing this truly hilly country. Reach a wood-and-stone picnic shelter, also built in the 1930s. It once offered a cleared view of the lake, but much of the forest has grown up since the park's inception. Keep climbing on a hillside, circling past an old roadbed before meeting Hilltop Trail. Coquina Trail heads downhill, making a shorter loop. Your loop turns right and ascends Hilltop Trail, which offers more vertical variation, both up and down, before meeting Laurel Group Trail. Laurel Group Trail leads both directions along Shanks Creek. Palmetto Trail leads right, away from the lake, running in conjunction with Laurel Group Trail, continuing for 8 miles through the adjacent Manchester State Forest. Turn left onto Laurel Group Trail, winding into small hollows before meeting Coquina Trail. Keep heading down along Shanks Creek before turning to cross it on a boardwalk. This small creek flows clear over a sand bed through lush bottomland that offers a real contrast to the steep hills bordering Levi Mill Lake.

The loop now turns downstream between the lake and the main park road. Reach a short pier leading into the lake, where you can look over lily pads lying silently on the water with cypress trees in the background. Park visitors can boat and fish in this quiet setting where gas motors are not allowed. You can rent a johnboat from the park at a very low rate, or bring your own canoe, kayak, or other boat, as long as you can carry it to the water, since there is no boat launch. Bass, bream, and catfish lie beneath the placid pond.

The trail continues along the lake then completes its loop after passing through the picnic area. Before coming here, consider camping at the state park. The campground is set high on a hill where pines, oaks, sweetgums, dogwoods, and hickories, draped in Spanish moss, stand over sandy sites. Ample ground vegetation divides the campsites and provides good privacy. Two bathhouses serve the campground, which has electric and nonelectric sites. Campsites are always available in the nonelectric loop. However, reservations can be made. Poinsett is a spring/winter/fall destination: Summer can be excessively hot, and there is no swimming here. Note also that you may experience noise from a nearby bombing range. The park stands adjacent to Manchester State Forest. This 25,000-acre forest has trails aplenty, besides the aforementioned Palmetto Trail, especially for mountain bikers. Three trails create loops covering more than 17 miles of pedaling. The Killer 3 Trail is the longest at 10 miles.

# Sesqui-centennial State Park Hike

Take a hike at this historic, scenic, and convenient state park situated amid greater Columbia. The preserve features rolling wooded terrain in the sandhills region, cut with clear, spring-fed creeks. Centennial Lake occupies the heart of the park, and this hike takes you by it. However, the hike starts by wandering through pines and turkey oaks before circling the scenic impoundment. From there you curve past more wooded hills and tributaries of the Jackson Creek. Explore the back 40 of the park—its remoteness will pleasantly surprise trail trekkers in the Midlands.

**TOTAL DISTANCE**: 4.8-mile loop

**HIKING TIME**: 2.5 hours

**VERTICAL RISE**: 85 feet

**RATING**: Moderate

**MAPS**: USGS 7.5' Fort Jackson North; Sesquicentennial State Park

**TRAILHEAD GPS COORDINATES**: N34° 5.507', W80° 54.487'

**CONTACT INFORMATION**: Sesquicentennial State Park, 9564 Two Notch Road, Columbia, SC 29223, (803) 788-2706, www.southcarolinaparks.com

## GETTING THERE

From Exit 17 on I-77 east of downtown Columbia, take US 1 North, Two Notch Road for 2.1 miles then turn right into the park. Continue past the fee booth, then, at .7 mile, turn left into the large trail parking area on your left.

## THE TRAIL

Sesquicentennial State Park came to be in the 1930s. It was originally developed by the Civilian Conservation Corps and thus has several historic structures still in use from those days. The park's name originates from its opening at the same time as Columbia's 150th birthday in 1936. Back then, Columbia was much smaller and Sesquicentennial State Park was located in the countryside but within easy striking distance of the South Carolina state capital. However, in the ensuing decades, Columbia has grown and its suburbs have enveloped the state park. Nevertheless, instead of thinking that civilization's arrival is a negative, rather think that the current situation makes the 1,400 acres of the state park all the more special. Not only

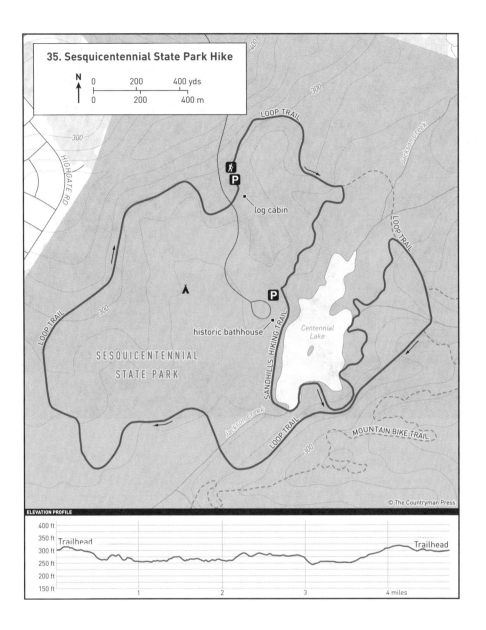

### 35. Sesquicentennial State Park Hike

N

| 0 | 200 | 400 yds |
| 0 | 200 | 400 m |

LOOP TRAIL

Jackson Creek

HIGHGATE RD

300

300

400

log cabin

LOOP TRAIL

historic bathhouse

Centennial
Lake

SANDHILLS HIKING TRAIL

SESQUICENTENNIAL
STATE PARK

300

LOOP TRAIL

Jackson Creek

LOOP TRAIL

300

MOUNTAIN BIKE TRAIL

© The Countryman Press

**ELEVATION PROFILE**

400 ft
350 ft — Trailhead
300 ft
250 ft
200 ft
150 ft

Trailhead

1    2    3    4 miles

have neighborhoods and businesses come out this way but also the interstate system runs very close to the park. This does add road noise but does not detract from the scenery as you make your circuit through the preserve. By the way, not only does "Sesqui"—as it is called by locals—have trails for hikers and mountain bikers, but it also has a sizable shady campground with water and electric sites as well as picnic shelters, fishing, canoeing, and kayaking. So consider making a day or weekend of it when coming here.

Join the loop trail near the trailhead kiosk. The fact that you are in the sandhills region becomes immediately evident, as the trailbed is sand and the

LOOKING OVER THE PARK'S LAKE

hillsides are partially sandy and dotted with pines and turkey oaks. A hillside drops off to your right, where a thickly vegetated clear spring branch flows toward Centennial Lake.

Hike under a power line at .1 mile. It isn't long before you pass the first of many unmarked spur trails. Most of these are unofficial paths, as official park trails are blazed. Stay with the blazed trails and you cannot get lost. Intersect a red-blazed access trail leaving left just a little distance past the power line. At .5 mile, after dropping off a hill, join Sandhills Hiking Trail, the park path that circles Centennial Lake. You are now in bottomland, despite the name of the path. Bay trees, brush and beard cane rise thickly. Bridge a spring branch at .6 miles via boardwalk. At .8 mile, a spur trail leads right to an alternate parking area.

Just ahead, you will see Centennial Lake. This 27-acre, man-made impoundment came to be during the development of Sesquicentennial State Park. Jackson Creek and its many tributaries feed it. You will undoubtedly see the historic bathhouse while coming alongside the lake. Unfortunately, no swimming is allowed these days. The state is trying to avoid lawsuits. Take note of the boats available for rent in this vicinity. After cruising along, the hike joins a concrete walkway that passes beside several picnic shelters as well as shaded picnic tables. Anglers may be seen bank fishing for bass, bream, or catfish.

The hike travels under the arched branches of waterside oak trees, then you span the outflow of the lake at 1.2 miles. Enjoy the view from the wooden bridge above the spillway. Sandhills Hiking Trail continues circling Centennial Lake and passes more picnic shelters. The lakeside brush thickens amid bottoms while curving around arms of the lake. Bridge trickling streams on boardwalks as well as wetlands in a particularly scenic area.

Rejoin the loop trail at 2.1 miles. Climb away from the lake on a mild hill, then, at 2.3 miles, Mountain Bike Trail leaves left and makes its own circuit in the hills above Centennial Lake. The hike undulates through drier hills divided by spring branches. Open onto a former parking lot and picnic shelter. Enjoy a few more lake views before turning away from the impoundment at 2.9 miles.

Return to Jackson Creek, crossing it at 3.2 miles. Jackson Creek is part of the greater Gills Creek watershed, which flows through heavily urbanized areas of Columbia en route to its mother stream, the Congaree River. Tributaries of Gills Creek, such as Jackson Creek, tend to rise and fall rapidly due to the natural draining of impervious surfaces

WALKING UNDER SHADED OAKS

such as streets, rooftops, and patios typically found in cities. The latest flood of Jackson Creek was in the fall of 2015, when heavy rains from a warm front merged with Hurricane Joaquin to produce 500-year flood levels caused by more than 20 inches of rain during the entire storm event. And the flood spread far beyond Jackson Creek. Numerous Columbia-area dams were breached. The city and much of South Carolina were thrown into a state of emergency. Here at Sesquicentennial State Park, the lake dam held, but Jackson Creek, flowing wildly, damaged the loop trail, where it crosses Jackson Creek below the dam.

This hike crosses Jackson Creek where the trail was damaged, at 3.2 miles. See if you can still see signs of flooding from this 2015 storm. Beyond there, the loop trail rises into sandhills in a lesser-developed part of the park. Pass within sight of the park campground at 4.3 miles. The last part of the trek winds through woods, and you reach the main park road at 4.8 miles. From here, the trailhead parking area is in sight, and your hike is concluded.

Consider checking out the log house nearby. It is said that the two-story structure was built in the mid 1700s, and it boasts of being the oldest standing building in Richland County. It was moved to Sesquicentennial State Park in 1969.

# Stevens Creek There-and-Back

**TOTAL DISTANCE**: 11.2 miles round trip

**HIKING TIME**: 5 hours

**VERTICAL RISE**: 100 feet

**RATING**: Moderate

**MAPS**: USGS 7.5' Clarks Hill, Parksville; Sumter National Forest—Long Cane District; Stevens Creek Trail

**TRAILHEAD GPS COORDINATES**: N33° 43.789', W82° 11.031'

**CONTACT INFORMATION**: Sumter National Forest, Long Cane Ranger District, 810 Buncombe Street, Edgefield, SC 29824, (803) 637-5396, www.fs.usda.gov/scnf

Stevens Creek is a scenic and preserved parcel of the Savannah River Valley. Its headwaters rise south of the town of Greenwood, in Greenwood County. From there, tributaries gather and Stevens Creek comes to be, forming the division between McCormick and Edgefield counties. This trail comes along the stream near Modoc, before Stevens Creek flows into Clarks Hill Lake. At this point, Stevens Creek is big enough to float down in a canoe, having carved quite a valley of its own. This well-maintained path travels the steep bluffs and rich bottomlands of Stevens Creek in the Long Cane District of Sumter National Forest, north of Augusta. Along the way, it winds through steep-sided valleys that feed Stevens Creek. Perhaps its most noteworthy feature is the size and preponderance of jack-in-the-pulpit wildflowers, which grow in this valley in a quantity I have never seen anywhere else.

## GETTING THERE

From the town square in Edgefield, take SC 23 for 16.5 miles to the trailhead, which is on your right just after the bridge over Stevens Creek.

## THE TRAIL

Leave the parking area and immediately enter an area of rich hardwoods of white oak, sugar maple, and beech. Ferns spread across the forest floor. Soon you'll cross the first of many wooden bridges that span feeder branches, including Key Branch. Some crossings are rock-hops, but all can be easily made, in times of normal flow. You may also notice that the trail winds around to minimize gradients. All these meanderings can be

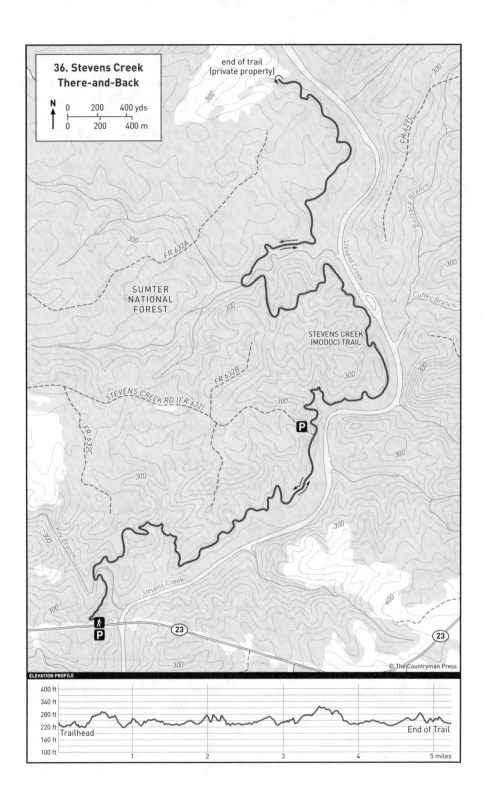

36. Stevens Creek
There-and-Back

N

| 0 | 200 | 400 yds |
| 0 | 200 | 400 m |

end of trail
(private property)

FR 429C

Buzzard Branch

300

FR 632A

SUMTER
NATIONAL
FOREST

Stevens Creek

300

Cuffey Branch

STEVENS CREEK
(MODOC) TRAIL

FR 632B

STEVENS CREEK RD (FR 632)

FR 632C

300

Key Branch

Stevens Creek

300

300

400

23

23

© The Countryman Press

ELEVATION PROFILE

| 400 ft |
| 340 ft |
| 280 ft |
| 220 ft |
| 160 ft |
| 100 ft |

Trailhead

End of Trail

1    2    3    4    5 miles

JACK-IN-THE-PULPITS GROW RAMPANT IN THIS VALLEY

along a shoulder above the creek, with bottomland to your right. In summer, the bottomland brush will be incredibly dense under tulip trees aiming for the sky. Wildflowers, jack-in-the-pulpit particularly, are abundant in this area and throughout the rest of the hike.

Jack-in-the-pulpits are normally green to whitish, and sometimes adorned with stripes, making them much less showy than other colorful wildflowers. Once you notice them, however, you will see them everywhere—this flower blooms in staggering numbers. Its prime bloom time here in Stevens Creek is mid-April to mid-May. "Jack" is the nodule that sits in the middle of the pulpit, which is called a spathe. The actual wildflower is inside the pulpit, clustered at Jack's base. These wildflowers sometimes have a carrion-like odor, which indicates they have been pollinated by flies.

At 2.1 miles, the path reaches a junction. Here, a spur trail leads left uphill to an alternative parking area on Forest Road 632. Modoc Trail leaves the junction and works onto the side of a sheer bluff. The watercourse has been pinched in by the bluff and sports noisy rapids. You can look through the trees below to see tan sandbars and rocky riffles.

At 2.4 miles, you'll pass a bridge to your left that seemingly leads nowhere. This is a relic of the old path, now rerouted. Hikers cross the bridge and make a short climb up the hill, making the path just beyond the bridge look well used, but if you continue, the trail peters out in overgrown woods. Instead, the correct rerouted track cruises down to a branch and crosses the stream just above a low waterfall. Curve into the edge of bottomland; cane crowds the footway. You can see the light gap cre-

explained by its increased popularity with mountain bikers, though it's still well used by hikers. The reroutes use more moderate grades in drier areas, which keep the trail packed and less prone to erosion. The trail is marked in 0.5-mile increments to keep you apprised of your progress.

While winding through the branches feeding Stevens Creek, watch for a couple of outlier patches of saw palmetto. This shrub is more commonly found in the Lowcountry, toward the coast. That makes its presence all the more ironic among the hardwoods so prevalent in the mountains. You begin to wonder where Stevens Creek is, as the trail continues to wander in these small hollows. At 1.1 miles, the trail saddles

TURTLE IN THE STEVENS CREEK BOTTOMS

ated by the 30- to 40-foot-wide creek to your right. It is possible to reach the stream by a short bushwhack at this point. Once again, the trail climbs onto a sheer bluff, dominated by oaks. The steepness of the terrain is impressive; there is no way anyone is going to the creek from up here.

At 3.6 miles the trail turns west and climbs onto a ridge dominated by pines mixed with a few cedars. At this point the path reaches its highest elevation, just above 300 feet. And now that the trail has gone up, it must come down. Leave the ridge and curve through some deeply incised land where beech trees thrive in the shady moist hollows. You cross a shallow rock-lined stream on a wooden bridge at 4.3 miles. The span is a good 8 feet above the stream, which may go dry in late summer and early fall. Regal pines reign over smaller hardwoods in this bottomland. The trail turns east, back toward Stevens Creek, opening to the largest expanse of bottomland yet. This is good deer country; you may see a buck or doe here in early morning or late evening.

Work back onto another sheer bluff. The creek can be seen below, rushing over rapids. Leave the bluff and wind amid more hollows before reaching the Modoc Trail's official end at private property at 5.6 miles. This is a good place to turn around and retrace your steps. Here, an old path enters the brush heading forward, and a much more heavily used trail veers west on a pine-lined old roadbed. The westbound track heads uphill along the national forest boundary to reach a power-line cut in 0.2 mile.

# Timmerman Trail at Congaree Creek

Part of the greater capital city's Three Rivers Greenway network, this greenway near the city of Cayce explores the bottomlands of Congaree Creek, much of it within Congaree Creek Heritage Preserve. The entire route has a concrete surface as you drop from uplands into deeply forested bottomland, then cross Congaree Creek on an impressive iron bridge. Walk beside well-preserved Confederate earthworks as well as the site of Fort Congaree, from the early 1700s. Make a side trip to view the big Congaree River before circling back along Congaree Creek through more notable forestlands.

**TOTAL DISTANCE**: 4.0-mile loop

**HIKING TIME**: 2 hours

**VERTICAL RISE**: 35 feet

**RATING**: Moderate

**MAPS**: USGS 7.5' Southwest Columbia; Three Rivers Greenway

**TRAILHEAD GPS COORDINATES**: N33° 56.520', W81° 2.678'

**CONTACT INFORMATION**: City of Cayce, 1800 12th Street, Cayce, SC 29033, (803) 796-9020, www.cityofcayce-sc.gov/riverwalk

## GETTING THERE

From Exit 2 on I-77 south of Columbia, head north on 12th Street Extension for .6 mile to a traffic light. Turn left on SCANA Parkway, then immediately turn right into the Timmerman Trail parking and Congaree Creek Canoe Access.

## THE TRAIL

The paths on this hike link to other paths on the greater Three Rivers Greenway, a system of trails traveling through the heart of Columbia around and along the Saluda, Broad, and Congaree rivers, as well as other corridors. Timmerman Trail primarily wanders along Congaree Creek, a tributary of the Congaree River. Luckily, the public lands of Congaree Creek Heritage Preserve were already here and it was simply a matter of putting in the trails. The city of Cayce did it; the concrete pathways are enhanced by two iron pedestrian bridges, allowing this loop to happen. The loop hike is popular with not only hikers, but also joggers and bicyclers. You can extend

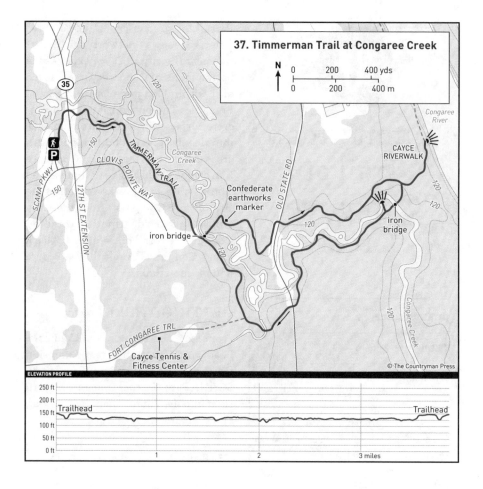

37. Timmerman Trail at Congaree Creek

this venture by simply continuing north along the greenway system up to and beyond the alternate trailhead at Granby Landing Road.

The Timmerman Trail access is also used by paddlers plying Congaree Creek. Leave the large and sometimes busy parking area and follow the concrete path into woodland. The trail immediately heads under 12th Street on a boardwalk, skirting the edge of the heritage preserve boundary. Curve past an office building, then drop into the Congaree Creek bottomland, where gum and cypress occupy the wetter terrain while oak, sweetgum, and pines

create a continuous canopy in drier situations. Of special note is the Atlantic white cedar tree, rare for these parts and part of the reason why the heritage preserve exists in the first place.

Come alongside Congaree Creek at .6 mile. You are on a bluff overlooking the swift, shallow stream, often crossed with fallen logs. Timmerman Trail occasionally bridges tributaries of Congaree Creek. Reach the loop portion of the hike at .8 mile. Head left here, spanning Congaree Creek on an imposing 300-foot iron truss bridge. Take good looks up and down Congaree Creek. Beyond the span, Timmerman Trail takes you

TRAIL BRIDGE OVER CONGAREE CREEK

past an interpretative sign detailing the Congaree Creek earthworks, erected shortly before the Civil War ended in 1865. A skirmish over the defensive line occurred in these woods on February 15, 1865.

Yet more history lies ahead. The trail cruises along the earthwork line, still in good shape. At 1.1 miles, a spur leads right and connects to the now-closed portion of Old State Road. This closed part of Old State Road is now a short-cut for the loop, and the Old State Road bridge over Congaree Creek is now used by bicyclers and hikers.

Our loop stays on the concrete green-way as it turns north and parallels Old State Road, then it crosses it at 1.2 miles. You are still paralleling the Confederate earthworks in seasonally flooded wetlands. These wetlands make you appreciate the concrete walkway that is Timmerman Trail—otherwise traversing these woods would be a muddy experience much of the year.

Span a seasonal tributary on a big wooden bridge at 1.6 miles. The site of old Fort Congaree is nearby. The English arrived here in 1718, establishing Fort Congaree, a defensive and trading post. Settlers soon followed and created a community known as Saxe Gotha, located a little west of the Timmerman trailhead. Lands were plotted out, and at one time hundreds of people lived in Saxe Gotha. Repeated Indian incursions scared the settlers into abandoning these lands. The site of Fort Congaree was discovered in 1989. The Congaree Creek area was also a site for Revolutionary and Civil War forts.

At 1.7 miles, reach a trail intersection. For now, head left, angling toward the Congaree River on the connector that links Timmerman Trail to the rest of the Three Rivers Greenway trail network. It is about a mile to the trailhead at Granby Landing Road. We can walk this path a bit and then come to a picnic table overlooking the Congaree River, a massive waterway that lies below the confluence of the Saluda River and the Broad River. This is a spot where you'll want to linger.

Backtrack, then resume the loop at 2 miles. Shortly, cross Congaree Creek on a shorter iron truss bridge above Congaree Creek. After the bridge, you turn upstream along Congaree Creek. At 2.1 miles, a spur trail leads right to an overlook of Congaree Creek. The stream has cut a steep-sided valley in spots, despite already being in bottomland. Continue the circuit, mimicking the curves of the creek. Come to the blocked-off segment of Old State Road at 2.7 miles. This portion of the road is closed, and its bridge over the Congaree is within sight. However, we stay straight on the concrete Timmerman Trail under shady hardwoods and pines.

Pass the straight spur leading left to the Cayce Tennis & Fitness Center at 3.0 miles, near a clearing. Stay with Timmerman Trail, crossing more tributaries of Congaree Creek. Complete the loop portion of the hike at 3.2 miles. From here, it is a 0.8-mile backtrack to the trailhead.

# Tates Trail at Carolina Sandhills Refuge

**TOTAL DISTANCE**: 5.1 miles round trip

**HIKING TIME**: 3 hours

**VERTICAL RISE**: 45 feet

**RATING**: Moderate

**MAPS**: USGS 7.5' Middendorf; Carolina Sandhills National Wildlife Refuge

**TRAILHEAD GPS COORDINATES**: N34° 33.259', W80° 13.282'

**CONTACT INFORMATION**: Carolina Sandhills National Wildlife Refuge, 23734 U.S. Highway 1, McBee, SC 29101, (843) 335-8350, www.fws.gov/refuge/ Carolina_Sandhills

The Carolina Sandhills are a unique part of the Palmetto State. Formed when the Atlantic crashed the shoreline 100 miles inland from where it is today, these hills are actually ancient dunes. Much of the area was settled, but the thin, sandy soils proved poor for agriculture and the land became badly eroded. In 1939, the federal government purchased the land. Ecosystem management and restoration efforts began immediately and continue to this day in these 45,000 hilly acres of forests, streams, and lakes. You can experience a slice of the refuge on the remote and quiet Tates Trail. It travels through the valley of greater Ham Creek, first dipping to Martins Lake, an impoundment important to migratory birds and other year-round residents, then heading up the valley in the margin between longleaf pine woods and the lusher bottoms, crossing Poplar Branch and circling poorly named Pool D, another lake, to reach a shaded overlook of the lake at some contemplation benches. A hat and sunscreen are recommended for this fall/winter/spring destination: Much of the trail is open overhead.

## GETTING THERE

From McBee, at the intersection of US 1 and SC 151, take US 1 North for 3.1 miles to Carolina Sandhills National Wildlife Refuge. Turn left onto the road leading to the visitor center. Continue beyond this center, taking the gravel road leading 0.5 mile to Wildlife Drive. Turn left and follow the paved Wildlife Drive 3.9 miles to a signed right turn for Martins Lake. Stay with the road to Martins Lake for 0.7 mile to dead-end in a loop at the trailhead.

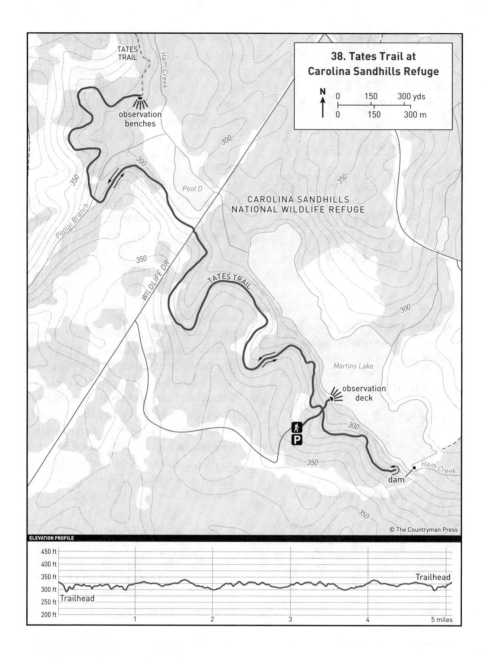

## 38. Tates Trail at Carolina Sandhills Refuge

CAROLINA SANDHILLS
NATIONAL WILDLIFE REFUGE

ELEVATION PROFILE

## THE TRAIL

Leave the trailhead, entering an area of longleaf pine mixed with turkey oak. The surprisingly sloping ground shortly descends to reach a junction. Tates Trail goes left and right, while another trail leads forward. Continue forward down steps past a seep to reach an observation deck, which the refuge refers to as a lookout tower. It is elevated and offers a good view of Martins Lake below, but it's

OVERLOOK AT MARTINS LAKE

hardly a tower. Still, the lake and fields beyond are visible, and in-season migratory birds will be visible on the lake.

Backtrack to Tates Trail, heading left as you return. Walk along a slope, soon crossing a small stream on a boardwalk. The area around the stream is thickly vegetated with ferns and other moisture-loving plants, which offer a great contrast to the drier sandhills through which they flow. Emerge from the boardwalk and travel the margin between the moist, dense shoreline of Martins Lake and the piney hills. You may see an older abandoned trail through the thick woods; the correct trail stays in more open country. Curve down to return to the lake near the dam that holds back Ham Creek to form Martins Lake. An

old boat ramp leads into the water here. Unfortunately, the trail dead-ends here, so you must backtrack. A loop around the lake would be better, but the trail as it is will suffice.

Cross the boardwalk a second time, passing the trail to the observation deck, and keep northerly. Tates Trail roughly parallels the lakeshore, which is well downhill. Another old abandoned trail travels below the newer, wider track that winds among longleaf pines. Turkey oaks grow in preponderance here, as the path begins circling around a seepage slope. The open nature of the longleaf woods allows unobstructed views of the surrounding forest. Longleaf pines once covered more than 90 million acres of land, from

TATES TRAIL OFTEN FOLLOWS THE MARGIN BETWEEN PINEY WOODS AND MOISTER WETLANDS

Texas to Virginia; natural fires kept the understory mostly clear, with scattered scrub oaks such as the turkey oak. These lightning fires started an average of every 2 to 4 years. Settlers and early park managers suppressed them, but now we understand the role fire plays in shaping ecosystems such as these. Just below the trail, the seepage-slope wetland, dense with moist vegetation, is not fire dependent and to this day offers a contrast of evergreen shrubs and deciduous bottomland hardwoods. The lakes here, such as Martins Lake, offer yet another ecosystem, albeit man-made. Carolina Sandhills Refuge has 30 lakes and ponds; more than 190 species of birds use this area for at least part of the year.

After you circle the seepage slope, Martins Lake once again comes into view. Turn away from the water, circling a second seepage slope. The sounds of nature dominate the woodland until you reach Wildlife Drive at 1.8 miles. Cross the paved road. The trail becomes grassier. You can now see uninspiringly named Pool D. A lake this scenic deserves a better name. It is filled with lily pads and tree snags. Nesting boxes on poles rise from the surface. Look for a large oak left over from what was likely a homesite by the trail. Wax myrtle, cane, and ferns border the water. The open track leaves the lake and reenters pines, circling up to cross Poplar Branch on a short wooden bridge. The name "Poplar Branch" refers to the tulip poplar trees that grow tall above the stream. Nowadays they are more commonly referred to as tulip trees, since they are not true poplars. Their leaves, which look like the outlines of tulips, turn bright yellow in fall. Tulip trees, quite showy, grow their own large green-and-yellow flowers in spring. They're uncommon in the Carolina Sandhills, thus whenever they were found somewhere, it was an unusual enough occurrence to warrant naming the creek for them. Notice this pretty little gurgling tributary of Ham Creek. It flows clear over a sand bottom and is hardly visible except at the trail crossing, due to the dense vegetation that surrounds it. The vegetation keeps it cool, which is important for the critters that live in and around it.

While traveling away from Poplar Branch, you can still hear it gurgling unseen. Keep circling the seepage of Poplar Branch. Look for sassafras and maple trees growing in the wetter margins. The trail curves back toward Pool D, which comes into view. The upper part of the lake is heavily wooded with cypress trees. Reach some observation benches under shady pines at 2.9 miles. This is a good spot to have a picnic or simply relax and enjoy the view. Tates Trail continues along up the Ham Creek Valley to nearly circle Lake 12; there's an alternative trailhead on SC 145.

The wildlife refuge offers more than just this trail. The visitor center, which you passed on your way in, is certainly worth a stop. Wildlife Drive is a scenic motorway allowing you to experience the refuge from your car. The lakes and ponds here are open for fishing; limited hunting is allowed, too.

# 39

# Turkey Creek There-and-Back

| | |
|---|---|
| **TOTAL DISTANCE**: 9.4 miles round trip | |

**HIKING TIME**: 4.5 hours

**VERTICAL RISE**: 120 feet

**RATING**: Moderate

**MAPS**: USGS 7.5' Parksville; Sumter National Forest—Long Cane District; Wine-Turkey Creek Trail

**TRAILHEAD GPS COORDINATES**: N33° 50.391', W82° 7.789'

**CONTACT INFORMATION**: Sumter National Forest, Long Cane Ranger District, 810 Buncombe Street, Edgefield, SC 29824, (803) 637-5396, www.fs.usda.gov/scnf

This hike explores the uppermost part of Turkey Creek. It's best in spring, but it's also a great fall destination. Located in the Long Cane District of Sumter National Forest, Turkey Creek Trail travels into a valley where hardwoods grow high and wildflowers bloom. Start descending on Wine Creek, a rocky clear stream, to meet the broad bottomland of Turkey Creek. Here you'll walk among regal hardwoods in lush bottomland overlooking bluff-sided Turkey Creek, lined with big cypress trees. The trail also climbs significant bluffs that tower over the creek before reaching Key Bridge, where this hike turns around. Trail treaders can continue for 7 more miles to the official end of Turkey Creek Trail. Backpackers will find good campsites along Wine Creek, Turkey Creek, and beyond. To backpack overnight, you must get a free permit from Sumter National Forest. Call (803) 637-5396.

## GETTING THERE

From the town square in Edgefield, take US 25 North for 4.1 miles to SC 283. Turn left onto SC 283 and follow it for 10.0 miles to the trailhead, located on your left, well after the Turkey Creek bridge (the trail starts along Wine Creek, not at Turkey Creek).

## THE TRAIL

Hikers and mountain bikers share this trail. Turkey Creek Trail leaves the parking area on SC 283 to enter pinewoods, aiming toward Wine Creek, whose valley is visible to your right. Notice white quartz visible on the forest floor. The ground is quite rocky here. Drift alongside Wine Creek, a clear stream about 5 feet wide, on the single-track dirt-and-

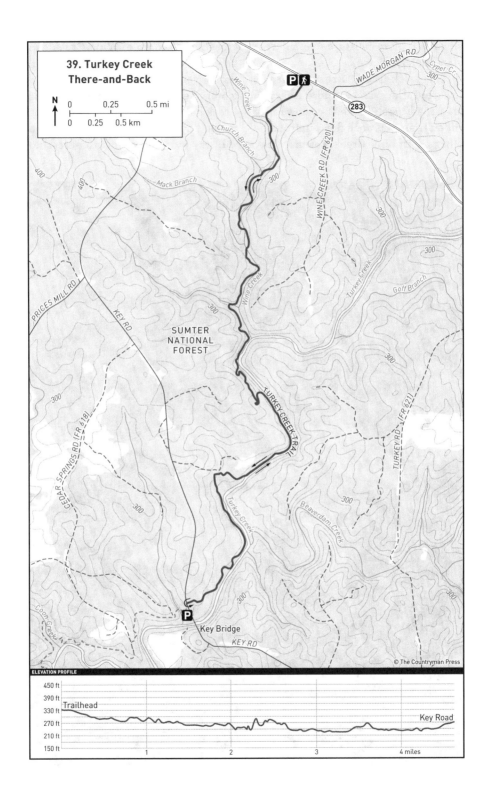

## 39. Turkey Creek There-and-Back

N

| 0 | 0.25 | 0.5 mi |
| 0 | 0.25 | 0.5 km |

Wade Morgan Rd.
Cyper Cr.
300
283
Wine Creek
Church Branch
Mack Branch
400
300
Wine Creek Rd. (FR 620)
Turkey Creek
300
300
Goff Branch
Prices Mill Rd.
Key Rd.
300
SUMTER NATIONAL FOREST
Wine Creek
300
300
Turkey Creek Trail
300
Turkey Rd. (FR 621)
Cedar Springs Rd. (FR 618)
300
300
Turkey Creek
Beaverdam Creek
300
Coon Creek
300
P
Key Bridge
Key Rd.
300

© The Countryman Press

**ELEVATION PROFILE**

| 450 ft |
| 390 ft |
| 330 ft |
| 270 ft |
| 210 ft |
| 150 ft |

Trailhead

Key Road

1    2    3    4 miles

stone path. More moisture-tolerant trees stand along the creek.

The rock-lined stream gurgles toward Turkey Creek and gathers in long, shady pools broken by noisy rocky riffles. Church Branch flows in from the other side of Wine Creek. Reach a rocky crossing at 0.6 mile. Wine Creek can be easily crossed here during normal flows. Notice the old rock pilings of a footbridge just above the crossing. Wine Creek has also demonstrated its ability to flood by destroying this bridge. You will stay in tight terrain after crossing

LILY IN THE BOTTOMLAND

the hardwood-bordered stream dominated by white oak, hickory, beech, and ironwood.

Streamside rock outcrops push the path to the water's edge, occasionally opening to wide flats before closing in again. Jagged rocklines cut across the creek. Tan sandbars gather on creek bends. In still other spots, logs and debris pile high from heavy rains. Wine Creek is quite a scenic Midland stream.

Turkey Creek Trail bridges a feeder branch, Mack Branch, coming in from your right, at 1.3 miles. Beard cane bor-

TRAILSIDE TRILLIUMS

ders the track in the bottoms. At 1.7 miles, the trail has turned away from Wine Creek and is curving into the watershed of an unnamed feeder branch, which it bridges at 1.7 miles. Note the large beech tree next to the footbridge. Bridge another branch before curving into the Turkey Creek Valley at 2.1 miles. A wide streamside flat opens, making you realize how tight the Wine Creek Valley was. In this flat, large tulip, beech, and sycamore trees tower over the terrain. Swing alongside Turkey Creek on a bluff, where you can glimpse the stream below. Bass and bream hide under logs and other areas of cover.

The Turkey Creek Valley can be much brushier than Wine Creek. Titi thickets border the path and close in on the trail. Titi is a brushy bush that grows along low-elevation streams and swamps from east Texas to Florida and then up to Maryland. It flowers in these areas in mid-April to mid-May. The blooms can form white clouds of fragrant flowers along the stream. This area is its westernmost distribution in South Carolina; it doesn't grow at all in the Upstate, but it does grow farther north in the Midlands and well into the Lowcountry.

Leave the bottom to wind up and onto a massive bluff overlooking Turkey Creek. The bluff is surprisingly precipitous, though the drop is but 100 feet or so. Loop back down to the bottom on a rerouted path that gradually takes you back to Turkey Creek. Notice the young buckeye trees and papaws, which add to the trailside brush. Many wooden bridges have been installed along intermittent streambeds coming into Turkey Creek, making the hike easier. The vegetation is quite thick where the path borders the stream. Wildflowers such as trilliums, mayapples, and more thrive here in spring, adding to an already lush valley. When possible, peer toward the stream, looking for the large cypress trees that grow on the water's edge.

The trail crosses a gas-line clearing at 3.2 miles. Your route stays in lush woods before opening to an area devastated by pine beetle damage. Fallen pine trunks are scattered like matchsticks over the terrain. A young forest of redbud, sweetgum, and tulip trees, however, are rising among the fallen pine. The brush will be thick here in summer, especially blackberry and honeysuckle. Return to woods, enjoying more massive tulip trees. Titi grows in clustered tunnels along the trail. Pass a trailside kiosk before reaching Key Bridge at 4.7 miles. This is a good place to backtrack. However, the trail continues south of the road and on for 7 more miles.

To continue the trail, cross the paved road at Key Bridge, then look for a dirt road leading down to an old bridge. A trail kiosk is located in the woods off the dirt road. From here, Turkey Creek Trail curves around Coon Creek then returns to Turkey Creek, alternating between bluff and bottom, spanning other feeder branches before reaching the confluence with Stevens Creek 4.5 miles beyond Key Bridge. Here it turns west, then northwest, passing a spur trail to reach Forest Road 617 and finally rising away from Stevens Creek to meet FR 617A at 12 miles. If you wish to avoid backtracking, you can spot a car at Key Bridge: From Edgefield, take SC 23 west to County Road 68, Key Bridge Road. Turn right onto 68 and follow it for 5.0 miles to Key Bridge. Parking is found on a dirt road on your left after the bridge.

# III.

# LOWCOUNTRY

**40**

# Awendaw Passage of the Palmetto Trail

**TOTAL DISTANCE**: 8.4 miles round trip

**HIKING TIME**: 4.5 hours

**VERTICAL RISE**: 20 feet

**RATING**: Moderate

**MAPS**: USGS 7.5' Awendaw; Awendaw Passage of the Palmetto Trail; Francis Marion National Forest

**TRAILHEAD GPS COORDINATES**: N33° 2.353', W79° 33.687'

**CONTACT INFORMATION**: Francis Marion National Forest, 2967 Steed Creek Road, Huger, SC 29450, (843) 336-3248, www.fs.usda.gov/scnf

Many consider the Awendaw Passage the most beautiful segment of Palmetto Trail. It's the easternmost passage of the entire state-long master path of South Carolina. The passage starts on the Intracoastal Waterway at Buck Hall Recreation Area, part of Francis Marion National Forest. It travels through piney woods and freshwater marshes before opening onto Awendaw Creek, a tidal stream offering extensive vistas of saltwater marsh and forests beyond. The trek continues along the creek in maritime forest of palm and live oak, often crossing saltwater tributaries on wide boardwalks that also offer more long looks as well as close-up views of the salt marsh. Palmetto Trail joins a bluff heading westward, drifting in and out of lush woods while often opening to more views of Awendaw Creek. The trail eventually turns away from the creek for good, a nice point to reverse course. It is every bit of 8.4 miles going out and back. However, you can turn around at any point: Enjoy as many of the saltwater vistas as you desire, then backtrack to Buck Hall. Note: Bring bug dope with you if you're traveling this trail during the warm season.

## GETTING THERE

From the intersection of US 17 and US 17A in Georgetown, take US 17 for 29 miles to Buck Hall Recreation Area on your left. Turn into the recreation area; the trail begins on your left just before the recreation area boat ramp. There is a parking fee. Alternative directions from Charleston: Follow US 17 north for 30 miles to Buck Hall Recreation Area, on your right.

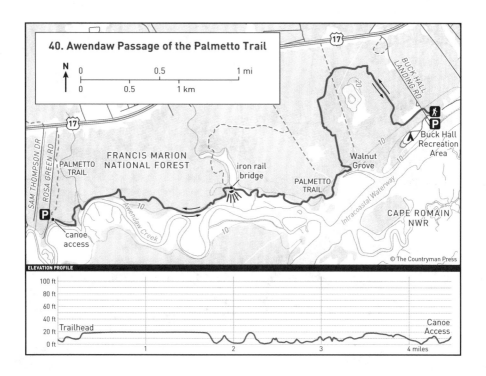

## THE TRAIL

The trail leaves the day-use parking area on a boardwalk, which circles a palm tree, symbolizing Palmetto Trail. The boardwalk angles through freshwater wetland before reaching dry land just before crossing the entrance road to Buck Hall. Keep southwesterly before curving right and passing the overflow parking lot for the recreation area. Cross a pair of long boardwalks over more freshwater wetlands. Keep forward on a wide track to pass under a transmission line at 0.6 mile. Ahead, the trail makes a left while the grassy track you've been following keeps forward. Bridge a canal and stay with the trail as it crosses a sand forest road. Pass under the transmission line for the second time at 1.1 miles.

The trail winds through pines that devolve into thick oaks, then maritime woods with cedars and palms, as you lose elevation. At 1.8 miles, the trail reaches a boardwalk with handrails, opening onto Awendaw Creek and the Intracoastal Waterway. This area is known as Walnut Grove. You can peer into the distance and see tidal marsh that seems to go on forever. Boats will be plying the waters in nice weather. This is where the trail really comes into its own, offering more than occasional views of the coast for the next 2-plus miles.

The trail passes through wetter portions, crossing small boardwalks in the dampest spots as it keeps along the edge of the marsh. At 2.2 miles, wind beneath a dense palm copse. Palms remain common along Awendaw Creek, along with live oaks, for the next segment of the trail, which crosses a wide-open boardwalk at 2.5 miles.

THIS BLUFF PROVIDES ELEVATED VIEWS OF TIDAL AWENDAW CREEK

At 2.7 miles you'll meet a grassy road-bed coming in from your right. Stay left here to span a major tidal tributary on an elaborate bridge with iron rails. The waters below you will be flowing toward the land or toward the sea, depending on the tide. Open, extensive views of the marsh, all the way to the Intracoastal Waterway, spread before you. The vista extends down the length of Awendaw Creek, where it meets the Intracoastal Waterway, and beyond, to Cape Romain National Wildlife Refuge. This is my favorite spot on the hike.

Palm trees decrease in number thereafter. The trail travels the margin where the saltwater marsh meets the forest, allowing you to look out on open tidal flats from the shade of live oak trees. Palmetto Trail turns away from Awendaw Creek at 3.1 miles, passing over a boardwalk then traveling through oak woods before opening to cross a transmission line at 3.4 miles, still heading through woods away from the bluff. Sweetgum and oak, with an understory of yaupon and wax myrtle, prevail. Occasional contemplation benches are set along the bluffs.

Pass three last boardwalks before coming along the bluff a final time at 3.8 miles. It's surprising how high this bluff is, so close to the sea. Enjoy more views of this special swath of South Carolina. Parts of the trail are open overhead toward the end. The trail continues on the bluff, offering stellar marsh vantage points before abruptly turning right at 4.2 miles. You are at the paddling access for Awendaw Creek and alternate trailhead for Palmetto Trail. This is a good stopping point, as Palmetto Trail heads toward US 17, toward the bulk of Francis Marion National Forest and the Swamp Fox Passage of the Palmetto Trail (Hike 50).

As you backtrack, imagine how it would feel to hike the entire Palmetto Trail, from the mountains of the Upstate, through the Midlands, into the Low-country, to the last few miles here. When it's completed, the trail will be around 450 miles long. Some of its segments are not yet open, but with the diligence shown thus far, the completion of South Carolina's master path is only a matter of time. For more information on Palmetto Trail and what you can do to help with the completion, please visit www .palmettoconservation.org.

Buck Hall Recreation Area is not only the eastern terminus of Palmetto Trail, but it also offers a quality campground with electricity for 14 RV sites; 5 tent-only sites overlook the Intracoastal Waterway. The campground also has water and hot showers. A boat ramp is available for anglers in search of salt-water species. A shaded picnic shelter and restrooms as well as a fishing and viewing pier are located at the trailhead parking area.

# Caw Caw Interpretive Center Loop

Caw Caw Interpretive Center is a Charleston County park that offers a first-class birding and wildlife locale. An interconnected network of trails traversing a variety of habitats gives you an extensive overview of the Lowcountry flora and fauna. The sheer number of trails will ensure repeat visits to this destination. The loop hike described here travels the outermost collection of trails and also visits every habitat within the park. Be apprised that the interpretive center run by Charleston County offers more than just trails.

**TOTAL DISTANCE**: 3.6-mile loop

**HIKING TIME**: 2.2 hours

**VERTICAL RISE**: 10 feet

**RATING**: Easy

**MAPS**: USGS 7.5' Ravenel; Caw Caw Interpretive Center

**TRAILHEAD GPS COORDINATES**: N32° 47.500', W80° 11.853'

**CONTACT INFORMATION**: Caw Caw Interpretive Center, 5200 Savannah Highway, Highway 17 South, Ravenel, SC 29470, (843) 889-8898, www.ccprc.com

## GETTING THERE

From Exit 212B off I-526 west near Charleston (the end of I-526 West), take Sam Rittenburg Boulevard a short distance to US 17. Turn right onto US 17 South and follow it for 10 miles. The park entrance will be on your right. Continue on the park road to end in front of the visitor center. The park is open Tuesday through Sunday, 9 a.m. to 5 p.m., closed Monday. There is an entrance fee.

## THE TRAIL

If you are interested in going on a guided bird walk here—they're held regularly—call ahead at (843) 889-8898 for exact dates and times. The visitor center is staffed during park hours, and personnel can answer other questions you may have. Water and restrooms are also available. Interpretive kiosks are spread out along the trail system. Leave the walkway between the two buildings of the interpretive center, shortly reaching a trail junction. A trail leads to your right to a rice field-overlook boardwalk, which is worth a look. Imagine this open swamp once having been irrigated into straight-line rice fields. Leave the junc-

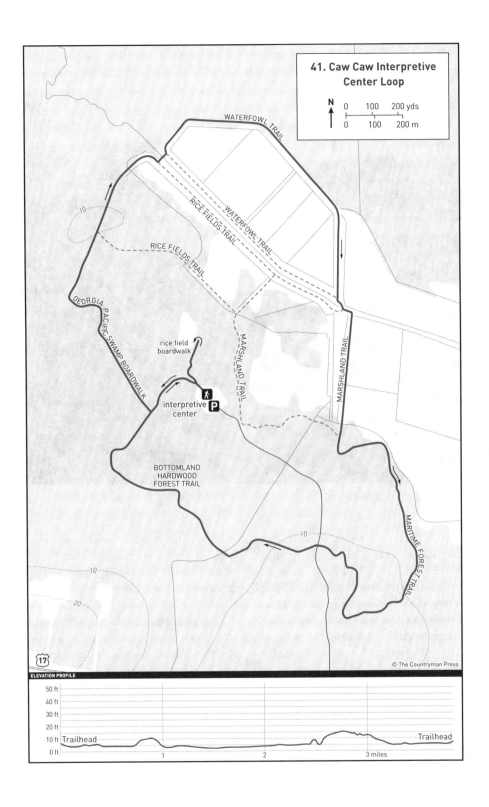

41. Caw Caw Interpretive Center Loop

N

| 0 | 100 | 200 yds |
| 0 | 100 | 200 m |

WATERFOWL TRAIL

WATERFOWL TRAIL

RICE FIELDS TRAIL

RICE FIELDS TRAIL

GEORGIA PACIFIC SWAMP BOARDWALK

rice field boardwalk

MARSHLAND TRAIL

MARSHLAND TRAIL

interpretive center

P

BOTTOMLAND HARDWOOD FOREST TRAIL

MARITIME FOREST TRAIL

10

10

10

20

17

© The Countryman Press

ELEVATION PROFILE

| 50 ft |
| 40 ft |
| 30 ft |
| 20 ft |
| 10 ft | Trailhead | | Trailhead |
| 0 ft |
| | 1 | 2 | 3 miles |

BOARDWALK OVERLOOKS FORMER RICE FIELDS

tion to your left, shortly intersecting Swamp Sanctuary Trail and Bottomland Hardwood Forest Trail. Begin your loop by leaving to the right to cross a bridge over a strand of Caw Caw Swamp. Notice how water levels are maintained by a water-control structure at this bridge. The marshes and swamps of Caw Caw are managed to maximize conditions for wildlife. Stay left again as you join the Georgia Pacific Swamp Boardwalk. There are seemingly innumerable trail intersections, but if you want to follow this outermost loop, just stay left from this point forward. The boardwalk trav-

els amid the cypress, maple, and gum trees of a seasonally inundated flood-plain where cypress knees and palmetto grow under the shadow of the swamp giants.

The boardwalk ends and you begin to follow a wide grassy road in shade. At 0.8 mile Slave Settlement Trail leaves to your right amid large live oaks. Nothing remains of the actual settlement, but this high ground under the oaks was the location where slaves lived while they worked the adjacent rice fields. And that makes sense: This ground is the highest around, and the oaks provide the shade that would have been needed after working open rice fields. Restrooms are located near the settlement site.

Join a dike and open area on a grassy track heading toward the waterfowl area, now on Waterfowl Trail. Span a bridge over a canal and join a second dike, which curves to the east and was originally created for the rice plantations. Swamp forest stands to your left, while open waters mixed with aquatic vegetation lie off to your right. The open wetlands are now managed for ducks instead of agriculture. Waterfowl will be visible here in what were once rice fields. At 1.6 miles, you'll pass a couple of water-control structures; stay left to join Marshland Trail, which travels across tidal marsh. Occasional benches stretch along the loop, usually in shady areas, where numerous trees grow: cedar, live oak, and Chinese tallow trees, an exotic invasive species nearly impossible to eradicate. Open watery expanses, with tidally influenced and not entirely fresh water, border the left side of the trail. The right side is fresh water. The aforementioned water-control structures also divide the fresh- and saltwater areas. The tides push up nearby Wallace Creek. Meet Maritime Forest Trail at 1.9 miles, which enters woods bordering a canal. Cedars are prevalent here as the trail winds through palmetto. Views extend across the canal.

Rejoin a roadbed under live oaks as the loop reaches its southernmost point. Leave the roadbed to your right, joining Bottomland Hardwood Forest Trail in thick woods of hickory and oak. Pass some wild tea plants, left over from when this area was a tea plantation. Later, vegetables were grown here; you can still see the crop rows and shallow ditches made to drain the fields. Short, low bridges span these little ditches. The fields are now grown up with trees, rising together in lush thickness exacerbated by vines. The footpath twists and turns in the trees, providing maximum contrast to the straight dike paths.

Cross the park entrance road at 2.8 miles, now on a wider track. The walking is easy, and soon you reach a junction located at a point where you were earlier. Follow the signs to return to the interpretive center at 3.6 miles. You may want to walk some of the other shorter interior paths, as well, while you are here. The ones nearest the interpretive center are immaculately groomed.

There are a total of 8 miles of trails here at Caw Caw, which adds up to 654 acres. The site was once part of a 5,000-plus-acre rice plantation from two centuries ago. In addition to the Wednesday- and Saturday-morning bird walks, Caw Caw has extensive environmental education programs covering habitats, plants, rice cultivation, Gullah culture, and natural resource management, among other subjects. The Charleston County park system is actively engaging residents and visitors in numerous other programs beyond the borders of Caw Caw, from canoeing and kayaking to backpacking to holding seasonal festivals. For more information about Charleston County Parks and its programs, visit www.ccprc.com.

# Dungannon Plantation Loop

| | |
|---|---|
| **OTAL DISTANCE**: 3.7-mile loop | |

**HIKING TIME**: 3 hours

**VERTICAL RISE**: 15 feet

**RATING**: Easy to moderate

**MAPS**: USGS 7.5' Ravenel, Wadmalow Island; Dungannon Preserve

**TRAILHEAD GPS COORDINATES**: N32° 44.856', W80° 11.694'

**CONTACT INFORMATION**: South Carolina Department of Natural Resources, Rembert C. Dennis Building, 1000 Assembly Street, Columbia, SC 29201, (803) 734-3893, www.dnr.sc.gov/

Part of the South Carolina Heritage Trust program, this land parcel is not only a hiking destination but an important wood stork nesting site. A network of trails exists, along with additional miles of closed roads used to access the preserve by official personnel. This hike takes you through a rich forest to swamplands, then to a boardwalk, where you can overlook significant wood stork nesting habitats. Springtime visitors will have the added visual delight of wildflowers. The hike is easy, as it mostly travels double-track trail en route to a bridge before finally culminating at the aforementioned boardwalk.

## GETTING THERE

From Exit 212B on I-526 west near Charleston (the end of I-526 West), take Sam Rittenburg Blvd. a short distance to US 17. Turn right on US 17 south and follow it for 7.3 miles to SC 162. Turn left on SC 162 and follow it for 3.9 miles to reach the trailhead on your right. Dungannon Heritage Preserve will be on your right.

## THE TRAIL

The state of South Carolina has become an important wood stork breeding ground as Florida's extensive wetlands continue to diminish. Wood stork nesting sites were first found in South Carolina in 1981. Following this discovery, Dungannon Plantation was purchased in 1995 to provide wood stork nesting habitat. Land that was flooded for rice fields more than two centuries back has now reverted to a place for nature's birds to thrive. Nesting wood storks are normally found at Dungannon between April and July, sometimes earlier in spring. Hikers, especially with binoculars, will likely spot storks here at that

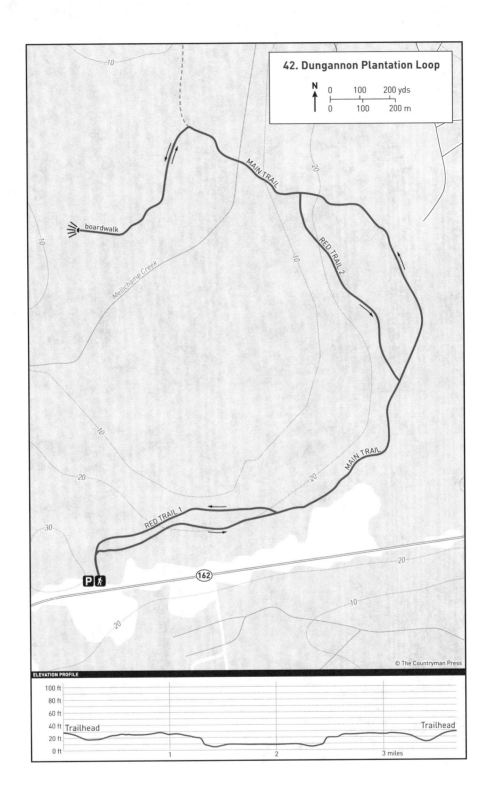

42. Dungannon Plantation Loop

N

| 0 | 100 | 200 yds |
| 0 | 100 | 200 m |

MAIN TRAIL

RED TRAIL 2

boardwalk

Mellichamp Creek

MAIN TRAIL

RED TRAIL 1

162

10

20

30

20

10

20

ELEVATION PROFILE

100 ft
80 ft
60 ft
40 ft
20 ft
0 ft

Trailhead

Trailhead

1          2          3 miles

© The Countryman Press

DUCK MOSS COVERS MELLICHAMP CREEK SWAMP IN FALL

FALL WILDFLOWERS GROW ALONG SWAMP'S EDGE

time, though the boardwalk found along this trek is usually closed then, to allow the birds to nest. In 2015, a total of 282 wood stork nests were counted at Dungannon Plantation Heritage Preserve, with an average of two chicks per nest.

The swamp at Dungannon presents favorable stork nesting habitat. The birds prefer living in cypress trees 50–150 feet tall, with open water underneath them. The rookery averages more than 100 nests annually, and it is South Carolina's largest wood stork nesting habitat. The wood stork's federal status was downgraded from endangered to threatened in 2014. In the late 1970s, wood stork populations had shrunk to only 2,500 total breeding pairs in the United States. However, due to establishment of places like Dungannon, between 15,000 and 20,000 breeding pairs of wood storks now thrive across the country, with around 2,000 wood stork nests in South Carolina alone.

The rice plantation-turned-swamp is also home to alligators, egrets, wood ducks, and blue herons, among other wildlife. So consider viewing other wildlife as well as plant species, too. For example, white swamp lilies color the woods in spring. The South Carolina Department of Natural Resources not only manages the plantation for swamp-loving creatures but they are also restoring other plant communities, too, including longleaf pine forests.

Leave the shaded Dungannon Preserve parking area in thick oak woods on a wide roadbed. Shortly head right on the blue-blazed Main Trail, as Yellow Trail and Red Trail 1 diverge. Main Trail is a double-track path rambling easterly along the edge of the preserve, working around the swamp formed when Mellichamp Creek was impounded generations back to facilitate Dungannon's rice-growing enterprise. This trail, along with the closed roads, is open to foot travel only, though the South Carolina DNR uses the roads for preserve management. After crossing an outflow of the swamp, use a dike to span the wetland.

At .4 mile, Red Trail 1 comes in on your left. Keep straight on Main Trail in pines and oaks. Houses and backyards on SC 162 are visible to your right. At 0.6 mile, walk by the lone marked grave of Matthew Sanford, then curve left, now heading north. At 0.9 mile, the narrow Red Trail 2 leaves left and is your return track. For now, keep straight on Main Trail. At 1.3 miles, drop off a hill and meet the other end of Red Trail 2. Cross a spillway on a footbridge. Keep straight on a dike. After making it across the wetland, Main Trail reaches an intersection at 1.6 miles. Here, Main Trail heads north for the remote far end of the preserve, while our hike exits to the left in flatwoods. At 1.8 miles, you will come to the boardwalk and wood stork nesting area. A small picnic area is situated near the boardwalk. Stroll the boardwalk, using your binoculars to look for wildlife. Remember the boardwalk is seasonally closed during nesting season. Wood storks are noted for being vulnerable to human disturbance. Backtrack on Main Trail after enjoying the boardwalk. At 2.3 miles, leave right from Main Trail to the single-track Red Trail 2, under tall forest. Rejoin Main Trail at 2.8 miles. At 3.3 miles, split right again, joining Red Trail 1. Along the way, try to identify the five species of orchids found at Dungannon before you arrive back at the trailhead at 3.7 miles.

# 43

# Hunting Island State Park Loop

---

**TOTAL DISTANCE**: 3.1-mile loop

**HIKING TIME**: 2 hours

**VERTICAL RISE**: 10 feet

**RATING**: Easy

**MAPS**: USGS 7.5' Fripp Inlet; Hunting Island State Park

**TRAILHEAD GPS COORDINATES**: N32° 21.716', W80° 26.708'

**CONTACT INFORMATION**: Hunting Island State Park, 2555 Sea Island Parkway, Hunting Island, SC 29920, (843) 838-2011, (843)838-4263, www .southcarolinastateparks.com/ huntingisland

---

Hunting Island State Park—South Carolina's largest island park—is a great beach destination that also offers good hiking trails, a quality campground, cabins, and one of the most beautiful lighthouses in the Southeast. The loop hike described here offers coastal scenery as it enters a dense forest of palms, pines, and live oaks, then travels along a tidal lagoon just on the backside of the Atlantic Ocean. The estuary is very attractive. Near the end of the lagoon, the trail curves back inland, undulating through ancient wooded dunes on old fire roads in a deep, dark forest where furtive deer bound away through thickets. This inland forest is markedly different from nearly every other hiking destination in this book, so enjoy it before you complete your loop.

The mosquitoes can be troublesome during summer on this trail, as will heat. The park is busy during summer with beachgoers, and if you choose to visit at that time, bring bug repellent and plan your trek for early in the morning. Late fall through spring is the preferable time to enjoy this hike, however. A side trip to the Hunting Island Lighthouse is a must if you come here. One more thing—parts of the movie *Forrest Gump* were filmed in the vicinity of the trail.

## GETTING THERE

From Exit 33 off I-95, take US 21 South for 42 miles through the town of Beaufort; stay with this road to Hunting Island. Pass the left turn to Hunting Island State Park Campground and continue to make a left turn into the main park. Continue beyond the side road to the visitor center to reach an intersection. North Beach Road leaves left. Continue forward at this intersection, not on North Beach Road, then stay right, passing beach accesses

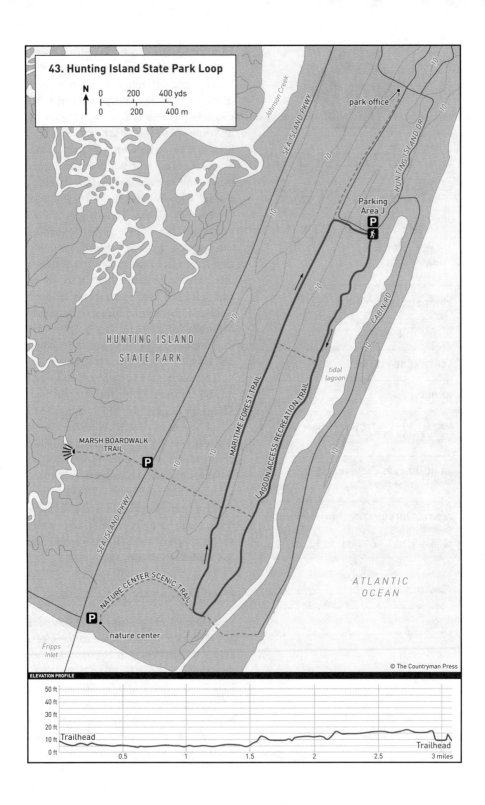

**43. Hunting Island State Park Loop**

N

| 0 | 200 | 400 yds |
| 0 | 200 | 400 m |

Johnson Creek

SEA ISLAND PKWY

park office

HUNTING ISLAND DR

Parking Area J

CABIN RD

HUNTING ISLAND STATE PARK

MARITIME FOREST TRAIL

LAGOON ACCESS RECREATION TRAIL

tidal lagoon

MARSH BOARDWALK TRAIL

SEA ISLAND PKWY

NATURE CENTER SCENIC TRAIL

ATLANTIC OCEAN

nature center

Fripps Inlet

© The Countryman Press

**ELEVATION PROFILE**

| 50 ft |
| 40 ft |
| 30 ft |
| 20 ft |
| 10 ft | Trailhead | | | | Trailhead |
| 0 ft |
| | 0.5 | 1 | 1.5 | 2 | 2.5 | 3 miles |

to reach Parking Area J. The trail starts at the road cut in the middle of Parking Area J, leading away from the Atlantic Ocean and the tidal lagoon. There is a park entrance fee.

## THE TRAIL

The actual trailhead can be hard to find, even when you do reach Parking Area J. Once you're at the parking area, you can follow the road as it curves around to reach the trailhead, or you can find the cut in the center of the long wooded parking area and then find the trail there. A signboard is located at the trail's beginning. You'll immediately enter the dense maritime woodland that makes this hike so special. Tall palms growing in huge numbers intertwine with needle-dropping pines and shade-bearing oaks, creating a deep, dark, fairy-tale forest.

Look for the trail leading left just beyond the trailhead and take it. Wind through the crowded woods to open onto the tidal lagoon. This narrow waterway separates you from the beach and the pounding surf of the Atlantic, easily audible from this distance. The outline of palms and live oaks on the far side of the lagoon contrasts with the open sky over the ocean. On this side of the lagoon palm trees hang over the water and a small sand beach borders the inlet. Fallen palm trunks line the water's edge. Palmetto and yaupon form thickets below the palms. Cacti grow where the sand drains fast. The scene is simply gorgeous. This is a popular fishing area, so don't be surprised if you see anglers idling away in chairs, pole in hand, vying for saltwater species. They use the trail and a shortcut from Parking Area J to access the lagoon.

Later, the thick forest gives way to a grassier shore; palms aplenty rise from the sand and grass. The trail here is a sandy track, and if rains haven't come lately, the footing can be loose; travel slows. But who is in a hurry in such a place? Salty breezes drift off the lagoon as you reach a trail junction at 0.5 mile. A cross trail bisects the greater loop. Keep forward, still hiking along the lagoon, to reach a second trail junction at 1.0 mile. Here the cross trail leading right continues across the loop to reach US 21, crosses it, and extends out to a wide-open marsh on a boardwalk. If you want to access the boardwalk, continue on the loop and catch it on the other end, because too much attractive lagoon trekking awaits.

In places, the lagoon widens. Pines stand behind the palm-lined shore. You will likely see shorebirds somewhere along the way. Ahead, the shore stays lined with grass; you travel the margin where palm trees grow from the grass, but not quite where the live oaks and pines form dense woods on the landward side. Reach a trail junction at 1.5 miles. A wide and sturdy bridge leads left over the lagoon. The path beyond it leads to a park cabin area. You are free to use this trail, but do not disturb the cabin users. You may choose to go this way and return via the beach, though you must pass beyond the parking area along the beach then find a beach access and walk a road. This must be done to get around the upper end of the lagoon. I recommend taking the deep-woods route back to the trailhead, then exploring the beach and the lighthouse later.

The loop curves away from the ocean, and then it reaches another junction shortly. Moving forward, the trail leads to a fishing pier and parking area near the bridge to Fripp Island, while the trail leading right bisects the heart of

HUNTING ISLAND LIGHTHOUSE

Hunting Island. Travel on an elevated track amid deeply wooded and surprisingly hilly terrain where the shadows are deep and deer will likely be seen. At 2.0 miles you'll once again meet the spur trail leading out to the marsh boardwalk. If you take this spur, it will lead through the dark woods to emerge onto blindingly open grassy marsh that looks like it could extend forever.

The main loop keeps in the deep woods of Hunting Island. The smells here—of pine needles, oak leaves, and pockets of fresh water—contrast greatly with the aromas of the salty lagoon. All too soon, you reach a trail junction. The main path continues forward to briefly hit a park road before continuing on to the visitor center; you take the side trail leading to your right, which passes through an open grassy area before ending at Parking Area J at 3.1 miles.

Hunting Island Lighthouse stands tall along the preserved coastline of 4 miles that fronts the Atlantic Ocean here in the 5,000-acre state park, one of the largest in the South Carolina system. The lighthouse was built in 1873. It replaced one that was built in 1859, but dismantled by the Confederates to confound Union ships as they plied the offshore shoals that mark the halfway point between Savannah, Georgia, and Charleston. It was moved to its present location in 1889 due to erosion, in use until 1933. The campground fronts the beach on the northernmost part of Hunting Island. The wooded setting of the widespread campground is very pretty and offers RV sites and walk-in tent sites. The campground fills every weekend during summer and occasionally during the week. Sites are usually available the rest of the year.

PALMS GROW AMONG GRASSES BESIDE THE ION SWAMP INTERPRETIVE TRAIL

# Ion Swamp Interpretive Walk

**TOTAL DISTANCE**: 2.0 miles

**HIKING TIME**: 1 hour

**VERTICAL RISE**: 10 feet

**RATING**: Easy

**MAPS**: USGS 7.5′ Ocean Bay; Francis Marion National Forest; Ion Swamp Interpretive Trail

**TRAILHEAD GPS COORDINATES**: N33° 0.278′, W79° 40.961′

**CONTACT INFORMATION**: Francis Marion National Forest, 2967 Steed Creek Road, Huger, SC 29450, (843) 336-3248, www.fs.usda.gov/scnf

The name Ion, in Ion Swamp, is unusual. It's actually a corruption of the word iron, as this hike takes place in Iron Swamp. Iron Swamp is on the upper end of the Wando River drainage, east of Charleston. The interpretive walk here, in Francis Marion National Forest, explains the workings of the Wytheywood rice plantation, and it tells you how a swamp can be changed from swamp to rice fields and back to swamp again. The walking is easy, and it offers a chance to explore a swamp without getting your feet wet. You may see alligators, herons, and other creatures in season. Birding is popular here.

## GETTING THERE

From Exit 30 on I-526 in Mount Pleasant, take US 17 north for 16 miles to Ion Swamp Road, FR 226. If you reach the Sewee Visitor and Environmental Education Center on your right, you have gone .2 mile too far. Turn left onto FR 226 and follow the gravel road for 2.4 miles. The trailhead will be on your left.

## THE TRAIL

Leave the trailhead on a narrow trail through thick, lush woods of sweetgum, oak, pine, and bay trees. Cross a short boardwalk to join a closed forest road leaving to your right. The trail is much wider here. On either side of the track, buttressed tree trunks reveal at least part-time inundation of the wetlands from which they grow. These buttressed trunks help the trees stay upright in wet or loose soils. You will soon see the first of many interpretive signs along the trail. This one gives a recipe for a rice plantation:

# Traditional Rice Dish

1. Clear swamp of all trees by hand
2. Dig ditches and build banks with hand tools
3. Build wooden floodgates to control drainage and water flow to rice fields
4. Cultivate rice by hand using mules wearing special rawhide boots that keep them from sinking in the mud
5. Perform the above tasks in extreme heat and humidity and periods of heavy rain, thick clouds of mosquitoes, and possibly with the threat of swamp fever, a.k.a. malaria

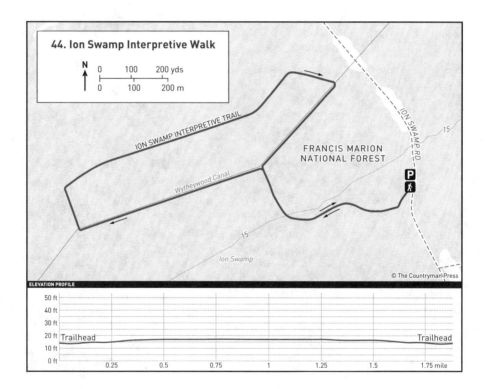

As you continue deeper into the swamp, more trailside water appears. You will also see metal relics left over from when the area was further altered after the plantation days. A system of metal water-control structures was installed to manage water levels for wildlife today. In plantation days, these structures were wooden dams with boards laid vertically and added or removed to change water levels. Today metal pipes and gates are most common,

CYPRESS KNEES GROW ALONG THE TRAIL

and hand cranks resembling steering wheels open or close the pipes.

Nesting boxes for wood ducks are scattered along the trail. You will see the wooden boxes atop posts; a circular galvanized metal barrier below the box foils predators like raccoons or rat snakes. These creatures will go after the duck eggs or even the nesting hen if given the opportunity. Wood ducks are one of the few reproducing species of waterfowl in South Carolina. In the East they are found from Minnesota to Florida and Texas. South Carolina is doing its part to help wood ducks; its Department of Natural Resources, along with Ducks Unlimited, has helped provide funding for more than 30,000 wood duck nesting boxes over the last two-plus decades.

At 0.4 mile you'll reach the loop portion of the hike and the Wytheywood Canal. Turn left here, with the canal to your right and wide swamp off to your left. The canal served two functions. First, it was used to irrigate the rice fields. Second, it was used for goods transport; as you look at the canal, imagine using a push pole to move a boat loaded with rice down the 7-mile, hand-dug canal to the Wando River and on down the Wando to Charleston to peddle the rice.

Wytheywood Plantation was established in the late 1700s, on the front end of South Carolina's heyday as a rice producer. The success of rice production here may have propelled further rice production in the Lowcountry. Rice production came into its own from 1839 through 1859, when South Carolina produced 70 percent of the nation's supply. The falloff in 1859 was caused by the Civil War, after which plantations couldn't function as well without slave labor. Before the war, imagine slaves clearing the land and building the levees upon which you

walk today. Consider the physical labor that took place here as you lightly toil on your walk in a place now reverted to back-of-beyond, where time and the healing hand of nature, with a little help from man, have turned this from a sunscorched, level field laced with dikes to a wooded wetland where nature's beasts, from the reptilian alligator to singing warblers, can thrive.

Nowadays trees line the canal, and grow in the middle of it. It has partly filled up with forest debris and couldn't be paddled today. But the canal itself is clearly visible and to this day brims with water in spring. At 0.8 mile the trail reaches a modern water-control structure. Notice also that old dikes have been reinforced in places. Here the loop crosses the canal and turns right, leaving the Wytheywood Canal to join another canal. Watch for cypress knees rising on the trail to trip the unwary walker.

Willow trees grow alongside the dikes. The waters are deeper here, and alligators will be seen during warmer weather. If you do hike this trail in warm weather, bring insect repellent. Tupelo trees, also known as gum trees, complement the cypress. Maples grow in the margins, which are moist but not inundated often. Sweetgum and oak occupy higher ground.

The trail turns again and passes through nearly pure red maple stands. As you look out on the wooded wetlands, try to pick out the grid pattern of the rice fields. A keen eye can see the elevated lines dividing the lower, wetter area despite the passage of two centuries. Continue through the deep, dark woods on an irregular dike that undulates up and down. The swamp around you, entirely freshwater, is quite close to the ocean, which makes it a more special

HERE, THE TRAIL TRAVELS ALONG WYTHEYWOOD CANAL

environment and more valuable to the wildlife of the Lowcountry.

The trail turns again, and at 1.3 miles, it crosses a boardwalk over a particularly wet section. Soon you'll cross the old Wytheywood Canal for the second time, on a bridge. The trail then parallels the Wytheywood Canal one final time. Wood duck nesting boxes are scattered in the woods in great numbers. Span another boardwalk just before completing the loop portion of the historic hike at 1.6 miles. Backtrack to the trailhead, completing the hike at 2.0 miles.

The Sewee Visitor Center, located on US 17 near the road to Ion Swamp, is well worth a visit. It offers interpretive information about Francis Marion National Forest, the South Carolina Center for Birds of Prey, and Cape Romain National Wildlife Refuge. Inside, a display area details the flora and fauna of the region, and a large map room creates a geographic sense of it. Interpretive trails and a live red wolf enclosure are located outside the main building. It's open Tuesday through Sunday from 9 a.m. to 5 p.m.

# Old Santee Canal Loop

**TOTAL DISTANCE**: 2.3-mile loop

**HIKING TIME**: 1.1 hours

**VERTICAL RISE**: 35 feet

**RATING**: Easy

**MAPS**: USGS 7.5' Cordesville; Old Santee Canal Park

**TRAILHEAD GPS COORDINATES**: N33° 11.615', W79° 58.313'

**CONTACT INFORMATION**: Old Santee Canal Park, 900 Stony Landing Drive, Moncks Corner, SC 29461, (843) 899-5200, www .oldsanteecanal.org

Old Santee Canal Park combines natural and human history in a beautiful setting on the edge of Moncks Corner. Before the United States was even a country, the fathers of nearby Charleston sought a way for crops to be shipped from the Midlands down to Charleston, avoiding a dangerous trip down the coast from the mouth of the Santee River to Charleston. If the Santee and Cooper Rivers could be connected, then goods could be safely floated directly to Charleston, which was good for the farmers and good for the traders of South Carolina's shipping center. With the blessing of one George Washington, the Santee Canal Company set about building the country's first "summit canal," a canal with locks that climbed and descended elevation along its length. The 22-mile waterway was finished in 1800 after 7 years, at which point it began its 50-year span of operation. Cotton and other goods were towed by mules and later with manpower, using push poles. The nineteenth century moved on, however, and the canal became obsolete with the establishment of railroads to ship goods to Charleston and points beyond. The canal was abandoned; later, most of it was submerged under Lake Moultrie, ironically named for the South Carolina governor who got the canal moving forward. This section of the canal is still intact, though, and along with the historic Stony Landing House, the modern Tailrace Canal, and the waters of Biggin Creek, it makes for an interesting destination to hike, explore some Palmetto past, and enjoy the beauty of nature.

## GETTING THERE

From Charleston, take US 52 west to Moncks Corner and a traffic light. At

**45. Old Santee Canal Loop**

N

| 0 | 100 | 200 yds |
| 0 | 100 | 200 m |

observation
point

Tailrace Canal

Biggin Creek

bird blind

boardwalk
overlook

STONY LANDING RD

interpretive
center

P

Berkeley Museum

Stony
Landing House

© The Countryman Press

**ELEVATION PROFILE**

| 100 ft |
| 80 ft |
| 60 ft |
| 40 ft |
| 20 ft |
| 0 ft |

Trailhead

Trailhead

0.5      1      1.5      2      2.5 miles

STONY LANDING HOUSE OVERLOOKS THE COOPER RIVER

Moncks Corner, with a CVS store at the light, 52 West goes left and 52 Bypass goes forward, as R.C. Dennis Boulevard. Keep forward on R.C. Dennis Boulevard, following it for 1.0 mile to reach Stony Landing Road. Turn right and follow Stony Landing Road for 0.6 mile to enter the park. Continue past the entrance station to reach the interpretive center. The hike actually starts at the back of the center, which can be reached after passing through the center itself. There is an entrance fee.

## THE TRAIL

A picnic area and restrooms are located outside the interpretive center. Enter the center through a replica of a canal lock made of brick. These locks were used to raise and lower flatboats as they traveled along the Old Santee Canal. Inside are historic and interpretive displays that are well worth your time. They describe the trials of building this historic canal using the tools of the day. Natural history information is displayed as well. Emerge from the back of the interpretive center to join a boardwalk, leaving to your left. The boardwalk travels above a watery wetland of cypress and open water. Interpretive information is posted on signs here. Stay left through what seems to be a maze of boardwalks around the interpretive center, and you'll soon join a hiking trail and dry land. Pass an old limestone kiln and hike alongside limestone bluffs, rare for

BUCKEYE BLOSSOMS ABOVE BIGGIN CREEK

these parts. Verdant ferns thrive at the base. The trail continues up the left bank of Biggin Creek, in the margin between the limestone bluff and the creek to your right. Magnolias, oaks, and other trees shade the path.

Surprisingly, the trail climbs steps to the top of the bluff. Who knew there was such steep terrain in this part of the Santee Cooper Country? Travel amid live oaks, beech trees, and palmettos. Bridge a small stream before drifting back down to the flats below the bluff. Ironwood thrives in these wetter spots, as do cane, holly, and fern. It's easy to see by the narrow boardwalks that this area floods at times.

Climb the bluff again and keep northbound to reach a trail junction. A boardwalk leads right, across Biggin Creek, and shortcuts the loop. A viewing platform that overlooks Biggin Creek is dead ahead. Keep left here, descending to the creek, joining a boardwalk to emerge onto the point where the creek and the Old Santee Canal meet. A trail to an observation point continues up the left side of the canal, while a boardwalk spans Biggin Creek. A rain shelter aids in times of precipitation.

The trail now curves to come alongside Tailrace Canal, the modern connector between what is now Lake Moultrie and the Cooper River. The old Santee Canal was 35 feet wide and 5.5 feet deep, and it seems tiny in comparison with the modern Tailrace Canal. A hill, likely from fill dirt from Tailrace Canal, pinches you in from the right. Reach the first of several spur trails leading away from the canal, over the hill and back down to observation points—bird-watching areas—on Biggin Creek. The total distance mentioned in this hike includes traveling these spur trails. Old Santee Canal Park is a big birding destination.

Sycamores and willows shade the path, which becomes a boardwalk in places. The next spur trail leads away from Tailrace Canal, over the hill of fill, over Biggin Creek, out to a boardwalk covered in black mesh, to end at a bird blind. Holes cut in the mesh allow photographers and other avian enthusiasts to add birds to their "life list," a record of all the species observed in the wild by ardent follows of winged creatures. Do not bypass this trip to the bird blind.

Resume the walk along Tailrace Canal, passing another spur trail leading right to Biggin Creek. Reach the boardwalk spanning a wide part of this stream; you intersected its other end earlier. Good views of the woods and water can be had from here. Bridge the outflow of Biggin Creek where it meets Tailrace Canal and Cooper River. The path opens onto the lawn of the Stony Landing House. This landing was an important trading location for South Carolina dating back to the 1730s. It was built in 1843. Later, during the Civil War, the landing was the site where the first successful underwater attack submarine, the CSS *Little David*, was built. The house and grounds are well preserved, filled with period furnishings, and open for tours.

Leave the grounds and return to the parking area, passing the interpretive center to your right. With your park entrance fee, you can also visit the Berkeley Museum, which focuses on the history of Berkeley County, South Carolina, from 12,000 years ago running up through the exciting time of the American Revolution and the Palmetto State's local hero, Francis Marion—the Swamp Fox—and on through the Civil War to the current day. Canoes are also for rent if you want to explore the area by water. Including the actual hike, you can easily spend an entire day here at Old Santee Canal Park.

# 46

# Sandpiper Pond Nature Trail and Beach Walk

**TOTAL DISTANCE**: 4.8 miles round trip

**HIKING TIME**: 3 hours

**VERTICAL RISE**: 5 feet

**RATING**: Easy to moderate

**MAPS**: USGS 7.5' Brookgreen; Huntington Beach State Park

**TRAILHEAD GPS COORDINATES**: N33° 30.575', W79° 3.747'

**CONTACT INFORMATION**: Huntington Beach State Park, 16148 Ocean Highway, Murrells Inlet, SC 29576, (843) 237-4440, www .southcarolinaparks.com/huntingtonbeach

Huntington Beach State Park is the setting for this coastal trek. Starting just inland from the Atlantic, the hike begins on Sandpiper Pond Nature Trail, passing through maritime coastal woods and along Sandpiper Pond, an interdune pond that has now been reconnected with the ocean. Observation decks and hilly dunes add vertical variety to the trail, which ends at a high observation tower overlooking the pond, where waterfowl and alligators may be congregating. You'll pass a parking area with facilities before following a boardwalk out to the ocean, then embarking on a beach walk—the crashing Atlantic is just feet away—to Murrells Inlet jetty, a place where anglers and boat-going ocean lovers gather when the weather is nice. In winter, the area is nearly deserted, making this a fine time to get back to nature on the most oceanic hike included in this guidebook. Make time to enjoy the other offerings here at Huntington Beach, detailed at the end of the hiking narrative.

## GETTING THERE

From Myrtle Beach, take US 17 south for 16 miles to the state park, on your left. Enter the park, passing the entrance station, and continue for 0.4 mile; then turn left onto the road leading to the education center, which is 0.2 mile distant on your left. Park here. The trail starts on the opposite side of the road from the education center.

## THE TRAIL

The education center is worth a visit. It focuses on the relationships among land, marsh, sea, and man. The roar of the ocean can be heard from the trailhead. Start the hike in a maritime for-

est to shortly reach a spur trail, on your right, leading to the state park campground. Traverse a boardwalk, entering cedar-pine woods with an understory of yaupon holly. The densely wooded dunes and swales of the terrain make the trail somewhat hard to follow, but the park has installed red-tipped wooden posts to indicate the way. This tree-filled, hilly country will surprise those expecting a perfectly level beach walk. Steps over some of the higher dunes prevent erosion from tearing them down.

The thick woods are broken by small clearings where light beams onto the path. Soon pass a spur trail leading to a dune top, where you can look over the ocean beyond Sandpiper Pond. Continue winding amid brushy thickets. The sandy trailbed can make for slow going, especially if it hasn't rained in a while. In places, a tidal creek is visible to your left. Bridge a waterway connecting the tidal creek to Sandpiper Pond at 0.5 mile. Just beyond, a trail leads left and connects to a park road.

The main path curves right, entering an area of live oaks, but be apprised that the trailside environment changes from minute to minute. You'll be hiking along a sandy path in an open area . . . then pine trees appear overhead, before

HUNTINGTON BEACH CAN BE VERY QUIET IN WINTER

evolving into a dark copse of live oaks. Pass another overlook of the marsh before opening to an elaborate tower-like overlook, the Maxwell Observation Deck. Here you can gain a linear look down at Sandpiper Pond and the marsh grasses that border it, as well as the woods that grow on the landward sides of the pond.

The hike reaches a parking area, picnic shelter, water, and restrooms at 1.0 mile. Stay to your right here and follow the boardwalk beach access. The boardwalk crosses the oceanside dunes and reaches the Atlantic. Depending on the day of the week, the season, and the weather, the beach can be crowded or deserted. Head left here, northbound on a wide sand swath bordered by sea oats and a rolling ocean. The Murrells Inlet jetty is visible in the distance, curving to the right.

Tan-gray sands slope into the sea, while to your left oat-covered dunes extend in an open area for some distance. The crunch of the sand, the sound of the waves, and flittering birds make for a classic beach walk. Continue angling for the jetty, reaching the rock structure topped with asphalt at 2.4 miles. This is a popular fishing area, so don't be surprised if you see boats in

Murrells Inlet and anglers tossing in a line from the jetty. In summer, the inlet can be full of people docking their boats, enjoying the scene. In winter, it's often completely desolate. On your way back, you can backtrack on Sandpiper Pond Nature Trail, or stay on the beach then cut through the campground, or walk the road back to the education center.

Keep in mind that there's much more to enjoy at Huntington Beach State Park. It offers a large campground, plenty of beachfront, and history in the form of Atalaya, the ruins of the house built by the Huntington family, who donated the property for this state park as well as Brookgreen Gardens, on the mainland side of US 17.

This 2,500-acre park has 3 miles of ocean frontage. The home of Mr. and Mrs. Huntington stands next to the day-use area. Back in 1930, the Huntingtons were traveling the Intracoastal Waterway and came upon the property that would become the state park. These New Yorkers bought it on the spot and began building the house with an eye for a wintering locale but also for preserving the area's natural attributes, from the open beach to the inland forests to what is now Brookgreen Gardens. The brick structure was erected without detailed plans but did take into account the potential for hurricanes. A great courtyard with a tower in the center and specific rooms built as studios for Mrs. Huntington, a sculptress, were unique attributes that make Atalaya worthy of a visit, whether you take a guided ranger tour or see the facilities on your own. It was last used by the Huntingtons in 1947. Later, Mrs. Huntington leased the property to the state of South Carolina for a park.

The campground has two large loops with a separate walk-in, tent-camping area. The first loop, the one with water, electric, and sewer sites, has camps closer to the beach in a mix of sun and shade from planted cedars and live oaks. These first 40 sites are popular with RVs and are reservable. The second loop offers sites farther from the ocean, most of them bordered with thick brush to create campsite privacy. Tent campers will enjoy the walk-in sites shaded by live oaks and pines. There's plentiful solitude back here, as brush thrives between sites. This popular state park stays busy throughout the warmer part of the year: It fills on weekends from March to September, and on many weekdays during the peak of summer. Campers crave the beachside sites, and proximity to ocean breezes will cut down on insects when they are bothersome, usually following rainy periods.

Brookgreen Gardens, founded by the Huntingtons, is across US 17 from the state park. Its 9,000 acres preserve the flora and fauna of the area, as well as displaying sculpture pieces. Upon admission, you can tour the gardens, focus on sculptures, see the zoo, or go on a trekker tour. More than 900 sculptures are scattered throughout the grounds. Take a boat trip on the Waccamaw River, view the historic rice plantations of old, and maybe catch a glimpse of alligators, birds, and other wildlife. Special events take place throughout the year.

# Santee Coastal Reserve Loop

**TOTAL DISTANCE**: 3.3-mile loop

**HIKING TIME**: 2 hours

**VERTICAL RISE**: 5 feet

**RATING**: Easy to moderate

**MAPS**: USGS 7.5' Minim Island; Santee Coastal Reserve WMA

**TRAILHEAD GPS COORDINATES**: N33° 9.227', W79° 22.065'

**CONTACT INFORMATION**: Santee Coastal Reserve, 210 Santee Gun Club Road, McClellanville, SC 29458, (843) 546-6062, www.dnr.sc.gov

This hike takes place in the Santee Coastal Reserve Wildlife Management Area, a locale that has seen many changes over the centuries. First, Santee Indians occupied it, then it became a rice plantation, and then the area became a private hunting retreat. Then the 23,000-plus acres of land were given over to The Nature Conservancy, which in turn deeded most of the property to the South Carolina Department of Natural Resources. The DNR manages the land today to maximize habitats for wildlife from shorebirds to sea turtles to waterfowl. The Nature Conservancy maintained ownership of a 1,000-acre tract and lake known as the Washo Reserve. It has a 200-year-old freshwater cypress lake and cypress-gum swamp. The Washo Reserve is the site of the oldest continuously used wading bird rookery in the United States. It also has the largest concentrations of nesting ospreys in the country. The Washo Reserve is co-managed by the Conservancy and the South Carolina DNR.

This hike primarily traces Marshland Trail, although it does touch on the Washo Reserve, first via boardwalk, then by trail to the open cypress lake, before resuming Marshland Trail, circling waterfowl habitat among other places. Mosquitoes can be troublesome here—bring insect repellent during warm-weather visits. Cooler days are the best times to visit. The reserve is open from 8 a.m. to 5 p.m. daily but is closed the first full week in October, the first 2 full weeks of November, the first full week in December, and Wednesday and Saturday between January 21 and March 1. Hunts go on at the reserve during these times. If you want to confirm that the reserve will be open, call (843) 546-6062.

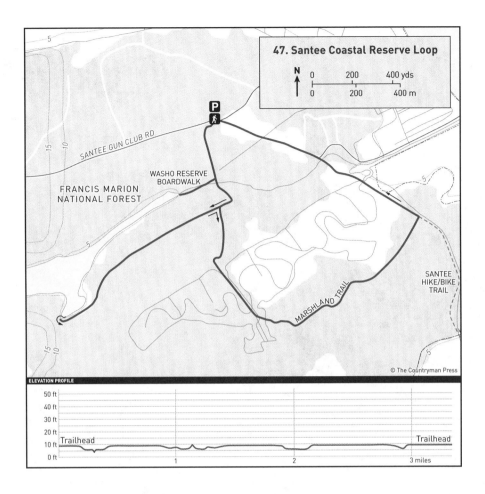

## GETTING THERE

From the intersection of SC 45 and US 17 in McClellanville, take US 17 north for 3 miles to the signed right turn for Santee Coastal Reserve, on Santee Coastal Road. Stay on Santee Coastal Road for 2.6 miles to reach Santee Gun Club Road. Turn right onto Santee Gun Club Road, shortly entering Santee Coastal Reserve, and then driving for a total of 2.7 miles to reach a parking area and gate on your left. Alternative directions from Georgetown: From the intersection of US 17 and US 17A in Georgetown, take US 17 south for 16.3 miles to South Santee Road. Turn left and follow South Santee Road for 1.4 miles to Santee Gun Club Road. Turn left again onto Santee Gun Club Road, then continue per the directions above.

## THE TRAIL

The beginning of Marshland Trail can be hard to find. From the parking area, a road leads forward beyond the gate. An information kiosk is here, too. As you face the kiosk, Marshland Trail heads into the woods along a ditch line to the right. Cross the open field along the ditch line to walk among live oak

WASHO RESERVE IS THE OLDEST CONTINUALLY USED ROOKERY IN THE UNITED STATES

trees. The track enters gorgeous swamp woods to reach the Washo Reserve Boardwalk. This boardwalk heads southwest for a distance to open onto a partially wooded swamp where you may see alligators or avian life, depending on the season. The Washo Reserve is an important birding area for night herons, ospreys, bald eagles, wood storks, and anhingas, among others. The endangered Bachman's sparrow resides in longleaf pine stands here.

Backtrack on the boardwalk and resume Marshland Trail, crossing an outflow of Washo Reserve. Marshland Trail keeps forward to reach an intersection at 0.5 mile. Stay right here and soon reach another intersection. Signs indicate that Marshland Trail leads left, but continue forward on the shaded roadbed. The westbound elevated track passes through woods that offer a little bit of everything, from holly to pines, live oaks, and swamp trees. Ferns dot the forest floor. At 1.1 miles, you will reach a large sign indicating the Washo Reserve boundary and a gate. To your right is the stunning Washo Reserve, the actual 200-year-old rookery that makes the place so important for wildlife. Breaks in the woods allow for open views of the lake and the cypress trees that border it. Pines grow tall above the cypress on higher ground. This is a good place to backtrack, as entrance into the actual Washo Reserve area is limited.

After returning to Marshland Trail, hang a right, continuing on a wide, shaded roadbed in piney woods. An open marsh lies off to your left. The piney woods give way to a shadeless dike with open marshes and evergreen thickets. Look to your feet for gator trails, crossing the dike from one wetland to another. The footing is uneven on this grassy track.

Reenter the woods, staying with the arrows that indicate the correct track. The trail continues to circle the greater marsh. At 2.6 miles, the Santee Hike/Bike Trail leaves to your right and makes a 7-mile loop. If you choose to hike this, have sunscreen and bug dope handy—much of the track consists of shadeless dikes. Many locals prefer to bike this trail rather than walk it. It does go along the Intracoastal Waterway and the South Santee River for much of its distance. There is also a 4-mile canoe trail out here that follows a canal and then loops through marsh.

Marshland Loop turns left at its junction with the Santee Hike/Bike Trail, and a logging road keeps forward. Stay left, joining a dike on the northeast end of the open marsh. Look for a boardwalk at 2.8 miles. It extends into the marsh and offers better views than does the dike. The path then leaves the marsh and passes through the maintenance area for the DNR. You will see buildings, tractors, and people, all part of the effort to keep the 23,000 acres in the best shape for Santee Coastal's flora and fauna.

Beyond the maintenance area the trail traces a road past the reserve office and other buildings, tucked away amid fields. The loop ends at the trailhead at 3.3 miles. The reserve also has another hiking trail, the 1.8-mile Woodland Trail, which travels through longleaf pines. It is located on the left-hand side of the road on the way to the main trailhead.

# Santee State Park Loop

| | |
|---|---|
| **TOTAL DISTANCE**: 7.3-mile loop | |

**TOTAL DISTANCE**: 7.3-mile loop

**HIKING TIME**: 3.5 hours

**VERTICAL RISE**: 40 feet

**RATING**: Moderate

**MAPS**: USGS 7.5' Saint Paul, Elloree; Santee State Park

**TRAILHEAD GPS COORDINATES**: N33° 32.870', W80° 29.889'

**CONTACT INFORMATION**: Santee State Park, 251 State Park Road, Santee, SC 29142, (803) 854-2408, www .southcarolinaparks.com/santee

Santee State Park is located on the shores of big Lake Marion, deep in Santee Cooper Country. In addition to camping, cabins, and other facilities, a pleasant loop trail circles the heart of the park. Open to hikers and mountain bikers, it travels along bluffs overlooking Lake Marion, running past old homesites and through rich woods before turning away from the lake to roughly parallel the park boundary, crossing a wetland on a boardwalk. Beyond, the path winds through a mix of pines and oaks to return to the trailhead.

The trail is blazed throughout. Spring and fall are the best times to enjoy this loop, although the park is busiest in summer, and many park enthusiasts do hike the trail then. If you're hiking here in summer, do so in the early morning, then go on the Fisheagle boat tour of Lake Marion, offered at the park in the afternoon. Winter brings solitude, both on the trail and on the lake beyond. The lake views are the highlight of the hike: You can stand well above the shoreline, where the ground gives way, dropping straight to the slender, sandy shore below. The park's picnic area, with water and restrooms, is accessible partway along the loop.

## GETTING THERE

From Exit 98 off I-95 near the town of Santee, take SC 6 west for 1.0 mile to the state park entrance on your right. Turn right onto State Park Road. Follow State Park Road for 2.3 miles to reach a four-way intersection. (The park picnic area and Cypress View Campground are to your right. All other facilities are dead ahead.) Keep forward here for 1.8 miles to reach the trailhead on your right. There is a parking fee.

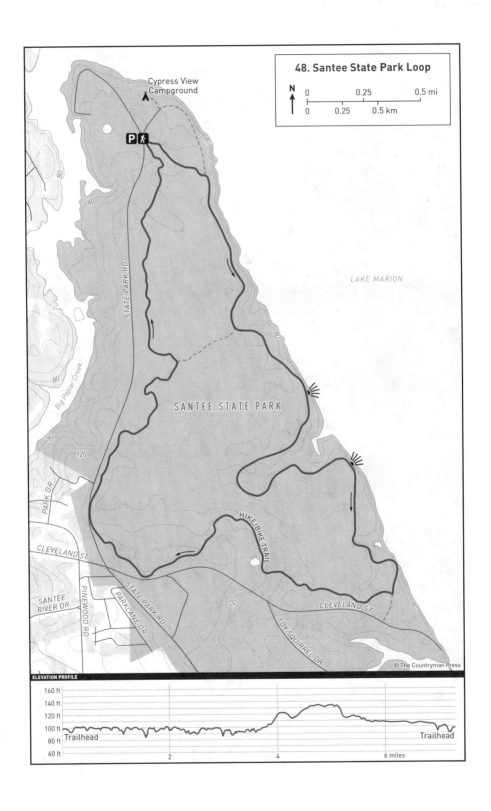

Cypress View
Campground

LAKE MARION

SANTEE STATE PARK

Big Poplar Creek

STATE PARK RD

80

80

80

80

120

120

80

PARK DR

CLEVELAND ST

SANTEE
RIVER DR

PINEWOOD RD

STATE PARK RD

PARKLANE DR

HIKE/BIKE TRAIL

FOX SQUIRREL DR

CLEVELAND ST

© The Countryman Press

N

| 0 | | 0.25 | | 0.5 mi |
| 0 | 0.25 | | 0.5 km | |

ELEVATION PROFILE

160 ft
140 ft
120 ft
100 ft
80 ft
60 ft

Trailhead                                                Trailhead

2            4            6 miles

SANDY SHORELINE OF LAKE MARION ON A CALM MORNING

## THE TRAIL

The Hike/Bike Trail leaves the sandy, pine-shaded parking area and passes through wooden vehicle barriers. The sand track enters a forest of pine, oak, and hickory with sweetgum mixed in. Spanish moss drapes the limbs. Drop to cross a small wetland on an elevated track before reaching a trail junction at 0.3 mile. To your left a trail leads to Cypress View Campground, one of two campgrounds here at the state park. The Hike/Bike Trail leaves right, tracing an old roadbed that was here long before the lake was a lake and the park was a park. Below the bluffs flowed the Santee River; this was just a country lane in South Carolina's sleepy coastal plain, where houses stood, sheltering families who moved on after the massive hydroelectric project that resulted in Lake Marion came to be. As you hike the trail, look for evidence of these former residents.

Lake Marion shimmers through the trees to your left. The wide, sand-and-soil southbound path makes for easy walking. The trail is mostly level, but dips where the land drains toward the lake. In these drains you may see logs piled together, along with limbs and other debris, left over from when the lake flooded in the past. Mostly shaded, the path is sometimes open where the trees are young, or in pine woods.

Continue dipping into richly wooded drainages and then rising into more piney woods, keeping a southerly track. Benches are occasionally set along the trail. At 1.5 miles, the Hike/Bike Trail saddles alongside the bluff above Lake Marion. From here you can look out on water as far as the eye can see. Below, the land drops off to a narrow shoreline, where a small sand beach backs against the lake bluffs.

Beyond the bluff, the path turns inland and begins working around the largest drainage flowing into the lake. Circle the slough, where wide-buttressed tupelo trees, along with bottomland hardwoods, grow along the stream shed. As you return to the lake, look for a bona fide swamp forest to the left of the trail. Tupelo and cypress rise from the water in this dark environ. Return to the lake bluff at 2.7 miles and gain more lake views. Cypress stands grow far out in the water. Lake Marion and its companion impoundment, Lake Moultrie, are the heart of Santee Cooper Country, covering 110,000 acres of watery expanse. The two lakes were created for hydropower; Santee State Park, at 2,500 acres, was established in 1949. The shores of these two lakes vary from bluffs, such as those here, to swamps, where cypress trees draped in Spanish moss overlook the expanse of water. Birds aplenty call the lake home—in some cases, a part-time home.

The trail continues southerly, dipping a couple more times over wetter locales before reaching a junction at 3.4 miles. The old roadbed you've been following continues forward and soon emerges on the road leading left just a short distance to the picnic/swim area. Across that road is Limestone Nature Trail, which makes a 1-mile loop in thick woods over rolling terrain. The Hike/Bike Trail leaves abruptly right from the junction, twisting and turning in thick woods on a single-track path. The forest closes in here, and the trail continues slaloming through trees before opening into a widely spaced, mature pine forest at 4.0 miles.

Continue into mixed woods, bisecting

several old roadbeds. The way is clear on your well-blazed path. At times the trail is on a slight slope leaning toward the lake. You may notice narrow, linear ditches cut into the forest. These are relics of agriculture, an effort to drain the land for crops such as cotton. At 4.7 miles, a park fee station is visible through the woods to your left. The trail curves north, running quite close to State Park Road to reach the long boardwalk at 5.3 miles over a wetland of tulip, ash, and bay trees rising from thick cane stands.

The Hike/Bike Trail turns away from the road at 6.0 miles, winding through thick forest and working around wetter areas of woodland. At 6.3 miles, it resumes a nearly due-north course through pines, and the walking is easy.

The Hike/Bike Trail veers off its straight line to circle a wetland just before completing the loop at 7.3 miles.

The Hike/Bike Trail and other shorter nature trails are but a few of the features of this state park. For lodging, it offers two campgrounds and cabins. Lake Marion is known for its fishing, and visitors can use the park boat launch or fish for bass, bream, and crappie from the park's pier. Get bait and tackle from the park store. Fisheagle tours are offered during the warm season. You can tour the lake and enjoy a narrated tour of Lake Marion's natural offerings. Stop in at the interpretive center to learn about the establishment of the lake and park. The park swim beach offers a place to dip into the waters of the lake, too.

# Spanish Mount Trail at Edisto Beach State Park

**TOTAL DISTANCE**: 3.9 miles

**HIKING TIME**: 2.1 hours

**VERTICAL RISE**: 5 feet

**RATING**: Easy

**MAPS**: USGS 7.5' Edisto Island, Edisto Beach; Edisto Beach State Park

**TRAILHEAD GPS COORDINATES**: N32° 30.259', W80° 19.330'

**CONTACT INFORMATION**: Edisto Beach State Park, 8377 State Cabin Road, Edisto Island, SC 29438, (843) 869-2156, www.southcarolinaparks.com/edistobeach

Edisto Beach State Park is primarily known for its palm-lined beaches, but the preserve also features some inland and maritime terrain that offers a good hike. Leave the park boat ramp on the South Edisto River and travel out to an overlook atop an old Indian shell mound, built up from years and years and years of eating shellfish and piling the remains along what became known as Scott Creek. From the mound, known as the Spanish Mount, you'll head easterly in woods along the tidal flats of Scott Creek, where you can gaze upon the stream and surrounding marshes. Continue to Forest Loop, where you circle back to Spanish Mount Trail and return to the trailhead. Be apprised that this hike is but one of the activities offered here at Edisto Beach State Park, with its two campgrounds, kayaking, fishing, and more.

## GETTING THERE

From Charleston, head south on US 17 for 20 miles to SC 174. Turn left, south, onto SC 174 and follow it for 20.5 miles to Palmetto Road (Palmetto Road is 1.2 miles before the main Edisto Beach State Park entrance to your left). Turn right onto Palmetto Road and follow it for 1.3 miles, then veer left onto a signed gravel road, Oyster Row Lane, and follow it to the park boat ramp. The trail starts at the parking area away from the boat ramp.

## THE TRAIL

This hike actually starts on Big Bay Trail, which is open to hikers and bicyclists. Pass around some vehicle barriers at the trailside kiosk to enter maritime woods of live oak, cedar, palm, and pine, adorned in Spanish moss. Shortly, you

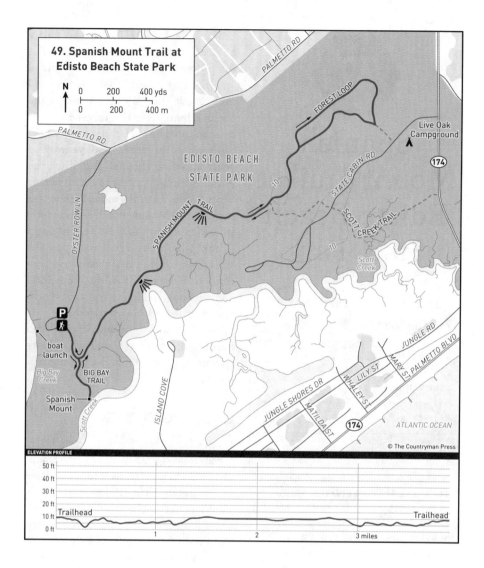

49. Spanish Mount Trail at
Edisto Beach State Park

N

| 0 | 200 | 400 yds |
| 0 | 200 | 400 m |

PALMETTO RD

PALMETTO RD

EDISTO BEACH
STATE PARK

FOREST LOOP

Live Oak
Campground

174

OYSTER ROW LN

SPANISH MOUNT TRAIL

STATE CABIN RD

SCOTT CREEK TRAIL

10

10

Scott
Creek

P

boat
launch

Big Bay
Creek

BIG BAY
TRAIL

Spanish
Mount

Scott Creek

ISLAND COVE

JUNGLE SHORES DR

WHALEY ST

LILY ST

MATILDA ST

MARY ST

JUNGLE RD

PALMETTO BLVD

174

ATLANTIC OCEAN

© The Countryman Press

ELEVATION PROFILE

| 50 ft | | | | |
| 40 ft | | | | |
| 30 ft | | | | |
| 20 ft | | | | |
| 10 ft | Trailhead | | | Trailhead |
| 0 ft | | | | |
| | 1 | 2 | 3 miles | |

will reach the spur trail leading right to the Spanish Mount, an Indian midden. This shell mound, built up in a circle and filled in the middle, came to be known as the Spanish Mount. It dates back at least 2,000 years. Mounds of shells at rich, estuarine areas are not uncommon in the Southeast, but the ringed shape of this mound and the name "Spanish Mount" are mysteries. It is, however, purportedly the second oldest pottery site in South Carolina. Others date the

Spanish Mount at 4,000 years old. A viewing platform has been installed, allowing you to look out onto Scott Creek and into a cut in the mound, showing layer upon layer of shells.

Backtrack to Spanish Mount Trail and head east on a level track with tiny gravel under your feet. Palms, magnolias, cedars, and oaks shade the tread and give the area the look an oceanside hike should have. The trail soon comes very near Scott Creek. Stop here and

LIVE OAKS SHADE SPANISH MOUNT TRAIL

SPANISH MOUNT TRAIL PASSES BY TIDAL SCOTT CREEK

gaze across the waterway and marsh grasses at Edisto Island, as well as beach houses beyond. At 1.2 miles, the trail leaves the lush forest and opens onto a boardwalk, which crosses a tidal tributary of Scott Creek. This allows another view of the marshlands to the south.

Reenter woods with many regal oaks, winding through the quiet heart of the park. Reach Scott Creek Trail at 1.4 miles. It leaves right to connect to a bicycle right-of-way bordering SC 174, which connects to the beach part of the park. Continue forward, meeting Forest Loop at 1.7 miles. Leave left on this natural-surfaced track, traveling through more live oaks with resurrection ferns and also passing beneath open pines. The walkway returns to Spanish Mount Trail at 2.2 miles. Turn right and begin your trek back toward the parking area.

On your way back you may consider

other activities here at Edisto Beach State Park. A trip here is like a trip back in time. This is a quaint park next to a small vacation village with no high-rises and very few chain stores. But it is growing, so enjoy the atmosphere while it lasts. Edisto Beach has been dubbed "Mayberry by the Sea" by visitors. This South Carolina coastal getaway between Charleston and Savannah, Georgia, should bear such a moniker with pride: The town contrasts mightily with other, more crowded destinations that have been homogenized by today's proliferation of chain hotels, motels, beach stores, and restaurants. Thankfully Edisto Beach, 20 miles off South Carolina's main coastal drag, US 17, is at the end of a dead-end road. Other easier-to-access destinations keep Edisto less populated. However, that doesn't make Edisto Beach unpopular. I call this park and community a place of return. Families come and camp here year after year and bring their kids, who in turn bring their kids.

Edisto Beach is on the northern tip of St. Helena Sound, a large bay where the Ashepoo, Combahee, and Edisto Rivers converge to meet the Atlantic Ocean with 1.25 miles of beachfront. The beaches are average in width and allow plenty of sunbathers and beach-combers to roam around. The sandy stretch extends north from the point where town and park meet. Low dunes at the park entrance back this beach. Picnic areas shaded by palms and oaks back the strand. The park office and gift shop are nearby. Farther down the shore, sea-oat-topped dunes give way to wind-sculpted, maritime vegetation atop dunes. The Edisto Beach State Park campground lies behind these dunes but is connected to the beach by five

accesses. Parkland ends and private property begins at Edingsville Beach. The village of Edisto Beach stretches south of the park. Houses mostly front the ocean here, but there are numerous public beach accesses along the 5 miles of beachfront.

Edisto Beach State Park has two camping areas with different atmospheres. The Main Camping Area is the more popular: It's just a dune away from the Atlantic Ocean with a creek on the mainland side of the campground. The Live Oak Camping Area, near Spanish Mount Trail, is less popular simply because it is farther from the beach, and you must drive to the ocean. The Main Camping Area will fill anytime during summer; reservations are highly recommended from June through August. The campgrounds also see an upsurge in business during spring break, but since alcohol is not allowed, a family atmosphere reigns. This is part of the reason families return year after year. The Civilian Conservation Corp (CCC) developed the original park facilities in the 1930s. But the number one attraction, the beach, was already here, and it is the primary draw of this park. Edisto Beach offers a chance to experience the quieter side of the South Carolina coast. Some visitors surf-fish in the Atlantic, while others will try the backcountry by boat, using the park boat ramp. Common catches include red drum, trout, and flounder. Still other folks paddle a canoe or sea kayak from this same launch. Charter-fishing operations are available in the town of Edisto Beach. Back at the park, daily interpretive programs are held in summer. So when you come here to hike, consider staying a while and enjoying all that Edisto Beach offers.

# Swamp Fox Passage of the Palmetto Trail

**TOTAL DISTANCE**: 48.1 miles end-to-end

**HIKING TIME**: 28 hours

**VERTICAL RISE**: 65 feet

**RATING**: Difficult

**MAPS**: USGS 7.5' Bonneau, Cordesville, Bethera, Huger, Ocean Bay, Awendaw; Swamp Fox Passage of the Palmetto Trail; Francis Marion National Forest

**TRAILHEAD GPS COORDINATES**: N33° 16.355', W79° 57.838'

**CONTACT INFORMATION**: Francis Marion National Forest, 2967 Steed Creek Road, Huger, SC 29450, (843) 336-3248, www .fs.usda.gov/scnf

This is the best long-distance hike in the Lowcountry and one of the best treks in the entire Palmetto State. The Swamp Fox Passage of the Palmetto Trail travels its entire length through Francis Marion National Forest, named for the American Revolutionary War hero who continually harassed British forces and then fled to the coastal swamps, only to attack again. And for his wily skills, Francis Marion was dubbed the "Swamp Fox." Originally simply Swamp Fox Trail when parts of it were finished in 1968 by Boy Scouts, then made part of Palmetto Trail, this trek from Lake Moultrie to the coast traverses longleaf pine woods, hardwood floodplains, evergreen shrub bogs, and blackwater swamps. Starting near Lake Moultrie, the trail heads east to span Wadboo Swamp, then travels past Cane Gully and Alligator Creek before reaching Witherbee Ranger Station. From here it traverses drier country before turning south and joining a railroad grade. It then comes along the deep beech forests of Turkey Creek before climbing to extensive longleaf woods. The pine and oak forests near Halfway Creek Campground are simply beautiful. The trail then stays mostly on level grades, passing through wooded swamps before spanning Steed Creek, a tidally influenced freshwater stream. The passage finally leaves Palmetto Trail to end at US 17.

The Forest Service has established primitive camps along the trail. If you wish to camp elsewhere, you must obtain a camping permit; call (803) 336-3248 for information. Campsites can be generally found in the uplands bordering streams and swamps. Note that major streams are bridged and boardwalks are established over most wetlands. Also, the hiking season for this trail is late October through April. The

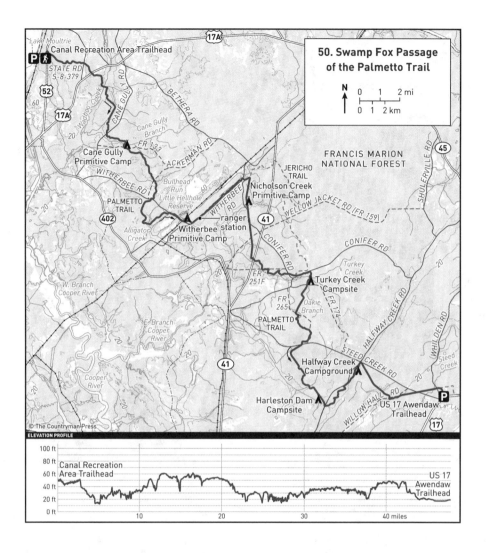

water will be down in fall. Spring offers wildflowers and more wet expanses. Do not attempt it in summer, and bring bug dope during the shoulder seasons. Also, not every gravel forest road crossing is noted in the following narrative. However, every paved road crossing is noted.

## GETTING THERE

US 17 trailhead: From the intersection of US 17 and US 17A in Georgetown, take US 17 for 32 miles to the trailhead in Awendaw, on your right. The trailhead lies below the road and is easy to pass, so be on the lookout.

Canal Recreation Area trailhead: To reach the Canal Recreation Area trailhead from the US 17 trailhead, go south just 0.1 mile farther on US 17 to Steed Creek Road. Turn right and follow Steed Creek Road for 12 miles to SC 41. From here, continue forward, now on SC 402 West; follow this road for 15.6 miles, turning right onto US 52/US 17A. Veer left as 52 and 17A soon split, staying with

HOODED PITCHER PLANTS GROW ALONG THE TRAIL

52 for 3.7 miles to reach Canal Recreation Area on your left. Try to arrange a shuttle ride from US 17 or park at nearby Bonneau if you can—Canal isn't the safest parking in the world.

## THE TRAIL

Canal Recreation Area has water spigots, in case you need to fill up. Leave north from Canal, bridging a small canal to reach Palmetto Trail. The path splits: The Lake Moultrie Passage of the Palmetto Trail heads left, while the Swamp Fox Passage (SFP) continues forward in pines to soon cross US 52. Curve east, passing under a power line and continuing in oaks and sweetgums. Bay trees grow in the wetter spots. Watch for potholes left in the trail by fallen and eroded pines. Elevated single-track boardwalks stand in wetter areas here and throughout the SFP. Cross paved Road 379-S at 2.2 miles before crossing US 17A at 2.9 miles. The SFP enters longleaf wiregrass woods, with myrtle and cane in wetter areas. The flora changes to wetter bottomland woods upon reaching Wadboo Swamp at 4.3 miles. Span the flowing swamp stream on a high bridge before entering the depths of the brooding and gorgeous swamp and a former rice-cultivation area. Keep forward on a slave-built dike in low woods. A trained eye will spot the grid pattern of the dikes and canals in this now wooded, formerly open wetland, rife with saw palmetto. Boardwalks cross wetlands in places. Leave left from the dike, climbing to drier woods with a grassy track, crossing two forest roads before stepping over small Callum Branch on a footbridge at 6.3 miles.

The Swamp Fox Passage continues easterly, bisecting more forest roads before coming along Cane Gully Branch, which it crosses on a long dike and bridge. A wide, wooded swamp is to the left of the dike. Just after the swamp outflow, at 7.7 miles, reach Cane Gully Primitive Camp, under pines. The SFP travels in pine flatwoods on a wide track, crossing a few more forest roads to traverse a boardwalk over Alligator Creek at 13.4 miles.

Enter mixed-age longleaf pines and wetter areas with pitcher plants before reaching paved Witherbee Road at 14.5 miles. The trail then passes through pine plantations broken by occasional short boardwalks over streamlets before dipping to densely forested Alligator Creek at 14.5 miles. Span this attractive area on a wide boardwalk before climbing into naturally dispersed longleaf woods. Recross paved Witherbee Road at 16.9 miles. Traverse open areas to come alongside Little Hellhole Reserve, a dammed waterfowl area, at 14.9 miles. Join Witherbee Road to cross the Seaboard Coast railroad tracks, then pass Witherbee Primitive Camp, set in shady oaks, at 15.4 miles. Soon cross Gough Branch then reach Witherbee Ranger Station at 17.3 miles. Water spigots, parking, and information are available.

The SFP keeps northeast on a level track, paralleling then crossing Witherbee Road a final time at 20.2 miles. Stay with the white blazes, as the trail becomes a bit confusing on old roadbeds before meeting Jericho Trail at 20.7 miles. Keep right here, joining an arrow-straight, brush-lined old railroad grade through wet areas. This grade is part of a 300-mile network of logging trams built in the late 1800s and early 1900s while lumber workers were timbering what became Francis Marion National Forest. Pass a spur trail to your left to Nicholson Creek Primitive Camp at 22.0

FALL ASTERS BRIGHTEN FRANCIS MARION NATIONAL FOREST

miles. This camp is partly open to the sun, since nearby pines were killed by the southern pine beetle. Shortly, you will span Nicholson Creek. The wooded swamp locale around the bridge is particularly attractive and is worth a stop. Keep forward on the grade before leaving it by turning left and crossing paved SC 41 at 24.7 miles.

Cruise east in the attractive Turkey Creek Valley, enjoying rich beech and tulip tree forests in the hilly margin between wetland and upland, occasion-

ally spanning small branches on bridges in the bottomlands. This is one of the most scenic stretches of the entire SFP. Return to open pine flatwoods before passing the other end of Jericho Trail at 27.8 miles, then briefly follow FR 166 before turning right to bridge Turkey Creek in swampy hardwood bottomland at 28.9 miles. Turkey Creek Campsite is in pine-sweetgum upland just beyond the watercourse.

Keep southwest in pines. Cross a forest road and proceed forward, walking an open grassy roadbed that you think may not be the trail, but is. Ahead, the trail returns to being a footpath at a grassy turnaround, bridging small Oakie Branch at 31.0 miles. Pass through younger woods with many standing dead trunks, victims of fire, before crossing paved Steed Creek Road at 33.6 miles. Enter thicker woods with pond pines. Join another logging tram heading southeast, passing through shrub bogs. At 35.7 miles, the trail leaves abruptly right from the tram and begins a reroute, eventually emerging onto Forest Road 170 to span Harleston Dam Creek on the road bridge at 36.8 miles. The SFP then reenters bottomland woods to your left to join the tram again, and makes the Harleston Dam Campsite, in younger pines and oaks, at 37.5 miles. You must carry your water from Harleston Dam Creek to this campsite.

Continue southeasterly, emerging to cross paved Halfway Creek Road at 38.0 miles, then turn northeast in tall long-leaf flatwoods. These high pines are the best species along the trail. There are limited numbers of mature pine trees here in Francis Marion National Forest because the area was devastated by Hurricane Hugo in 1989 and is still recovering. Reach Halfway Creek Campground at 41.1 miles. This auto-accessible, live-oak-shaded camp no longer has a pump well. Bring your own water. The SFP soon turns back southeast, joining another grade through evergreen shrub bogs and other wooded wetlands as it passes through some of the unusual Carolina bays, oval-shape wetlands with no known origination. The rail ties are still visible in the grade here. Join FR 224 at 44.0 miles, only to leave left again at 44.6 miles.

Pass through open woods to rejoin the grade yet again, tunneling under a bottomland swamp forest. Cross Steed Creek Road at 46.5 miles, still in lush wet woods. Span Steed Creek on an iron truss bridge at 47.3 miles. Look for pilings of old bridges here in this tidally influenced freshwater stream. Reach the spur trail to the US 17 parking area at 47.6 miles. Palmetto Trail continues forward; you stay right on the spur trail to reach the lot at 48.1 miles.

# INDEX

*Italicized numbers indicate illustrations.*